THE SACRED LITERATURE SERIES

THE SPIRIT OF ZOROASTRIANISM

THE SPIRIT OF
ZOROASTRIANISM

Introduced, translated, and edited by

PRODS OKTOR SKJÆRVØ

PUBLISHED IN ASSOCIATION WITH
THE INTERNATIONAL SACRED LITERATURE TRUST

YALE UNIVERSITY PRESS
NEW HAVEN AND LONDON

For information about the Sacred Literature Series and other Yale University Press publications please contact:
U.S. Office: sales.press@yale.edu   yalebooks.com
Europe Office: sales@yaleup.co.uk   www.yalebooks.co.uk

Set in Arno Pro by IDSUK (DataConnection) Ltd
Printed in Great Britain by Hobbs the Printers Ltd, Totton, Hampshire

Library of Congress Cataloging-in-Publication Data

Skjærvø, Prods O.
    The spirit of Zoroastrianism / Prods O. Skjærvø.
        p. cm.
    Includes bibliographical references.
    ISBN 978-0-300-17035-1 (cl : alk. paper)
    1. Zoroastrianism–Sacred books.   I. Title.
    BL1510.S55 2011
    295–dc23

                                                                          2011041889

A catalogue record for this book is available from the British Library.

10 9 8 7 6 5 4 3 2 1

The International Sacred Literature Trust was established to promote understanding and open discussion between and within faiths and to give voice in today's world to the wisdom that speaks across time and traditions.

What resources do the sacred traditions of the world possess to respond to the great global threats of poverty, war, ecological disaster, and spiritual despair?

Our starting-point is the sacred texts with their vision of a higher truth and their deep insights into the nature of humanity and the universe we inhabit. The publishing program is planned so that each faith community articulates its own teachings with the intention of enhancing its self-understanding as well as the understanding of those of other faiths and those of no faith.

The Trust especially encourages faiths to make available texts which are needed in translation for their own communities and also texts which are little known outside a particular tradition but which have the power to inspire, console, enlighten, and transform. These sources from the past become resources for the present and future when we make inspired use of them to guide us in shaping the contemporary world.

Our religious traditions are diverse but, as with the natural environment, we are discovering the global interdependence of human hearts and minds. The Trust invites all to participate in the modern experience of interfaith encounter and exchange which marks a new phase in the quest to discover our full humanity.

CONTENTS

PREFACE

The only comprehensive collection of translations of Zoroastrian texts is that by E. West in the Sacred Books of the East from about 1900. Since then, the only anthology of Zoroastrian literature in English is that by W. W. Malandra, which, however, contains only Avestan and Old Persian texts. In this book, I have tried to follow a number of key concepts from their earliest appearances in the *Gāthās* and the *Young Avesta* through the Pahlavi literature, including, in particular, texts illustrating priestly thinking and discussions about the faith, leaving out many of the better-known Avestan texts, which are included in Malandra's anthology. All the translations are my own, although I have, of course, consulted existing translations and discussions.

Some readers might have wished for more explanations, but the size of the book was limited, and I decided texts were more important. The bibliography contains suggestions for further reading. Additional information on individual terms can also be found in the *Encyclopædia Iranica* and its on-line version www.iranica.com/newsite. West's translations, useful although outdated, together with others, are now on-line, as well, at avesta.org, where texts on rituals are also to be found.

ACKNOWLEDGEMENTS

I am grateful to my long-time friend and collaborator Ursula Sims-Williams for bringing me into this project by suggesting my name and to Malcolm Gerratt for inviting me to do this volume and for his support. I would also like to thank the International Sacred Literature Trust, whose aim is to publish "the great songs, poetry, stories and teachings from the spiritual heritage of humanity" to enable us to "draw upon the spiritual wisdom of the past in developing wisdom for the future." I am grateful for being allowed to be part of this project. Finally, I must thank Yale University Press for producing this attractive volume.

EDITORIAL NOTE

As the "abstract" vocabulary denoting divine entities is likely to be confusing, such terms are in upper case, e.g., Good Thought (as opposed to "a good thought," etc.), Wrath (as opposed to "wrath, anger"), Tradition (the *dēn*, as opposed to "many traditions," etc.). Many of the divine names probably retained their full meaning in the Old Avestan texts and have been translated here. They were probably just names already in the Young Avestan texts, where they have not been translated, for instance, Ahura Mazdā, Angra Manyu, Sraosha, etc. The original meanings of the Pahlavi forms Ohrmazd, Ahrimen, Srōsh, etc., were obviously no longer recognizable.

Original Avestan and Pahlavi terms have sometimes been added in parentheses for the benefit of the specialists, for instance "perception (?)" (*wīr*). See also pp. 6–8.

Uncertain translations are sometimes marked by (?) or, when left out, by "...".

Transcriptions have been simplified and normalized throughout: a macron denotes long vowel (*ā*); *w* is used for Avestan *v*; *kh* is used for the guttural of German *ach*, Persian *khāne*; and *zh* for the voiced sibilant of English *leisure*, French *jour*, Persian *zhāle*.

The superscript numbering in the texts is that of standard editions or translations. References in the Introduction and the List of Texts Translated (pp. 261–2) take the form [3:4] = Section 3, paragraph 4. Omitted text is indicated by "..." or "(...)." In the inscriptions, square brackets [ ] indicate illegible text.

INTRODUCTION

1 ZOROASTRIAN LITERATURE

Background

Zoroastrianism, one of the oldest world religions, originated in the second millennium BCE among Iranian tribes in Central Asia. Their religion is commonly called Zoroastrianism in the West, after the Greek form Zoroaster for Avestan Zarathushtra (here: Zarathustra), but also Mazdaism after Ahura Mazdā, their supreme god. Later, after they moved south onto the Iranian Plateau, this religion became that of three great Iranian empires, the Achaemenids (550–330 BCE), the Arsacids/Parthians (247 BCE–224 CE), and the Sasanians (224–650). No longer a state religion after the Arab conquest of Iran, it lost importance, but is still practiced in Iran and in western India (the Parsis), as well as in the diaspora.

Iranians are here defined as speakers of Iranian languages. These include the ancient languages Avestan, Old Persian, Middle Persian = Pahlavi, and others, from which modern Persian (Farsi), Kurdish, Pashto (Afghan), and many others are descended. Their closest non-Iranian relatives are the Indo-Aryan (Indic) languages (Sanskrit, Hindi, etc.). These "Indo-Iranian" languages are in turn part of the Indo-European language family, which includes most of the languages spoken in Europe.

The close relationship between the languages and literatures of the ancient Iranians and Indo-Aryans proves they were once a single people, who probably lived in Central Asia east and southeast of the Aral Sea as far back as the third millennium BCE. While the

Indo-Aryans had long since begun migrating into what is today northern Pakistan and northwestern India, the Iranians remained until splinter groups began moving onto the Iranian Plateau. Ethno-geographical names in the *Avesta* cover the area from the Aral Sea via the Helmand river valley in southern Afghanistan to the area southeast of the Caspian Sea, modern Gurgān [cf. 12:13–14; 64:67]. The Persians and Medes entered the history of western and southwestern Iran in the Assyrian royal annals from the ninth century BCE, and the other Iranian peoples, many known from the *Avesta*, the Achaemenid inscriptions from 520 BCE, and the writings of the Greek historians Herodotus, Ctesias, Xenophon, and others from the fifth century BCE onward.

The *Avesta* and Other Zoroastrian Literature

Zoroastrian literature thus spans over three thousand years. The oldest texts are those contained in the *Avesta*. There is no identifiably historical information in the Avestan texts, but the language and contents are similar to those of the Rigvedic hymns, the oldest of which can be dated to approximately 1500–1000 BCE. It is therefore likely that the oldest part of the *Avesta*, the *Old Avesta* (including the *Gāthās*), had reached its final form by about 1000 BCE and the *Young Avesta* before the Achaemenid period, perhaps during the Median period (ca. 700–550 BCE).

The indigenous history of the *Avesta* is described in the ninth-century Pahlavi texts, among them the *Dēnkard* [1–2; 30:47–48, 40.19], according to which the *Avesta* was divided into twenty-one *nasks* (literally "bundles" ?), corresponding to the twenty-one words of the *Ahuna Wairiya* [110:13]. Of the books listed in the *Dēnkard*, only the *Videvdad* is still complete, while others are incomplete or lost. Earlier references to *nasks* are found in the Avestan hymn to Haoma [47; 74; 90; 108; 111] and the third-century CE inscription of the Sasanian high priest Kerdīr (after 276) [85].

The terms *Avesta and Zand* and *Zendavesta* were used in the West already in the seventeenth century to refer to the Zoroastrian sacred texts on the model of the Bible and the Koran, but there was never a single book (or manuscript) with all the texts. Rather, the manuscripts contain only individual texts or groups of texts. These manuscripts are from the thirteenth to nineteenth centuries, the history of a few of which can be followed back to about 1000 CE. Some contain the "plain" (*sade*) Avestan text, others the Avestan texts accompanied by a Pahlavi translation with commentaries, the *Zand*.

Later literature includes the Old Persian (Achaemenid) and Middle Persian (Sasanian) inscriptions, the "Pahlavi (Middle Persian) Books," and modern literature from Iran and India in Persian and Gujarati.

Early Zoroastrian literature as oral compositions

The Avestan texts were the results of a millennia-long transmission of oral compositions. As time passed and its composers moved from place to place, their language was adapted to the spoken languages, while the contents stayed fairly stable. At some time, however, for some reason, certain texts came to be regarded as sacred and immutable, and, by and by, the Young Avestan-speaking priests no longer understood the compact and allusive *Gāthās* composed in a language long since dead. There must therefore have existed oral translations and explanations of the texts, the *Zand*, which no longer rendered the original accurately and which, over time, became part of a larger exegetical tradition that was transmitted down through the generations and was constantly adapted to new times and places. We see these local traditions surface in the Achaemenid and Sasanian inscriptions.

By the first centuries of Arab domination, a large corpus of oral traditions had been accumulated, which was referred to in the Pahlavi literature as the Tradition (*dēn*). Even after writing became common, the oral tradition was considered superior [cf. 136:12–13], and the authors more often refer to what is "said in the Tradition" than to what is "written".

There was also an unwritten epic tradition, fragments of which are preserved in the *Avesta* and the Pahlavi books, but which was written down only from the tenth century on in New Persian by Ferdowsi (the *Shāh-nāme* "Book of Kings") and others [Intro. section 3].

Avestan texts

Excerpts from the following texts are included here:

The *Yasna* in seventy-two sections (*Yasna* 1–72) was mainly recited during the morning ritual (*yasna*). It includes the *Old Avesta*, comprising the *Yasna Haptanghāiti*, the "Sacrifice in Seven Sections" (*Yasna* 35–41) and the five *Gāthās*, "songs": the "Song of the New Life" (*Yasna* 28–34), "Song of the Wishes" (*Yasna* 43–46), "Song of the Life-giving Spirit" (*Yasna* 47–50), "Song of the Good Command" (*Yasna* 51), and "Song of the Good Ritual" (*Yasna* 53). The first and last strophes of the *Gāthā* collection, the *Ahuna Wairiya* (Pahlavi *Ahunwar*) and the *Airyamā Ishiyō* (*Yasna* 54.1), as well as two short texts based on the first strophe of *Yasna* 43, the *Ashem Wohū* , "Order (is) Best," and the last of *Yasna* 51, the *Yenghyē hātām*, "of him among those who are," were considered especially sacred and powerful and were recited throughout the *Avesta* and at all kinds of official and private rituals [110:13–15].

The *Videvdad* (or *Vendidad*) in twenty-one chapters, Avestan *vī-daēwō-dāta*, "the law (*dāta*) for how to keep the evil gods (*daēwa*) away (*vī*)," deals mainly with pollution and purification [chap. 8].

The *yasht*s are short and long hymns to individual deities. Some were recited at certain seasonal festivals: the *yasht*s to Mithra at the Mihragān festival at harvest time; that to Tishtriya at the Tīragān around mid-summer; and that to the *frawashi*s, "pre-souls," at the Frawardīgān at New Year about April 1 [17:49–52; 136:26, 26a].

The *Khorde Avesta*, "little *Avesta*," of which most Zoroastrians possess a copy, contains miscellaneous short texts in Avestan, Pahlavi, and Persian, such as confession texts (*patīt*) and prayers recited when tying the *kusti* and before eating and urinating. The *Niyāyishn*s, "invocations" to the sun, Mithra, moon, waters, and fire are recited daily or monthly.

Achaemenid-, Seleucid-, and Parthian-period inscriptions

The Achaemenids (the dynasty founded by Cyrus the Great) were, to our knowledge, the first Iranians to use writing, inspired by their literate neighbors, Elamites, Assyrian–Babylonians, and Arameans.

Most of their inscriptions (in Old Persian) come from Iran, but some from as far away as Suez in Egypt. The earliest known is the Bisotun (Behistun) inscription (520 BCE), in which Darius I (522–486 BCE) narrates how he came to power and united the Iranian lands. In his later inscriptions, he talks about his various achievements, as well as his relationship with Ahura Mazdā. His son and successor, Xerxes I (486–465 BCE), followed his father's example, while most of the inscriptions of subsequent kings (e.g., Artaxerxes II, 405–359) contain little more than their ancestry and a list of the lands of their empire. Most of the inscriptions are trilingual in Old Persian, Elamite, and Babylonian, and of the Bisotun inscription there is also an Aramaic version on papyrus. The inscriptions contain numerous Avestan echoes and, probably, more or less direct citations [83].

Coins and a few inscriptions remain from the Seleucid (330–247 BCE) and Parthian periods, as well as from the rulers of Pārs (Greek Persis, modern Fārs, whence *Persia, Persian,* and *Farsi*), the homeland of the Achaemenids and the Sasanians.

Sasanian inscriptions
Most of the third- and fourth-century Sasanian kings, beginning with Ardashīr I (224–240), left inscriptions. Ardashīr's son Shāpūr I (240–70) left a long trilingual (Persian, Parthian, and Greek) inscription (260) describing his empire, his battles with three Roman emperors, the fire-temples he founded, and his relationship with the gods [124]. His son Narseh (291–302) left a long bilingual (Persian and Parthian) inscription (293), which narrates how he was chosen king by the dignitaries of the realm in the place of his great-grand-nephew, who, still very young, was, allegedly, under the influence of an evil conselor.

The inscriptions of the high priest Kerdīr, whose career lasted from Shāpūr I to Narseh I, date from the beginning of Shāpūr's grandson Warahrān II's rule (274–91). In them he details his career and beliefs [84; 130] and recounts his visionary journey into the beyond [85].

The Pahlavi books

Parts of the Zoroastrian Tradition were written down from the ninth century onward. The earliest dated text is the *Dēnkard*, "what is done according to the Tradition" (?), in nine books (the extant manuscript begins in book 3). It was begun by Ādurfarnbay, son of Farrokh-zād [1:7], a leading high priest in the early ninth century featured in several Pahlavi texts, among them a narrative of a debate with Abālish, a heretic, in the presence of the Abbasid caliph 'Abd-Allāh al-Ma'mūn (813–33) [135]. The *Dēnkard* was completed by Ādurbād, son of Ēmēd [1:9].

Other named authors include the two late-ninth-century brothers Zādspram, high priest of Sīrgān, a city south of Kerman, and Manushchihr, high priest in Shiraz and Kerman. Zādspram is credited with the *Wizīdagīhā*, "Selections" of texts on cosmology, eschatology, and other issues, while Manushchihr wrote several *Letters* to his brother, as well as the *Dādestān ī dēnīg*, "Judgments according to the Tradition" (completed 881). Appended to the latter in the manuscripts is the *Pahlavi Rivāyat*, a collection of information on various topics. The *Bun-dahishn*, "first creation," texts on cosmology, eschatology, and other issues, was written by Spandyād son of Māhwindād son of Rustom Shahriyār, about whom nothing else is known.

The old manuscript MK (1322) contains a miscellany of texts, among them the *Book of Deeds of Ardashīr, son of Pābag* [p. 28], the *Memorial of Zarēr* [p. 29], the *Book of Advice of Zarathustra* [92], *The Coming of Shā-Wahrām* [68], and *Some sayings of Ādurbād son of Mahraspand* [94].

Some texts are in question-and-answer form, including several of the above and the *Dādestān ī mēnōy khrad*, "Judgements of the Divine Wisdom" [93] and the *Pursishnīhā* "questions."

Visions of the beyond, aimed at verifying the contents of the Tradition, include those of Kerdīr [85], Wishtāsp and Zarathustra, and Ardā Wirāz.

Issues of religious and secular law are discussed in *Shāyist nē shāyist*, "What is proper (to do) and what is not" [113], and in the Pahlavi commentaries in the *Videvdad* [114–118], as well as in the *Hērbedestān*, "handbook for priests," *Nīrangestān*, "handbook of rituals," and the law book, *Book of a Thousand Judgements*.

On the translations

Zoroastrianism is known from a period of several millennia, so its world view must have changed over time as the Iranians moved and met other peoples. One problem in interpretating the texts is therefore how to define the central terms in the various periods. Another is the difficulty presented by English terminology that suggests modern concepts that should not be applied to the original texts. I have therefore avoided standard religious terminology, which, I feel, inappropriately suggests similarities with modern religions, as is the case with the translations in the *Sacred Books of the East, Pahlavi Texts* (www.sacred-texts.com/zor) and many modern translations. To achieve this, I have used terminology that will seem unfamiliar to those already acquainted with Zoroastrian literature in translation, but which will, I hope, cause the reader to think about what the terms could have meant to the people who used them. Thus a certain willingness on the part of the reader to be thus steered toward the past is required.

Note, in particular, that the frequent term *sacrifice* does not refer exclusively to animal sacrifice [112–113; 136:23], but also to the ritual consecrating and offering of gifts to gods, including water libations and food offerings [Intro. section 8].

The *Gāthās* are complex poems with multiple levels of reference: the human and divine worlds; the sacrifice, which connects the two; and the world of the poet. What precisely the Gathic poets understood by their terminology very often escapes us. Here, the translations from the *Gāthās* have been fleshed out to be readable (according to my concept), but without necessarily marking added words by parentheses. To understand the translations, the Introduction section 8 should be read first. A not so obvious reference of the important term *manyu* is to the poet's world, where it may refer to the (divine) inspiration.

Divine names have been translated for the *Old Avesta*, but, for the *Young Avesta*, Ahura Mazdā, Angra Manyu, Sraosha, etc. (Pahlavi Ohrmazd, Ahrimen, Srōsh, etc.) have been kept.

Translations of incongruous-looking Pahlavi terms that render Avestan are sometimes marked by quotes.

The style of many of the Pahlavi authors can be awkward and cumbersome and very difficult to render. Some of the translations here may still reflect the original style to some degree, although I have mostly rendered such texts relatively freely, often leaving out incomprehensible words and passages. Note that explanations of (Pahlavi) translations from Avestan are often introduced by "i.e.;" see, especially, the ritual texts in chapter 8.

2 Creation and the Divine World

Cosmic Contrasts and the Two Spirits

In the *Avesta* we see a universe divided between the worlds of gods and living beings and caught up in a battle between good and evil. The other world, that "of thought," can only be apprehended by thought, while this world, that "of living beings" (Young Avestan *gaēthiya*, Pahlavi *gētīy*) or the world "with bones", is conceived and born as a living being. The two worlds (Avestan *ahu*) oscillate between the states of good and evil, light and darkness, health and sickness, life and death, and, in this two-by-two scenario, all things in the universe, including gods and men, belong in one or the other camp in the conflict. The return to the state of light and life is effected when, strengthened by the sacrifices offered by humans, Ahura Mazdā regains command of the universe, the good deities overcome the evil ones, and the universe is healed and reborn [107; 110:1–2].

The origins of good and evil are two Spirits (Avestan *manyu* "mental impulse, inspiration"), depicted as "twin 'sleeps' (= sleeping things)," presumably twin fetuses embodying contrasting and irreconcilable potentials for good and evil. When these two Spirits "come together" (in battle), the next existence will be determined [6]. At that point, all beings, including the gods, must declare for good or evil by *choosing* either Order or chaos [6:5], as must every Mazdayasnian by uttering the *Frawarānē* [109], compare *Yasna* 10.16, "I belong to the sustainer of Order, not to the one possessed by the Lie, and that will be so until in the end, when the victory between the two spirits comes about."

Yasht 13 to the *frawashi*s contains a brief descripion of the primordial conflict between them and the final victory of the good Spirit over the evil one [17:12–13], and more detail is found in the Pahlavi texts. A reference to the initial defeat of the Evil Spirit as told in the Pahlavi texts is preserved in the hymn to Best Order: "He fell headlong from under heaven, the most lying of the evil gods, the destructive Evil Spirit. He howled: 'Woe to me! Blast Best Order! He will smite the worst of the illnesses (that I made)'" (*Yasht* 3.13–14).

The good Spirit is "Life-giving" (Avestan *spenta manyu*, Pahlavi *spenāg mēnōy*), a characteristic of all good entities in the world of thought. The underlying idea is "swelling," that is, with the juices of fertility and fecundity, which the Sasanian scholars understood as "making increase" (the translation as "holy" obscures the meaning). Thus, in the *Old Avesta*, the purpose of the battle is to revitalize the world by making it *frasha* "Juicy" [p. 30].

The other spirit is *angra*, which may originally have meant "dark, black." The Sasanian scholars understood his name as the Foul Spirit, referring to the *stench* coming from evil beings (cf. Old Persian *gasta* "foulness" [120:5; 124:2; 129:8]), but also interpreted *angra* as "killing" [71:101]. Here, *angra* is translated as "Dark" in the *Gāthās* and Angra Mainyu as "Evil Spirit" in the young Avestan texts.

In the *Young Avesta*, the other world is thought of as controlled by one or the other spirit and is called "that of the Spirits" (Avestan *manyawa*, Pahlavi *mēnōy*).

The two worlds can be simply referred to as "divine" and "human," but the common translation of *manyawa* (*mēnōy*) as "spiritual" should be avoided, as it is likely to evoke ghosts or ancestor spirits. The world of living beings or "with bones" can be referred to as "material" in the sense of "concrete."

Order and Chaos

Ahura Mazdā's first world was an ordered world, where everything was in its proper place. The principle of the cosmic order was Avestan *asha* (or *erta*, Old Indic *rta*), here rendered as "Order," the literal meaning being probably "something (harmoniously) fitted together." It was produced by Ahura Mazdā's thought [7:7], and its visible form is the day-lit sky with the sun.

The texts also suggest that the cosmic order was thought of as a perfectly woven "fabric" (*dāman*). This fabric contained all the original divine "models" (*ratu*, Old Indic *rtu*) for the cyclical recreations of the two worlds [p. 35].

The term *asha* is often rendered as "truth," but this English word can be misleading, since *asha* never means "truth" in the usual sense, as in he "spoke the truth," which is expressed by words meaning "straight" or "real."

The opposing principle is the cosmic deception or Lie (*drug*, *druj*, Old Persian *drauga*), which deceives men and gods as to the true nature of the universe, making them think the wicked are good, and so on: *Yasna* 43.15, "For *they* claim that all the Dark (*angra*) ones are sustainers of Order." Again, this word is not used in the common sense of English "lie," although "to lie" is *drujya-*, literally "deceive (by words)." Untruth is expressed by terms meaning "crooked" and "devious" or "unreal."

Those on the side of Order are called "sustainers of Order," those on the side of the Lie "possessed by the Lie." In the Pahlavi texts, I have occasionally used these translations, but also Righteous(ness) and wicked(ness), although the reader should keep in mind the original meanings. For "sustainer of Order," "living by Order" and similar renderings are sometimes preferable. It may help to think of the cosmic Order as governing everything that functions according to the divine laws of the Ordered cosmos.

Cosmos and chaos are also represented by Good Thought as the sunlit day sky, contrasted with Wrath as the dark, sunless night sky, in which the deities of the good creation are seen as stars battling against darkness: Yasna 48.7, "Let Wrath be tied down and Obstruction cut back, O you who wish to stretch hither and fasten the covering of Good Thought!" (cf. [46:4]).

The pair asha–drug clearly continues the old Indo-European concept of cosmos and chaos. In Iran, the original state of the universe before Ahura Mazdā ordered it was darkness, implicit in the statement that Ahura Mazdā caused the spaces to be suffused by light [7:7]. Chaos was a subversion of Ahura Mazdā's cosmos, caused by the supremacy of the powers of evil when strengthened by the sacrifices of those opposed to Ahura Mazdā, including evil poets and sacrificers (the Gathic kawi and karpan, Pahlavi kays and karbs).

At the end of time, asha will "have bones," and the cosmos will be permanently ruled by asha [p. 29].

Creation

Things come into existence by birth; by being fashioned, as by a carpenter or another artisan; or, simply, by being made. Once produced, things are set in place (dā-), which is the most generic Avestan term to denote creation (there is no creation "from nothing"). Evil things are "whittled" into existence, that is, inexpertly fashioned. Since the terms "create" and "creation" today mean different things to different people, it may be useful to think of the Old Iranian creations as artistic creations and Ahura Mazdā as the master artisan, who creates by his artistry [4:1; 5:3], while Angra Manyu's creations are inexpert and shapeless. Most commonly, it was Ahura Mazdā who set in place the creations [3; 4; 8; 17: 1–11], but the two Spirits and, sometimes, other gods also have this function [17:29, 76]. In Videvdad chapter 1, Angra Manyu makes his evil creations (pollution, illnesses, natural disasters, etc.) as Opponents (paitiyāra, Pahlavi petyārag) of those of Ahura Mazdā.

In the *Old Avesta*, creation by birth, involving father and mother, both cosmic and human, is frequently referred to [8:3; 44:5]. For the bodily constituents, see pp. 30–2.

According to the Pahlavi texts, the history of the world began when Ahrimen threatened Ohrmazd, which prompted him to create the two worlds and assign a temporal duration to them. Once the world of living beings had been born, Ahrimen assaulted it and polluted it with his evil creatures, upon which the creations were set in motion [17:53–57; 24:35; 27:23]. The duration of the created universe is 12,000 years = 3000: creation of the world of thought; 3000: creation of the world of the living in the world of thought (like a fetus), without the Opposition, and its birth; 3000: the Mixture, the world of the living after the Assault, with the Opposition, as a battle field between good and evil; and 3000: return to the origins, without evil [2.4.6–7].

Gods

In the *Old Avesta*, divine beings are referred to as "lords" (*ahura*, Old Indic *asura*), among them the heavenly fire, Ahura Mazdā's son, but they are mostly anonymous. In the *Yasna Haptanghāiti*, the heavenly waters, as well as various ritual objects of female grammatical gender, are invoked as "Ahura Mazdā's Women (*gnā*)" and as "ladies (*ahurānī*) of the divine lord" [5].

The Young Avestan term for "deity, god" is *yazata*, literally "worthy of sacrifices" (only male deities), which is an epithet of Ahura Mazdā in the *Old Avesta* (*Yasna* 41.3).

The Old Persian term was *baga* (Pahlavi *bay*) which, in the *Young Avesta*, still probably meant "distributor, apportioner," said of Ahura Mazdā and the Moon. The stars were set in place by him (*Videvdad* 19.23), as were Ohrmazd's dwelling [30:50] and the paths of the heavenly bodies [14:35; 17:54]. The Sasanian inscriptions have both *bay* from Old Persian and *yazd* from the Avestan [125; 130:9]. Pahlavi uses *yazd*, while *bay* is used as a title, Lord, Majesty (of kings).

Ahura Mazdā and the Life-giving Immortals are the principal deities and among those most frequently invoked. Only these and Airyaman are mentioned explicitly by name in the *Old Avesta*.

Young Avestan deities are as numerous as the stars [16:1], and several deities are identified with stars, many of the others, no doubt, also with constellations. This led earlier scholars to assume that they were survivals from pre-Zoroastrian times that resurfaced as the Prophet's teachings were forgotten and distorted. There is no textual or historical basis for this assumption, however. A few of them still have their old Indo-Iranian names, but most of the Zoroastrian gods and demons are deified abstract notions, especially emotions. The origin of this nomenclature is no doubt to be found in the macro-/micro-cosmic (ritual) correspondences the ancient (Indo-)Iranians saw in the world.

The Achaemenid kings Darius and Xerxes invoked only Ahuramazdā by name in their inscriptions, while acknowledging there were others [119:62–63; 121:3–4], but later kings also invoked Mithra and Anāhitā [124:2]. Similarly, the early Sasanian kings Ardashīr and Shāpūr invoked only Ohrmazd by name, but also referred to "(all) the gods" [125], and Narseh mentioned Anāhīd and "all the (other) gods."

Ahura Mazdā

The supreme deity was Ahura Mazdā, literally, "the All-knowing (ruling) Lord," where *maz-dāh* is an adjective meaning approximately "he who places (everything) in his mind" (not "wisdom," as commonly rendered). In the *Gāthās*, the two epithets are still independent words, while, in the *Young Avesta*, Ahura Mazdā had become a single name, and it is doubtful whether the original meaning was still known. By the Achaemenid period, the name was one word, Ahuramazdā, which in turn became Middle Persian Ohrmazd, Hormazd, and similar.

Ahura Mazdā ordered the cosmos and upholds the cosmic Order, and he is the benevolent ruler of the ordered cosmos. He is said to be the father of several gods: in the *Gāthās*, Good Thought, Order, and Ārmaiti–Humility; in the *Young Avesta*, all the Life-giving Immortals, as well as several other deities [7:8; 8:3; 9:4; 10:2; 13:2;

19:3]. His abode is the House of Song (*garō-dmāna, garō-nmāna,* Pahlavi *Garōdmān*) [19:3; 26:8; 30:16, 34; 61:14; 62:17; 69:39; 82:32; 88:11; 135:9].

Ahura Mazdā also sees to it that his fellow deities, who are all needed for victory over the forces of darkness and the good functioning of the cosmos, receive their share of sacrifices and praise; by sacrificing to them himself, he provides Zarathustra with the model for humans to do likewise [14:1; 15:17–19].

The Life-giving Immortals
Ahura Mazdā was closely associated with the Life-giving Immortals (Avestan *amesha spentas,* Pahlavi *amahrspands, ameshāspands* [26: 14–22]):

1. Good (Best) Thought (*vohu manah,* Pahlavi *wahuman, wahman*);
2. Best Order (*asha vahishta,* Pahlavi *ashwahisht, ardwahisht, urdwahisht*);
3. Well-deserved Command (*khshathra wairiya,* Pahlavi *khshahrewar, shahrewar*);
4. Life-giving Humility (*spentā ārmaiti,* Pahlavi *spandarmad*);
5. Wholeness (*haurwatāt,* Pahlavi *hordad*);
6. Undyingness (i.e.,) (*amertatāt, amertāt,* Pahlavi *amurdad*), probably "not dying before one's time" (rather than "immortality").

The six were probably brought into existence by Ahura Mazdā's primordial sacrifice: Good Thought (~ the sunlit sky) was the ordering principle which brought forth Best Order (~ the sun and the sunlit spaces); the Well-deserved reward for this creation was the royal Command; his daughter, Life-giving Ārmaiti-Humility (~ the earth), was also his consort, who, together with her father and spouse (as god of heaven), brought forth Wholeness and Undyingness (~ water/rain and plants).

In the *Young Avesta,* the six are normally listed as a group, which often includes Ahura Mazdā and is then referred to as "the Seven Life-giving Immortals."

The six also represent man, fire, metals, the earth, water/rain, and plants, respectively, who are also their helpers [26:14–22], and their names are sometimes used alone to refer to these elements [cf. 12:125; 57:37].

Avestan *ārmaiti* is rendered here as Humility, that is, as an obedient spouse and daughter (also, *humility* is from Latin *humus* "earth"). The literal meaning may be "thinking in right measure," contrasting with "thinking beyond the right measure, disrespect, scorn" (*tarōmaiti*, Pahlavi Tarōmad). The common rendering as "right-mindedness" may produce wrong associations.

Instead of Well-deserved, *wairiya* is often rendered as (something) "to be chosen," but the word is most common as an epithet of rewards and is never used as a verb.

In Pahlavi, the original meanings of these terms were obviously no longer apparent, and they are left untranslated here.

Airyaman

Airyaman (Pahlavi Ērman) was the god of healing and harmonious unions. He is invoked in the *Airyamā Ishiyō*, the last stanza of the *Gāthā* collection [104] and in the last chapters of the *Videvdad* [p. 36]. He also participates in the Perfectioning of the world [70:18].

Other divine beings

Sraosha (Pahlavi Srōsh), literally, perhaps, "readiness to listen," the willingness of gods and humans to listen to one another, was already in the *Old Avesta*, apparently, a warrior god with the ancient epithet *verthra-jan* "obstruction-smashing" (*Yasna* 44.16).

In the *Young Avesta*, Sraosha, "with the defiant mace," is a warrior god, whose main function is to destroy evil gods and other harmful beings, especially Wrath (*aēshma*), who smashes the sun with his "bloody mace" and bathes the sky in blood. The hymn to Sraosha (*Yasna* 56–57) is therefore recited just before sunrise to invigorate him for the showdown with the powers of darkness.

Sraosha was also the first sacrificer and the first to recite the *Gāthās* in the world of thought (*Yasna* 57.8), and, according to the later tradition, he presided over the punishment for sins in the hereafter.

Ashi (also Ashish Wanghwī "good Ashi"; Pahlavi Ard, Ahlishwang, Ashishwang), Sraosha's companion (*Yasna* 43.12), was goddess of "the sending off," presumably of the rewards. She was Mithra's charioteer [12:66–67] and also, apparently, that of Zarathustra in his fight with the Evil Spirit [49:21].

She was closely associated with Sraosha, as his epithet *ashiya* "accompanied by Ashi" (?) implies (Pahlavi Srōsh-ahlī, whose meaning was no longer understood, was replaced by Srōsh-ahlaw "righteous Srōsh"). She was often accompanied by Abundance (Pārendī, Pahlavi Pārand) [12:66].

Mithra and Rashnu (Pahlavi Mihr, Rashn) are not mentioned explicitly in the *Old Avesta*, but may be encrypted in *Yasna* 46.5: *MITHRAibyah . . . RASHNā* "by virtue of contracts, by straightness."

Mithra, whose name is distantly related to English *mutual*, was the overseer of obligations inherent in deals and contracts between gods and men, and men and men [12:2–4]. He was invoked by warriors before battle to make him strike fear into the hearts of those who break peace treaties. He would never sleep, had an inordinately large number of eyes and ears, and was able to survey vast areas like a shepherd, as implied by his epithet "having wide pastures" (Avestan *vouru-gaoyaoti*, Pahlavi Frākh-gōyōd, where the original meaning was no longer apparent). He dwelt in a house fashioned by Ahura Mazdā and the Life-giving Immortals on the top of Mount Harā, the mountain in the middle of the earth (around which heaven turns), which is unsullied by evil (*Yasht* 10.50–51). At dawn, he would go forth from there in front of the sun to clear its path [12:13]. He was identified with the morning star, Aphrodite (Venus), according to Herodotus (1.131).

Rashnu, "the straightener," was the god of everything straight, including straight (not crooked) behavior and spinning and weaving. According to the Pahlavi texts, he was one of the judges in the beyond [86:117]. See chapter 6. A related deity with unclear function was Rectitude (Arshtāt) [26:22].

Ardwī Sūrā Anāhitā (Old Persian Anāhitā, Pahlavi Ardwīsūr or Anāhīd) was a female deity identified with the heavenly river, probably the Milky Way. Her hymn is *Yasht* 5. She is named by her epithets "lofty, rich in life-giving strength, unattached" (or: "unsullied"), which qualify an implied noun "water" (explicit in *Yasna* 65.1).

Tishtriya (Pahlavi Tishtar) was the Iranian name of the star Sirius (the Dog Star), who fought drought personified as the demon Apaosha, and the Witch of Bad Seasons, as well as the "witches" who fall from heaven (shooting stars). In his hymn (*Yasht* 8; [14]), his battle with Apaosha to release the waters is described, in which he is aided by the star Satawaēsa (Fomalhaut) [14:9].

Werthraghna (Pahlavi Warahrān, Wahrām) was the victorious warrior god and one of Mithra's companions [12:66, 70–71], who would smash (*-ghna*) the obstruction or valor (*werthra*) of his opponents (*Yasht* 14). He had ten different shapes, all powerful males: the impetuous wind [14:33–34], a bull, a white horse, a rutting camel, an aggressive male boar, a man of fifteen, etc.

Wāyu (Old Indic Vāyu, Avestan Wayu, Pahlavi Wāy), originally, perhaps, the god of the wind that blows through the space between heaven and earth, was the god of the intermediate space itself [24:5–6], through which the souls of the dead must travel [86:115; 87:23]. Wāyu was therefore associated with inflexible destiny and had both a good and a bad side. *Yasna* 53.6 probably contains an allusion to Wāyu, where the poet tells the rivals that their compositions (differently from the *Gāthās* [111:2]) will be "foul food for you traveling through (or: mounted on) Wāyu." He plays an important part in Pahlavi cosmogony [24:5–6, 44–45, 53; 26:5, 17; 30:31].

Haoma (Pahlavi Hōm), the deity of the sacrificial drink *haoma*, is not mentioned explicitly in the *Old Avesta*, a fact that was long taken as an indication that (the historical) Zarathustra had banished its use. Haoma's ancient epithet *duraosha* is mentioned, however, the meaning of which is contested, but later understood as "the one who keeps death away." He is also, perhaps, encrypted in *Yasna* 29.7 in a list of sacrificial foods: "he, the lord, fashioned the poetic thought of the libation (*āzuti*) for the cow, as well as the milk (*khshwid*), he *who has the same taste* (*hazaoshah*), *the All-knowing one*, as Order," where HAzAO*shah* MAz*dāh* contains *haoma* and *hazaoshah* rhymes with *duraoshah*.

The hymn in praise of Haoma (*hōm-stawan*, *Yasna* 9–11 [p. 2]) is recited during the preparations for the pressing of the *haoma*-plant (Indic *soma*), which occurs at *Yasna* 27 [110]. The juice of the *haoma* had numerous positive effects [108:16–28].

The identity of the original plant is still disputed, but may have changed throughout the history of the Iranian and Indo-Aryan tribes. Today *haoma* is made from the ephedra plant.

The Fire (Avestan Ātar, Pahlavi Ādur) was the heavenly fire, the sun, son of Ahura Mazdā, but also inherent in the ritual fires.

The divine Fortune or munificence (Avestan *khwarnah*, Old Persian *farnah*, Pahlavi *khwarrah*) is an elusive entitity. Its Young Avestan hymn (*Yasht* 19) describes how the Fortune of the Poets (*kawis*) followed the heroes of the first ages and how the "unseizable (?) Fortune," which, when hidden in the Wourukasha Sea, was desired and fought over by gods, including the two Spirits, as well as by heroes and villains [34; 36; 39]. According to the hymn to the Sun (*Yasht* 6; [16]), when the sun shines, innumerable deities (the stars?) distribute it over the earth for the benefit of living beings.

In the Pahlavi literature, the Fortune is sometimes associated with royalty, but also with birth, notably those of Zarathustra and the mountains [23:5; 57:2–3, 46]. In the Pahlavi texts it is defined as "fulfilling one's own work," that is, one's specific duties according to one's social position [31:8; 57:5]. The adjective "endowed with Fortune" is rendered here as "Fortunate" or "munificent." Because it is often associated with luminosity, the word is commonly rendered by the potentially misleading term "Glory."

The divine "pre-existing soul" or "pre-soul," *frawashi* (Pahlavi *frawash, frawahr, fraward*)—fashioned by Ahura Mazdā (or the Amahrspands) according to the Pahlavi texts—enters into the fetus of every individual at birth, where it helps weave the bodily tissues inside which the innards are contained [17:11; 57:14, 46]. At death, they return to heaven, where, similarly, they assist Ahura Mazdā and the Life-giving Spirit in giving birth to the living cosmos [17:1–4], and they return to earth at New Year to be generously treated and reinvigorated for their participation in the rebirth of the cosmos [17:49–52]. All things in the good creation have a pre-soul, beginning with Ahura Mazdā, the Life-giving Immortals, and the sun, and ending with Astwad-erta, the final Revitalizer [17:80–145; p. 29]. They are depicted as female warriors fighting evil, as well as distributing rain to the fields of their supporters, but there is no reason to regard them as "guardian spirits (or: angels!)" as is often done. Their hymn is *Yasht* 13, and they are frequently invoked in the rituals.

In the Pahlavi texts, the expressions "having a good *fraward*" and "to whose *frawahr* we sacrifice" are used of Zarathustra and other ancient leaders of the Tradition.

The *Daēnā māzdayasni*, the Mazdayasnian Daēnā or Tradition, literally, the Vision(-soul) of those who sacrifice to Ahura Mazdā, is the cosmic Girdle (*kusti*), who is also among the battling gods [12:68, 126; 13:16; 90; 98–101]. The fortress Awareness-of-the-Righteous, made from the Fortune of the Tradition and guarded by *frawashis*, surrounds the sky to contain the forces of evil [29:6a3; 71:100; p. 31].

The Life-giving Word (*manthra spenta*, Pahlavi Mānsr-spand, Mahr-spand) was probably Ahura Mazdā's (poetic) thought expressed in words. It is identical with his (breath-)soul [17:80] and is also (the courser of ?) the chariot of the sun [90].

The Righteous (or Expert) Man and Expert Invitation (Avestan *dahma nar* and *dahmā āfriti*, Pahlavi Mard ī ahlaw and Dahmān Āfrīn) hold up the sky [23:4]. The latter is also the name of a text (*Yasna* 60.2–7) and appears in the shape of a camel (*Pursishnīhā* 31).

The *dāmi* is an elusive Old Avestan entity [7:7–8; 8:4]. If the word is related to Persian *dām* "net," he may be the Web-keeper (thus here) in charge of the orderly cosmic web; if it is related to Old Indic *dāman* "tether" he could be in charge of the heavenly horses, among them those of the chariots of the sun and Mithra. The *Young Avesta* knows a deity called the One in the likeness of the Web-keeper [12:66, 68,

127]. He is associated with the Expert Man and the Expert Invitation in the *Yasna*.

Other divine entities include several who have hymns dedicated to them, such as the sun (*Yasht* 6) and the moon (*Yasht* 7) and the goddess Druwāspā, "she who has healthy horses *or* keeps the horses healthy" (*Yasht* 9), as well as some who do not, including the Scion of the Waters (Avestan, Old Indic Apām Napāt, Pahlavi Ābān Nāf), deity of the fire in the clouds [14:4, 34; 48:95]; Nairya Sangha, Nairyō-sangha (Pahlavi Nēryōsang), "the heroic announcement," the divine messenger [17:85; 31:5; 57:21; 62:15; 65:61]; Pahlavi Gōshurūn, the Gathic *gēush urwan*, "soul of the cow (or: bull)," in Pahlavi the soul of the Bull set in place alone, whose complaint to the gods prompted the appointment of Zarathustra [26:17; 28; 132:5]; and others.

Demons

Avestan *daēwa* (Old Persian *daiva*), unlike Old Indic *deva* (Latin *deus*), no longer referred to good gods. According to the *Gāthās*, the *daēwas* lost their divine status when they were deceived and made the wrong choice [6:6]. Thus, the Old Indic *devas* Indra, Sharva, and the twin Nāsatyas are the Young Avestan *daēwas* Indar, Sāuru, and Nānghaithya (Pahlavi Indar, Sāwul, Nānghaith), who try in vain to kill Zarathustra in *Videvdad* 19 [20:6–9; 24:54].

The memory of the good *daēwas* lingered, however [8:20], and their original status apparently survived in the expression "gods and men" (*Yasna* 29.4). According to the *Young Avesta*, the old gods interacted with men until Zarathustra forced them underground [47:14–15].

In order to suggest the gradual demonization of these entities, Old Avestan *daēwa* will be rendered as "(bad) old god," Young Avestan *daēwa* as "evil god," and Pahlavi *dēw* as "demon."

The ruler of the world of darkness is the Dark Spirit [9:2], Angra Manyu (Pahlavi Ahrimen), a name that, like Ahura Mazdā, becomes fixed only in the *Young Avesta*, when the original meaning of the name had probably been lost (here rendered as the Evil Spirit). In Pahlavi, he is called the Foul Spirit (Gannāg Mēnōy) and is said to have produced, in particular, Akōman (from Avestan "evil thought"), Indar, Sāwul, Nānghaith or Tarōmad ("scorn"), Tawrij, and Zairij to oppose the six Amahrspands [20; 56:43; 95:4–6].

Other demons include Wrath (Aēshma, Pahlavi Heshm), embodiment of the night sky; the evil Wāyu, through whom the souls of the wicked must travel to hell; the Bone-untier (Avestan *astō-widātu*, Pahlavi Astwihād), who separates body and soul [27:24; 30:68; 86:114–117; 92:31]; Akatasha (Pahlavi Aktash), "fashioner of evil things" [20:24–25]; Greed (? Waran) [20:30; 24:47; 80:1b; 95:5]; the female arch-demon Lust (? Āz) [20:31; 27:19]; the demons Drag-off and Drag-away (Pahlavi Frazisht and Wizisht, Avestan Wizarsha), who drag the souls of the wicked off to hell; and others [20:22; 27:19; 30:31].

The Creation of Living Beings

The *Avesta* contains no explicit description of the making of humans. In the *Avesta*, the first two living beings, the first Man, living but mortal (Avestan Gaya Martān, Pahlavi Gayōmard), and the Bull set in place alone (Avestan *gao* [*aēwō-dāta*], Pahlavi *gāw* [*ēk-dād*]) are mentioned in lists of *frawashi*s (*Yasna* 23.2, 26.5, *Yasht* 13.86–87) and in a list of entities to whom homage is paid and sacrifices are offered (*Yasna* 68.22, *Vispered* 21.2), in all of which they precede Zarathustra. The Bull set in place alone is also mentioned in the hymns to the moon, which is said to contain its "seed" (*chithra; Yasht* 7, *Niyāyishn* 3).

In the Pahlavi texts, however, we find more detailed stories about the two and their deaths after the Assault and how they became the ancestors of men and domestic animals [23:15, 28, 36–37; 25:12–14; 27:19–26; 29e–f; 31:1–5; 32:9].

The history of mankind in the golden age ruled by Yima is told in the *Videvdad* [18]. Living beings being immortal, to avoid overpopulation Ahura Mazdā sends floods that decimate them, but tells Yima to build a kind of bunker (*wara*), in which specimens of living beings are preserved. According to the Pahlavi texts, the bunker will be opened to repopulate the earth when the world again suffers depopulation caused by catastrophies during the last millennia of the world [65:56; 67:36].

The mythical setting of these stories is the Aryan Expanse (Avestan *airyanam vaējō*, Pahlavi Ērānwēz) of the Good Lawful River (Pahlavi the good Dāitī), the first of the lands Ahura Mazdā made (*Videvdad* 1.2) and where Ahura Mazdā [!], the ancient heroes, and Zarathustra all fought the powers of evil [15:17; 18:20; 23:13, 15; 25:12; 47:14; 62:3].

3 Mythical History and the Zarathustra Myth

Hero-sacrificers of the First Ages

Several of the longer *yashts* (5, 9, 15, 17, 19) contain lists of characters who sacrificed to the great gods in some specific location, on a mountain or by a river, asking the god to grant him or her a wish. The few who were not granted their wish are the villains in the post-Avestan epic.

The *Avesta* gives few details, but the standard nature of the lists and the character of the scanty references render it likely that we are dealing with ancient Zoroastrian–Iranian epic tradition. Parallel motifs in Indic epics suggest that some of the details go back to Indo-Iranian epic tradition, even to Indo-European traditions.

In the Pahlavi texts, the mythical past has become the mythical history of the kings of Iran from the creation of mankind via the birth and death of Zarathustra during the reign of King Kay Wishtāsp and onward to the historical reigns of the Achaemenids, Arsacids, and Sasanians until the Arab conquest. In the Persian epic, Ferdousi's *Shāh-nāme* "Book of Kings," this mythical history is told in even greater detail. Its central character Rostam, however, is still barely mentioned in the Pahlavi texts [40:10; 68].

The earliest myths

Haoshyangha (Pahlavi Hōshang) is the one who preceded all the others (Avestan *para-dāta*, Pahlavi/Persian *pēsh-dād* "set in place before (the others)"). In the *Avesta*, he is said to have ruled over (old) gods and men in all lands in the seven continents of the earth [12; 12; 23:9], and he was granted the ability to strike down two-thirds of the old gods. In the Pahlavi literature and the Persian epic, he is descended from the first two humans, and, in the Persian epic, his epithet becomes the name of the first royal dynasty.

Taxma Urupi (Pahlavi Tahmōraf) did much the same as Haoshyangha, but, in addition, "rode the Evil Spirit changed into the form of a horse for three hundred years around both borders of the earth" (*Yashts* 15.12, 19.29). In the Persian Zoroastrian literature, this is but part of a longer narrative, which involved his also being swallowed by Ahrimen and then being rescued by Jamshīd (Yima), who pulled him out of the devil's behind. This caused Jamshīd's hand to become leprous, and it was not healed until a cow urinated on it, which revealed the healing properties of cow's urine (Avestan *gao-maēza*, Pahlavi *gōmēz* [116; 135:6; 136:27]).

Yima or Yima khshaēta, "radiant (?) Yima" (Pahlavi Jam and Jamshēd), is related to the Old Indic Yama, who became king of the land of the Fathers (the departed ancestors). The Avestan Yima, however, became the first king of the earth, king of the golden age, chosen by Ahura Mazdā himself [18:4–6]. He sacrificed to the gods to be granted the ability to make living beings immortal and the climate temperate [47:4–5]. He was granted his wish, but, then, in some way, committed a transgression by lying or exhibiting hybris and, according to the later tradition, was cast down from his throne and roamed the earth until he was cut in half by Spitiyura (assisted by Dahāg), a shadowy character mentioned in the *Avesta* (*Yasht* 19.46 and said to be Jam's brother in the later literature (*Bun-dahishn* 35.3–5).

Azhi Dahāka, "the Giant (?) Dragon" (Pahlavi Azhidahāg/Azh-dahāg, Dahāg, Persian Zohhāk), is the villain of the first act of the mythical history, who sacrificed for ability to depopulate the earth, a wish that was not granted. The sacrifice was offered in the land of Babri, which may mean "of the beaver," but was later identified with Babylon, where he is in the Pahlavi tradition. Still later, the Persian epic made him an Arabic king. Even this late, his serpentine nature was remembered: two snakes grew from his shoulders, which needed to be satiated daily with fifteen male and fifteen female youths, reminiscent of the story of the Minotaur.

Thraētaona (Pahlavi Frēdōn) is the Iranian dragon slayer, who captured Azhi Dahāka, and, according to the Pahlavi tradition [35; 40:2; 41:26; 47:8], chained him in Mount Dumbāwand, Iran's great volcano, modern Demāvand northeast of Tehran. He also liberated two beautiful women, Sanghawāchī and Arnawāchī ("she who utters announcements" and "she who utters faults"?), who, in the later tradition, are said to be Jamshēd's sisters [35]. Thraētaona had three sons, who, according to the Pahlavi tradition, were to divide the earth among themselves after their father's death: Salm got Rome, Tūz Turkestan, and Ērij Iran [40:3; 41:26]. The two elder sons, however, killed the youngest, but were in turn killed by Manushchihr in revenge. Frēdōn became prematurely old for scorning Ohrmazd [62:9].

Thraētaona/Frēdōn was invoked for healing, and his name may be related to that of Thrita, the first human healer [30:26, 67].

Kersāspa (Pahlavi Karsāsp, etc.; Persian Garshāsp, Sām [Narīmān]) was a curly-headed youth who slayed several dragons, as well as the creature *gandarva* that lived in or by the Wourukasha sea. According to the Pahlavi texts, he lies asleep till the end of time, when he is awakened to slay Azhdahāg, who breaks loose from his bonds. [47:10; 63:61; 67:40–42; 69:31]

The Kawis

A series of characters with the epithet *kawi* (Pahlavi *kay*) are involved in fighting the arch-enemy of the Iranians, Frangrasyān (Pahlavi Frāsiyā[b], Persian Afrāsiyāb), the villain of the second act of the mythological history and a Turian/Turanian, a term contrasted with Aryan [39; 40:5–14].

Eight *kawis* are listed together in the *Avesta*: Kawāta, Aipiwohu, Usan (Usadhan), Arshan, Pisina, Biyarshan, Siyāwarshan [40:11–13; 41:38], and Haosrawah [36].

Kawi Usan (or Usadhan, Pahlavi Kāy-Us, Persian Kāvūs, Qābūs), about whom no details are given in the *Avesta* other than the standard wish to become ruler over the good and the bad, has narratives in the Pahlavi tradition, and the name is closely related to the Old Indic Kāvya Ushan [40:8–12; 41:37].

Kawi Haosrawah (Pahlavi Kay Husrōy, Persian Kay Khosrow) is the last of the old *kawi*s [37; 40:14; 41:39]. According to the Pahlavi tradition, he does not die, but lies asleep until the end of time, when he is awakened to fulfill his destiny [41:40; 69:31–33].

Haoma (Persian Hūm) is featured in this tradition as the hero who captured Frangrasyān and brought him to Kawi Haosrawah [38]. Compare the hymn to Haoma (*Yasna* 11.7): "May Haoma not bind you like he bound the villain, the Turian Frangrasyān, in the middle third of this earth, fettered in iron!"

Kawi Wishtāspa and the war against the Khiyonians

The third act of the mythical history features Zarathustra and several characters mentioned in the *Gāthās*, often referred to as "the Gathic circle," but without details. In the *Young Avesta* and later, they are involved in a battle against the Khiyonians and their king Arjad-aspa (Pahlavi Arzāsp) over the *daēnā* of Zarathustra of the Spitāmas, foremost among them Kawi Wishtāspa (Gathic Wishta-aspa, probably "he who give his horses free reins"; Pahlavi Kay Wishtāsp, Persian Kay Gushtāsp), son of Luhrāsp [2:14; 40:14–16; 41:41; 52; 54; 55].

Zarathustra and the Gathic characters in the Old Avesta

In the *Gāthās*, Zarathustra ("he who has angry *or* old camels"?) is presented as the first sacrificer in the world of the living and the other named characters as being in Ahura Mazdā's house [43; 45:14].

We find Zarathustra in the third, second, and first persons, and, if we look at the structure of the *Gāthās*, we see that the most significant third-person references are in the introduction and conclusion of the collection, which suggests that the Gathic poet is telling the story of Zarathustra, probably an early version of the Pahlavi Zarathustra narrative.

In the introduction to the first *Gāthā*, the narrator introduces the subject of his poems, expecting divine support such as that given to Zarathustra, by which he, too, overcame the forces of evil [42:6] and for which he will later request a reward [103]. Next we are told how Ahura Mazdā chose Zarathustra to perform the sacrifice in the world of the living [42], and, after a while, we see Zarathustra in the process of performing the sacrifice [102].

At the beginning of the second *Gāthā*, Zarathustra in the first person introduces himself as Ahura Mazdā's praise-singer [44:7–8; cf. 59:55–57]. He then imagines himself as the winner of the poetic contest and as receiving his rewards in Ahura Mazdā's House of Song together with Wishtāspa and other poet-sacrificers of the past, including the Huwagwa brothers Frashaoshtra and Jāmāspa (Gathic Frasha-ushtra "the one with fat camels" and Jāma-aspa "the one with scrawny horses) [45:14]. In the last stanza, the poet expresses the hope for a successful sacrifice, worthy of Zarathustra, and a handsome reward from Ahura Mazdā [45:19]. The sacrificer is now proabably playing the role, as it were, of Zarathustra, as does the sacrificer in *Yasna* 8 [107:7].

Toward the end of the third *Gāthā*, the poet again invokes the example of Zarathustra for divine support and rewards [46:12].

In the fourth *Gāthā*, the third-person references to Zarathustra accumulate, as the poet assures us that he is faithful to the example of Zarathustra (*Yasna* 51.11), that he can expect opposition on his (i.e., the sacrifice's) way to the divine presence, as happened to Zarathustra (*Yasna* 51.12), but that he trusts Zarathustra's promise of rewards (*Yasna* 51.15). This *Gāthā* contains a long list of members of the "Gathic circle" following a reference to the "fee" (*mizhda*) promised long ago by Zarathustra and with which Ahura Mazdā comes forward in the House of Song.

In the fifth *Gāthā*, the poet states the obvious: Zarathustra's sacrifice was, as told and praised, the best (*Yasna* 53.1). To succeed, the sacrificer must therefore follow his example, become a "son of Zarathustra," as did others, among them Wishtāspa (*Yasna* 53.2). Zarathustra's youngest daughter, Pouru-chistā ("the one noticed/noted by many"), like her father and Wishtāspa one of the Spitāmas, aids her father in chasing darkness and produce the new dawn (*Yasna* 53.3).

The *Gāthās* come to an end with the descent of Airyaman (*Yasna* 54.1; [104]), who brings support to those with Zarathustra's good thought.

Zarathustra and the Gathic characters in the Young Avesta

In the *Young Avesta*, we find Zarathustra—often addressed as *spitāma*, "of the Spitāmas," or "Spitāma-son"—sacrificing, praising Ahura Mazdā, and fighting the evil gods and the Evil Spirit by reciting the sacred utterances [47:13–15; 49:19–20; 56]. He is imitated by the current sacrificer, who also refers to himself as "Zarathustra", or a "Zarathustra-son" [107:7; 109].

In the hymn to Haoma, his birth is described as the reward his father Pourushāspa ("he who has grey horses") received for pressing the *haoma* [47:13]. In the hymn to the fravashis, all creatures are said to have rejoiced at his birth, and Zarathustra is presented as the proto-type of three social divisions, especially the successful sacrificer [48:87–90]. In several hymns, Ahura Mazdā is portrayed as sacrificing to other deities (including himself, *Yasht* 1.9) to give them the strength to fulfill their cosmic functions, thus providing Zarathustra with the model for his own successful sacrifice [12:119; 15:1].

Zarathustra also appears in the list of mythical sacrificers who sacrificed to obtain certain rewards. Zarathustra's requests include the ability to make both Wishtāspa and Hutaosā (Wishtāspa's queen in the later tradition) help his *daēnā* along with their thoughts, words, and deeds [51; 52:26].

Zarathustra's wife Hwōwī sacrificed to Chistā [53:15] for a good husband, and his mother Dugdōwā is mentioned in an Avestan fragment. There are also references to Zarathustra's sons, among them the three Revitalizers who will be born from their father's semen, preserved at the bottom of Lake Kansaoya [56:5; 63:62; 64:66, 92]. Zarathustra had other sons, as well [65].

Wishtāspā also sacrificed to Druwāspā to let him bring home from the Khiyonians Humāyā [52:32], who, in the later tradition, became Dārāy's mother (see below). Hutaosā, for her part, sacrificed to Wāyu so that Wishtāspa would make her mistress of his house [55].

Zarathustra and the Gathic characters in the Pahlavi texts and later

Here we find a fully developed Zarathustra legend, including the divine plan for him, his miraculous birth, his meeting with Wahman who brought him before Ohrmazd, his enemies, and the birth of his three eschatological sons [57–62]. The assembling of the components of Zarathustra is described as a *yasna* ritual [57:46–47; cf. 105:1; p. 35].

The story of how Wishtāsp received the Tradition (*dēn*) and his battle with the Khiyonians is also narrated in the *Memorial of Zarēr*, a heroic epic-style narrative of the war between Wishtāsp and Arzāsp over the Tradition brought by Zarathustra.

The historical period in the Pahlavi texts

In the Pahlavi texts, the historical dynasties follow after this. Wishtāsp's son Spandyād's daughter or grand-daughter (daughter of Wahman) Humā becomes Dārāy's (Darius) mother, perhaps because the Achaemenid Darius's father was also called Wishtāspa [119:1; 122–124].

Dārāy is followed by Dārāy, son of Dārāy, and Alexander. These early reigns, too, are by now legendary, strongly influenced by the earlier myths [40:19].

From the 500-year rule of the Arsacid kings, only the memory of a Walakhsh survived in the Pahlavi tradition.

Also from the early Sasanian centuries, few historical facts were preserved [40:20–26]. In *Bundahishn* chapter 33, only Ardakhshahr (Ardashīr) is mentioned from the third century and is followed directly by Shāpūr (II), son of Ohrmazd (II) [son of Narseh], while, in chapter 35, he is said to be descended directly from his namesake Ardaxshahr (memory of the Achaemenid Artaxerxes), son of Wahman, son of Spandyād. Elsewhere, however, Shāpūr, son of Ardakhshahr, is also mentioned, and the *Book of Deeds of Ardashīr, son of Pābag* contains the story of Ardashīr and his son Shāpūr, as well as the birth of his grand-son Ohrmazd (I).

4 ESCHATOLOGY AND THE END OF THE WORLD

Zarathustra's revelation initiates the last three millennia and the count-down to the end of the world. His three sons, the Revitalizers (Avestan *saoshyant*, Pahlavi Sōshāns), born from the semen preserved in Lake Kansaoya (Pahlavi Kiyānsī), will appear at intervals of a thou-sand years each to bring the world closer to the end: Ukhshyad-erta, "who makes Order grow" (Pahlavi Ushēdar); Ukhshyad-nemah, "who makes homage grow" (Ushēdar-māh); and Astwad-erta, "who gives Order bones" (Sōshāns) [63:128–129; 67:43–45]. We may note that, by the traditional count, 2000 CE would be about the middle of the millennium of Ushēdar-māh.

During this time, various disasters will depopulate the world, which will then be repopulated from Yima's bunker [66; 67:36]. Azhdahāg (Dahāg) will run free, but be slain by Kersāspa [67:40, 42; 69:31]. Wishtāsp's son Pishyōtan (Avestan Pishishyaothna) will lead a troop to destroy the idol temples [67:33].

Finally, Astwad-erta, the Saoshyant *par excellence*, will raise the dead [61:6; 70:3, 6–7, 16, 23; 92:15], and they will gather in the Assembly of Isad-wāstra, "seeker of pasture" (Pahlavi Isadwāstar [61:2; 65:56]), another son of Zarathustra [70:10–15]. The heavenly dragon (Gōchihr) will fall down and set the earth on fire [70:17]. Finally, after passing through a river of molten metal, mankind will all be purified of their sins and go to paradise [70:18–19; p. 33].

Sōshāns and his father will complete the chain of sacrifices in the world of the living [69:32–33; 70:23], cf. *Dēnkard* 9.33.5 "At the time of the Perfectioning, Zarathustra, being of the three times, will act as chief priest (*zōd*) for this whole world ... and Wishtāsp of the Nōdar family will act as the supervisory priest (*srōshāwarz*)."

Ahura Mazdā will then perform the last sacrifice assisted by Srōsh and so produce the Final Body, that is, the final, permanent existence, and the world will be permanently *frasha* "Juicy," that is, filled with the juices of fertility and fecundity [6:9; 45:19; 61:6; 69:34; 70:29; 71:100; 92:15; 103:15]. [For the later texts, when the original meaning of *frasha* had been lost, I have used the terms Perfect and Perfectioning; Renovation is also commonly used.]

It is unclear how much of the later eschatology is already in the *Old Avesta*, but the daily renewal of the world may have been thought to lead up to a final judgement and a final renewal, when Order would have bones and the world would be permanently *frasha*.

5 BODY AND SOUL

Man's basic bodily constituents and mental faculties are listed frequently in the *Avesta*, although we cannot always identify them. In the *Old Avesta*, they are mentioned as part of the gift exchange between god and man: they were given to man by god and, in their sacrifices, men return the gifts god gave them, but which belong to him.

Man consists of a tangible body and various intangible mental parts. Darius is particularly careful to point out that Ahuramazdā bestowed upon him both good mental and bodily qualities, and the punishments he inflicts consist in taking away the basic bodily functions [76].

Death occurs when consciousness and bones are wrenched apart and the consciousness leaves the body [92:23].

In the *Old Avesta*, two principal constituents of the body are "bones" (*ast*) and "life breath" or "vitality" (*ushtāna*), but there are also others, among them "form" (*kerp*) and "breathing" (*anman*), consciousness (*baodah*, Pahlavi *bōy*), as well as three that are not well understood: *ahu*, which usually refers to the macrocosmos, *gaēthās*, which usually means "living beings, herds," "tissue connectedness, texture" (*uta-yuti*) and "(tissue) strength" (*tawishī*), which appear to keep the body together [7:11; 103:13–14; cf. 72–73].

Few other aspects of the body are discussed in the *Avesta*. Already in the *Gāthās*, Life-giving Humility is said to purify mortal women after birth (*Yasna* 48.5), and we are told that Ardwī Sūrā Anāhitā purifies men's semen and women's wombs for conception, as well as the milk in females [15:2].

Avestan man has three "souls": the *frawashi*, "pre(existing)-soul"; the *urwan* (Pahlavi *ruwān*), "(breath-)soul"; and the *daēnā* (Pahlavi *dēn*), "vision(-soul)" [7:11; 72–73; 78–79]. Later there is also Pahlavi *gyān* (*jān*) "soul," without which there is no life [19:7; 26:15; 29e:3; 31:3; 71:100; 87:9; 92:15, 23; 97:13; 135:9; 136: 19a, 26].

The pre-soul is made in the world of thought and pre-exists the person, being sent down to the world of the living when a person is conceived to assist in the making of the fetus and at the birth [17:11]. It returns to the other world when the person dies. Zarathustra's *frawashi* had special importance, and Zarathustra often has the epithet "whose *frawashi* is revered." In the Pahlavi books, we have more detailed descriptions of the formation of children in the womb [70:5].

The (breath-)soul leaves the body at death and wanders into the beyond to be judged. In Pahlavi, the soul that keeps the body alive is the *gyān*, while the *ruwān* goes into the beyond [chapter 6].

The *daēnā* is what allows man to "see" in the world of thought, but she also appears to the (breath-)soul in the form of a woman representing the totality of a person's thoughts, words, and deeds in life, which determines how she looks and for which the soul is judged in the beyond [82; 87:15–16, 19–20]. The word is often translated as "religion," but this only applies to certain uses of *dēn* in the Pahlavi literature and there is no reason to think that the word may have had the modern meaning of religion in the *Avesta* and early Sasanian times. Here, it is left untranslated or rendered as Tradition, that is the (oral) Zoroastrian tradition [pp. 35–6].

Among mental faculties, "thought" or "mind" (*manah*) contrasts with speech and actions and primarily refers to thoughts, but also the mind, where thoughts are made and kept.

The mind contrasts with "wisdom" (*khratu*, Pahlavi *khrad*), which contains the accumulated "knowledge" or "learning" (Pahlavi *dānishn, dānāgīh*) and "awareness" (*āgāhīh*) of the world and guides in deciding what to do [76]. It has two components, the wisdom one is born with (*āsna khratu*, Pahlavi *āsn-khrad*) and the wisdom one acquires through experience, what one has "heard through the ear" (*gaoshō-sruta khratu*, Pahlavi *gōshōsrūd-khrad*) [13:2; 19:5; 80:56; 97:41; 99:2; 135:9]. See also [45:3–4; 103:14; p. 34].

In the *Young Avesta* and Darius's inscriptions, we see how removing basic mental and bodily faculties is used as punishment [74–76].

The texts list other faculties, as well, which are at times hard to define. For instance, Avestan and Old Persian *ushi* may originally have meant "ear," then something like "ability to hear" [74; 76], but Pahlavi *ōsh* (*ush*) appears to mean "intelligence" or "memory" and modern Persian *hūsh* is "consciousness," which was Avestan *baodah*, Pahlavi *bōy*, homonymous with "smell" (Avestan *baodi*, Persian *bū*).

In the Pahlavi texts, in addition to *ōsh* and *gyān*, there are some new terms that can only be tentatively defined from the contexts: *wārom*, some deep-seated organ, "core," *okh* (Avestan *ahu* and *ahwā*, the meaning and function of which are unclear), *khēm* "character," *khōg* "temperament, disposition," *wīr* "perception," *gōhr* "essence," *ēwēn* "(bodily?) frame," and others [19:7; 79–81;135:9; see also the references for "souls", p. 31].

6 DEATH, REWARDS, AND PUNISHMENT

At death, the body dies, but the pre-soul returns to heaven, while the (breath-)soul hovers at the bed of the dead for three nights. Then, at dawn, it starts its journey into the other world, accompanied by its *daēnā* (*dēn*) in the form of a woman [82:30; 85–87]. She takes the soul to the Ford of the Accountant (Pahlavi "Chinwad bridge" or "passage of lamentations") [45:10; 82:30; 85–87], where its thoughts, etc., are weighed by Rashn on a perfectly just balance [85:27; 86:119–120]. According to the weight of its good and bad thoughts, etc., the soul will then either cross that bridge, now as wide as long, and go on to the Best Existence [19:5; 60a:1; 108:19] and become "one with Order," or fall down from it into hell when it becomes as narrow as a razor's edge.

The souls of the wicked will be tortured in hell until the end of the world, when the dead will be raised and pass through a river of molten metal, which will burn out all remaining sins [70:16–21; cf. 71; p. 29].

As with the eschatology, it is not certain how much of this myth is already in the *Old Avesta*, but see [45:10–11].

Certain persons were able to visit the other world by means of a "twin," who would travel there to verify the truth of the Tradition [2:22; 136:19c]. Examples include Kerdīr [85].

7 ETHICS

Zoroastrian ethics are simple: what contributes to the future victory of good over evil is to be recommended and rewarded, above all straightness or honesty, truthfulness, generosity, and moderation; what does not is to be avoided and punished, notably crookedness, deviousness, deceit, and miserliness or greed. These basic values are repeatedly stressed and detailed [95; 96; 131:73; 131; 135]. Among the most important values are care of the poor and fairness: treating all the same, whether high or low. The principle of moderation, neither over-doing nor under-doing, is paramount. Opposite these are greed, lust, desire, hate, envy, etc. The most generic terms are *frārōn* and *abārōn*, approximately, "morally good and evil." Being truthful and honest, in particular, includes abstaining from slander.

Marrying one's closest relatives (parents, siblings, children) was said to be one of the foremost good deeds (Pahlavi *khwēdōdah*), the model for which was provided by three divine and mythical unions: Ohrmazd and his daughter Spandārmad (the earth), Gayōmard and his mother

Spandārmad, and the two first humans Mashī and Mashiyānī [97]. The historicity of such unions has been much discussed, and, although there is concrete evidence for them, it is not clear to what extent they were practiced in the general population at various times.

At the age of fifteen, a Zoroastrian assumed responsibility for his or her own behavior, when the sacred shirt was donned and the sacred belt fastened for the first time [14:13; 99–101]. By their symbolism, these two make explicit the nature of man as a microcosmic analogue to the macrocosmos [100; 101:9–23]. The shirt represented the sky and Good Thought and the belt the cosmic Girdle, the Daēnā Māzdayasni (Pahlavi Dēn Māzdēsn) [88; 101:14–18, 22].

The totality of a person's law-abiding actions was referred to as "work and law" [31:11; 57:35] or "work and religious acts" [92:50].

8 RITUALS

The Yasna, a Ritual Re-Creation of the World

The *Yasna*, literally, "sacrifice," was the text acompanying the morning ritual (*yasna*), performed to recreate the world of light after a period of darkness. It is formed as a gift-exchange between guest-friends, in which the sacrificer offers up to Ahura Mazdā all that is needed for him to re-produce the new, fertile world, including bones and life breath, in return for which Ahura Mazdā recreates the world and remunerates his sacrificer.

In the *Old Avesta*, it is clearly suggested that the ordering of the universe was achieved by a divine sacrifice, but only the Pahlavi texts mention the primordial sacrifice explicitly. In *Yasna* 29, when Zarathustra is chosen by Ahura Mazdā to be the first human sacrificer, his task is to bring down among the living the ingredients of the sacrifice already fashioned by Ahura Mazdā [43:7].

The regeneration of the sun-lit sky is achieved by the bulls that pull the chariot of the sun across the sky, which are identified with the poet-sacrificer's "guiding wisdom" (*khratu*), while his rivals only achieve the opposite effect by their pathetic efforts [45:3–4, cf. 103:14]. When the sacrifice is successful, Order will be revived [44:16].

The Young Avestan *yasna* is a reperformance of the first sacrifices, performed by two priests, the *zaotar* "libator" (Pahlavi *zōd*), the only one mentioned in the *Old Avesta*, and his assistant, the *rāspī* (Pahlavi for unattested Avestan **rāthwiya*, the one in charge of the *ratus*).

The *Yasna* begins with statements affirming the sacrificer's appurtenance to the good world and his determination to help bring it back, which is followed, in *Yasna* 1–7, by the announcing and assembling (*niwaēdaya- hankāraya-*, Pahlavi *niwēy- hangerd-*), then ordering of the divine model constituents (*ratus*) of the world so as to represent the primordial creation [105].

The models are presented in a relatively fixed list containing the five divisions of the day, beginning with the period preceding dawn, and associated elements, altogether thirty-three. There follow the models of the months (new moon, full moon, the moon of the 23rd day) and the seasons (spring, mid-summer, harvest, fall, mid-winter, New Year); and the years.

The sacrificer then apologizes for any faults made that might antagonize the deities [106].

In *Yasna* 8, the priest states the purpose of the *yasna*, which is to place Ahura Mazdā back in command of the world, and prays for comfort for the good, but discomfort for the wicked [107]. There follow a hymn in praise of Haoma [108] and the *Frawarānē* [109], in which the priest declares for the good powers against the evil ones by praising Order and scorning the evil gods. Finally, he presents to Ahura Mazdā his vision-soul, who will convey his sacrifice up to the divine world and will successfully combat the forces of darkness on the way (*Yasna* 12.9; cf. [17:154; 73]). *Yasna* 26 contains a long invocation of the pre-souls, crucial in the battle against the powers of darkness, as well as in the rebirth of the cosmos.

Yasna 27 accompanies the pressing and offering of the *haoma* juice and introduces the *Old Avesta*, which then follows [110]. Subsequently, the *Gāthās* are praised and sent up toward the divine realm, while providing food and clothes for the (breath-)soul on its way to Ahura Mazdā's abode [111]. These texts were especially effective for fighting darkness and pollution; the *Ahuna Wairiya*, in particular, could send even the Evil Spirit back to hell [24:28–31; 47:13–15; 49:19–20; 56].

Sraosha, the divine fighter against the powers of darkness, is then praised (*Yasna* 56–57). The *Ahuna Wairiya* and other sacred texts are sent up to the divine realm (*Yasna* 61), and the heavenly fire is praised in *Yasna* 62–64, which (originally) coincided with sunrise. The waters are praised, both the cosmic waters out of which the sun is reborn and the heavenly waters, which produce fertility on earth (*Yasna* 65). The forces of good are again praised and so strengthened, while the forces of evil are scorned and rejected, until the cosmos is completely reborn (*Yasna* 66–72), the sacred texts playing a decisive role in overcoming the forces of darkness (*Yasna* 71.6–8).

Important ingredients are the fire, which conveys the sacrifice to the gods; the *haoma* (Pahlavi *hōm*); the *barsom* (Avestan *barsman*), twigs of certain plants [15:9; 114:16; 136:17]; and water for cleaning and for libations (Avestan *zaothra*, Pahlavi *zōhr*) [15:9; 91–95; 23:12]. Animal sacrifice was also practiced (*ātash-zōhr*) [112; 113].

The Videvdad, a Ritual Purification of the World

The *Yasna* is also recited in the *videvdad sāde* ritual, a purification ritual recited from midnight till after sunrise, in which another six priests were originally involved, but whose roles are today played by the *rāspī*. Here, parts of the *Yasna* are replaced by a set of texts called *Vispered*, and the *Gāthās* are expanded by the twenty-two chapters of the *Videvdad*.

The *Videvdad* in twenty-one chapters, Avestan *vī-daēwō-dāta*, "the law (*dāta*) for how to keep the evil gods away (*vī*)," contains rules for how to avoid and remove from Ahura Mazdā's creation pollution caused by dead matter and bodily refuse and is framed by mythical narratives. Chapter one contains the story of how Ahura Mazdā established the lands and how the Evil Spirit fashioned the evils now plaguing them; chapter two contains the story of Yima, first king in the world of the living, and the Iranian "flood story" [18; p. 23]; chapter nineteen contains the story of Zarathustra's tryst with the evil gods and the Evil Spirit and how he exorcised them by performing a purification ritual [56]; and chapters twenty to twenty-two contain the story of how, with the help of Nairyō-sangha, the Life-giving Word, and Airyaman, Ahura Mazdā and the world were healed of the innumerable diseases brought upon them by the Evil Spirit.

Other Rituals

Among smaller rituals are the homage (Avestan *nemah*, Pahlavi *namāz*) [19; 101; 136:15]; the offering to certain deities of the *drōn* (Avestan *draonah*), originally parts of the sacrificial animal [112:4; 113], later also bread [136:17]; the *barshnūm*, a stringent purification ritual [116]; and the *sag-dīd*, viewing by a dog [116; 136:28].

9 ON KINGSHIP

The qualities of kingship occupy a central position in Zoroastrian ethics. The Achaemenid kings used the cosmology to define their own divine place in the cosmos as god's chosen representative in this world [3; 76], and, in both the Achaemenid and Sasanian inscriptions, the relationship between god and king and king and subjects is portrayed as one of mutual ownership, obligations, and indebtedness: the king belonged to god and god to the king [122; 125], the subjects were the king's bondsmen and would abide by the king's and Ahura Mazdā's law [119:8; 83:7=129:7]. Whatever good was done in the empires had the support of god *and* the king and was done for *their* benefit. A good king would keep the realm healthy and make it prosper, while a bad or corrupt king would cause it to deteriorate and be destroyed [119:54–55].

The king's victory over his enemies, who are also god's enemies, was regarded as matching god's victory over the evil one. Moreover, the king set an example for his successors, but also for his subjects in general [119:55, 64; 125]. His work was Perfect (*frasha*), matching that of Ahura Mazdā [76:1; 123; p. 30].

10 DOCTRINAL ISSUES

In the Pahlavi literature, disagreements among scholars, several of them known by name, are commonplace, but even in Young Avestan times, there appear to have been diverging traditions. One, in particular, was learnt by Frashaoshtra from Zarathustra regarding a non-standard order of the invocations in the *Yasna* [127–128]. We know from the Pahlavi literature, in fact, that Frashōshtar was regarded as an early authority [2:14].

In the *Avesta*, especially the *Videvdad*, those who sacrifice to Ahura Mazdā (*mazda-yasna*) are contrasted with those who sacrifice to the evil gods (*daēwa-yasna*) and are sometimes described as second-rate citizens. For instance, learning surgery involved experimenting on *daēwa-yasnas* before being allowed to treat a *mazda-yasna* (*Videvdad* 7).

Later, beginning with the Achaemenid inscriptions, we find statements regarding gods and which gods to worship [129] and, in the Sasanian period, diverging traditions and beliefs.

In the high priest Kerdīr's inscriptions, we have for the first time direct evidence for concerns about the correctness of the Tradition. To obtain confirmation that what was being done was the right thing, Kerdīr staged a trip by his double (twin) into the beyond. He also tells us how he dealt with other religions and non-conformist practices in the far reaches of the Sasanian territories [130:14–18].

The Pahlavi books contain the exposition of the good Tradition and often discuss what is according to the Tradition and what is not. In several texts, we find the Tradition contrasted with other views, notably those of Christians and Muslims [131; 136]. One authority often mentioned is Ādurbād, son of Mahrspand, high priest under Shāpūr II (309–79) [94]. The dispute between Abālish (reading uncertain) and Ādurfarnbay, son of Farrokh-zād, is set at the court of al-Ma'mūn (ruled 813–33), son of Hārūn al-Rashīd [135].

✦

CHAPTER ONE

TEXTS ON THE HISTORY OF THE SACRED TRADITION

From the Pahlavi Texts

1 About the book of Dēnkard (Dēnkard III, 420)

[2] The written *Dēnkard* is a section of what is manifest in the Mazdayasnian Tradition, which is adorned with the knowledge of all things.

[3] Firstly, there are extracts from the good Tradition of the Teachers of Old, the first pupils of Zarathustra of the Spitāmas, who brought the Word containing the knowledge (*dānishn*) and awareness (*āgāhīh*) of all issues as manifested in the good Tradition and obtained by Zarathustra by asking and listening to Ohrmazd, like light from the original Light.

[4] And it tells how that exalted ruler Kay-Wishtāsp commanded that the original questions and decisions be set down in writing from beginning to end, that they be consigned to the gubernatorial treasury, and that copies be distributed as was appropriate. From then on, copies of the awareness it contained were sent to the Fortress of Books and kept there.

[5] During the disasters that the miserable villain Alexander brought upon Iran, the Tradition, and the kingdom, the copy in the Fortress of Books was burned, and the one in the gubernatorial treasury fell into the hands of the Romans. It was also explained in Greek language from the awareness that was transmitted by the ancients.

[6] Then his majesty, king of kings, Ardashīr, son of Pābag, came to restore the kingdom of the Iranians, and this book was brought back from the scattering to one place. The righteous Tansar (or: Tōsar) came, one of the Teachers of Old and chief instructor, and the king

ordered him to compare the book with the evidence of the (oral) *Avesta* and complete it from that evidence. And so it was done. He commanded that it be kept in the gubernatorial treasury as if it were a piece of the blaze of the original Light and that a copy of the awareness it contained be distributed far and wide as was appropriate.

[7] Then, after the harm and destruction the Arabs brought upon both the archive and the national treasury, Ādurfarnbay, son of Farrokh-zād, leader of the Mazdayasnians, reassembled with renewed strength those scattered copies in the anthology (*dīwān*) of the court. By inspecting and comparing them with the *Avesta* and *Zand* of the Good Tradition and the words of the Teachers of Old, he then returned it, as it were, to a glimmer of what had once been a blaze.

[8] After the horrible turmoil and harm that befell Zardusht, son of Ādur-farnbay, leader of the Mazdayasnians, that anthology, too, was destroyed, that book was torn up, scattered, and damaged, fell into disuse, and began deteriorating.

[9] Since then, I, Ādur-bād, son of Ēmēd, leader of the Mazdayasnians, urged by the gods, with the help of the Mazdayasnian Tradition, with renewed strength, turned to seeking out and examining, at great pains, this book that had been recovered from that worn and dirty anthology, now in many pieces, some illegible, which had been returned, then carried off and stolen and once again brought back. I made selections from it with the aid of my inquiring wisdom to guide me, again comparing it with what the ancient Teachers of Old had said and done and what was manifest in the *Avesta*, enlarged from the knowledge of the Good Tradition. I arranged it in chapters and subjects, as a spark of the glimmer of that blaze from the light of the original Light. Thus I assembled, guided by the Good Tradition, this, which was named, as a proxy (*stūr*), as it were, of that great original, the *Dēnkard* of a thousand chapters.

2 History of the sacred books (Dēnkard IV)

[14] When he was done with the battle with Arzāsp, King Wishtāsp sent messengers and various writings culled from the Mazdayasnian

Tradition, which is adorned with knowledge of all things, with many kinds of skills and learning to the principal rulers about accepting the Tradition. A priest whose tongue was particularly skilled accompanied them in this work. He also sent Spidag, Arzrāsp, and others outside Khwanirah to inquire about the Tradition. They came to Frashōshtar, who dispatched them when he had made them fully aware of it.

¹⁵ (The Achaemenid) Dārāy, son of Dārāy, having committed to writing the entire *Avesta* and *Zand* as it had been received by Zarathustra from Ohrmazd, commanded two copies to be made, one to be kept in the gubernatiorial treasury and one in the Fortress of Books.

¹⁶ The Arsacid Walakhsh ordered a memorandum to be made and sent to the various provinces with orders for the safe-keeping of the *Avesta* and *Zand* as it had come down in unadulterated form, as well as of the teachings, to the extent each had escaped the harm and chaos caused by Alexander and the pillaging and robbing by the Romans and were now scattered throughout Iran in writing, but also remained authoritative in the oral transmission.

¹⁷ His majesty, king of kings, Ardashīr, son of Pābag, guided on the straight path by Tansar, asked that all those scattered teachings be brought to the court. Tansar took charge: some he accepted, and some he left out as non-authoritative. ¹⁸ And he issued the following order: "As far as we are concerned, any exposition that differs from that in the Mazdayasnian Tradition, but which provides awareness and knowledge, is not inferior to it."

¹⁹ Shāpūr (I), king of kings, son of Ardashīr, brought back together the writings outside the Tradition on medicine, what the stars say and their movements, time and place, nature and accident, becoming and decay, and the many other crafts and skills that were scattered in India, Rome, and other lands. He compared them with the *Avesta* and ordered any copy not contaminated by different ways to be given to the gubernatorial treasury. And he put up for discussion whether to place with the Mazdayasnian tradition all those that were not contaminated.

[20] Shāpūr (II), king of kings, son of Ohrmazd, brought everything that was said (in the Tradition) up for discussion and examination in the quarrel regarding what constitutes "contamination of the waters."

After Ādur-bād (son of Mahrspand) escaped unharmed by the word of the ordeal, he said this too (in dispute) both with all those with different ways and those with different ways who were able to enumerate (the contents of) the *nask*s of the Tradition: "Now, whoever we have seen in this world, except those who refuse to leave the evil Tradition, we shall work on him diligently." And so he did.

[21] The present majesty, Husrōy (Khusraw), king of kings, son of Kawād, it is told, when he had overcome heresies and false doctrines by fully opposing them, he increased, according to what was manifest in the Tradition, in every heresy greatly the awareness and detailed examination of the four branches (priests, soldiers, farmers, artisans).
[22] And he also said: "Those endowed with intelligence can know firmly the truth of the Mazdayasnian Tradition by examination. But it is not principally by examination that it is seen in this world to be superior and to make things increase; rather, it is possible by purity of thought, speech, and action and by sacrificing to the gods while uttering well, in pure fashion, the divine word as it was spoken in the other world.

And We shall be able to call "priest (*mowbed*) of Ohrmazd" those whose ability to see in the other world has been manifested among us and, by it being shown to Us, too, that there is a broad means to see the other world after the measure of this world, we shall be able to request from them both kinds (of sight?) in full.

[23] And also, in the way that the gods provide "irrigation and cultivation," especially for the Iranians, their land has progressed by teachings from the Mazdayasnian Tradition, which is the accumulated (*hangad*) learning of the ancients, which has now permeated all of Khwanirah. There is no dispute among those aware of these things about different views; so greatly has the *Avesta* been kept oral in pure saying, adorned with writing from tales in books, and, to put it in the

manner of the common people, been "drained" (and cultivated), in making people aware of what it says.

And so, the entire knowledge comes from "wells" in the Mazdayasnian Tradition for this reason, which We have come to know: if all is in doubt and something is to be examined outside of the Mazdayasnian Tradition, the whole world will come to this place to seek it anew and examine it.

✦

CHAPTER TWO

TEXTS ON CREATION AND THE DIVINE WORLD

From the Old Persian Inscriptions

3 Darius praises Ahuramazdā's creation (DE)

Ahuramazdā is the great god who set in place this earth, who set in place yonder sky, who set in place man, who set in place happiness for man, who made Dārayawahush king, one king over many, one commander over many.

I am Dārayawahush, the great king, king of kings, king over lands of many kinds, king over this earth, son of Wishtāspa (Hystaspes), a descendant of Hakhāmanish (Achaemenes).

From the Old Avesta

4 From Yasna 37

[1] In this manner, we are sacrificing to the All-knowing Lord, who, by his command, greatness, and artistries set in place the Cow and Order, the good waters and the plants, the lights and the earth, and all good things.

5 To the waters (Yasna 38)

[1] We are offering up in sacrifice, together with its divine women, this earth which carries us. These women who are yours, O All-knowing Lord, well-deserved (rewards) in accordance with Order, those we are worshipping: [2] O Milk offerings, Purifications, Juicifications, Humilities. [Cf. p. 12]

We are offering up in sacrifice the good reward on account of these divine women, the good invigoration, the good fat oblation, the good fame, the good fecundity.

³We are offering up in sacrifice the waters, glittering and nectar-pouring, which flow forth, ladies of their divine lord, whose art works they are, with good fords, good flooding, and good washing places, we offer you all (as gifts) to both worlds. ....

⁵We call you hither, O best ones, most beautiful ones, also named waters, milk-giving cows, mother cows, not to be harmed, nourishers of the poor, and giving everybody to drink!

6 On the two Spirits (Yasna 30)

¹Now, I shall speak, O you who wish to come, those words to which even a knowing man should pay attention: the praises and ritual performances of my good thought performed for the Lord, O well-attentive ones, and for Order, on account of which, through the lights, gladdening things (the sun, rewards) are being seen.

²Listen, all of you, with your ears to my best utterances! Observe, all of you, through the flame (of this fire) by your thought the choices of discrimination made man by man for his own body, before the great (heavenly) Audition, for them to be announced to *us* in return when you perceive ours.

³Thus, those two Spirits in the beginning, renowned as the twin "sleeps" (= sleeping things), the twin thoughts and speeches—they are two actions: a good and a bad. Between those two, those who give good gifts have discriminated rightly, not those who give bad gifts.

⁴Whenever the two Spirits come together, one determines for the first time that there will be life for the good and lack of survival for the bad and also how their existence shall be at last. The Worst Existence will be that of the wicked, but for the sustainer of Order there will be Best Thought.

⁵When these two Spirits made their choices, you, the one possessed by the Lie, would produce the worst things. The most life-giving Spirit (inspiration), which is clad in the hardest stones, chose to

produce Order, and so do whoever by their *true* actions shall obtain the favor of the Lord, him, the All-knowing one, again and again.

[6]The old gods especially did not discriminate straight between these two, as deception would come over them while consulting, so they would choose the worst thought. Thus, together they would scramble to Wrath, with which mortals sicken this existence.

[7]But to this one he comes with command and Order on account of his good thought. Texture gives him form, Humility gives him breathing (saying): "Of these rewards there shall be for you there (at the judgement) according as you shall request them, if first in line, on account of your . . .!"

[8]When the retribution comes for these sins, then, O All-knowing one, he shall constantly present the command to you by his good thought for you to announce it to these, O Lord, who shall be placing the Lie in the hands of Order. [Cf. 119:54]

[9]May *we* be (the men of ?) those who shall make this existence Juicy, O All-knowing one, and you, the lords, by the bringing of . . . and by our Order, when one's thoughts shall be in one and the same place where one's clear sight (?) shall at first be one way, then another.

[10]For at that time there will come down upon you, O wicked ones, the deflation of the tumescence of the Lie. But the fastest coursers shall be harnessed up to the good dwelling of Good Thought, that of the All-knowing one and of Order, who shall be leaving the others behind in the race for good renown.

[11]Because you now master (?) the deals that the All-knowing one establishes with you, O mortals, regarding both good going and non-going and what is long-lasting harm for the wicked and what are the life-giving strengths for the sustainers of Order, therefore, henceforth, by those deals wished-for things shall be for you.

7 *From Yasna 31*

[7]He who was the first to think those thoughts: "The free spaces are blending with the lights"—it was by his guiding thought that he, the Web-keeper (Weaver?), thought Order, by which he upholds Best

Thought. By that Spirit/inspiration you grow, O All-knowing one, who still here and now are the same, O Lord.

⁸Thus, I now think with my thought of *you* as being the first, O All-knowing one, yet youthful, father of Good Thought, since I have grasped *you* in my eye as the true Web-keeper of Order and seen you in the actions of this existence as the Lord.

⁹Humility was with you. *Yours* was the Spirit (inspiration) of great guiding thought there (in the form of?) the Fashioner of the Cow, O All-knowing Lord, when you were giving her the choice of paths: to come to the forager or to him who shall not be a forager for her—

¹¹when you, O all-knowing one, for the first time fashioned, by *your* thought, for us our beings (*gaēthā*) and vision-souls (*daēnā*), as well as our guiding thoughts (*khratu*), when you would place in us life breath (*ushtāna*) with bones (*ast*), when you would place our actions and announcements where a man is now obtaining (?) what he chooses and wishes for.

8 *From Yasna 44*

³I am asking you this: Tell me straight, O Lord! Who is, I wonder, the first birth father of Order? Who first set in place the road of the sun and the stars? Who is he through whom the moon is now waxing then waning? Just those things I wish to know, O All-knowing one, as well as these others.

⁴I am asking you this: Tell me straight, O Lord! Who first held up the earth below and the clouds above, keeping them from falling? Who fashioned the waters and the plants? Who yoked the two speedy coursers to the wind and the clouds? Who, O All-knowing one, is the Web-keeper of Good Thought?

⁵I am asking you this: tell me straight, O Lord! Which artisan first set in place light and darkness and, for man, sleep and wakefulness? Who is he through whom there is dawn, noon, and night . . .?

. . .

²⁰Did the old gods, O All-knowing one, really ever have the good command?—I must really ask—they, who are now withholding

their wish from these our men. By your actions, you, the "mumbler" and the "priest," knowingly give the Cow over to Wrath and by utterances which the "poet" utters in lamentation to the wind. They do not care for her, in order to further her pasture by the Order (of their rituals).

9 On the two Spirits (Yasna 45)

[1]And so I shall proclaim! Now hear! Now listen, both you who are approaching from near and from afar! Now, pay attention to it, all of you, for it is brilliant! May not the one whose announcements are bad destroy this existence a second time by his bad preference, the one possessed by the Lie, impeded (?) by the utterances of his tongue.

[2]Thus, I shall proclaim the two Spirits at the beginning of this existence, of which two the Life-giving one shall tell the Dark one: "Neither our thoughts nor announcements, neither guiding thoughts nor preferences, neither utterances nor actions, neither vision-souls nor breath-souls go together."

[3]Thus, I shall proclaim the *first* (announcement) of this existence, the (ordinance?) which the knowing one, the All-knowing Lord, has now spoken to me. Those of you who shall *not* produce this poetic thought in this way, in the way this (ordinance?) is and (in the way) I shall think and speak it, for those the last word of this existence will be "woe!"

[4]Thus, I shall proclaim the *best* announcement of this existence in accordance with Order: He is "the All-knowing one" because he knows him who set it in place to be the father of the Good Thought that invigorates you, while his daughter is Humility whose works are good. He is "Lord" because he keeps an eye on all things for them not to be deceived.

[5]Thus, I shall proclaim, for it to be heard, the word that the most Life-giving one tells *me* and which is the best for mortals: Whosoever shall give Readiness to listen (*sraosha*) to this one of mine shall come to Wholeness and Undyingness. By the actions of his good Spirit the Lord is All-knowing.

⁶Thus, I shall proclaim the greatest one of all, praising *him* with Order who, through his Life-giving Spirit, is generous to all those who are. Let the Lord, the All-knowing one, listen, he, in whose hymn I debate with my good thought. Let *him* teach me the best (thoughts/utterances/actions) by *his* guiding thought,—

⁷he to whose Life-giving strengths of generosity they shall wish to come who are now living, those who have been, and those who shall become, as well as the breath-soul of a sustainer of Order, strong in the race for Undyingness and Texture—strengths which come down as "disaster!" upon the men of the one possessed by the Lie.

¹⁰It is *he* with whom I am here wishing to exchange gifts by our sacrifices, the actions of our Humility, him, the All-knowing Lord, who is now made renowned on my breath. When one has assigned, by one's Order and one's Good Thought, Wholeness and Undyingness to *him* for them to be in *his* command, *they* shall give to this one Tissue strength and Texture to be his.

10 From Yasna 47

¹Through the Life-giving Spirit and Best Thought in accordance with Order, by action and speech, they shall give to this one [=me] Wholeness and Undyingness. By his command, the All-knowing one together with Humility is the ruling Lord.

²He produces the best of this most Life-giving Spirit (inspiration) by the utterances of his Good Thought to be sped along by his tongue, and the works of Humility by his hands, through *this* understanding: He, there, is the father of Order: the All-knowing one.

11 Airyaman (Yasna 54.1)

Let speedy Airyaman come here with support for our men and women, with support for Zarathustra's good thought, by which his vision-soul may gain a worthy fee! I am now asking for the reward of Order, which the All-knowing Lord shall deem worthy of being sped hither.

From the Young Avesta

12 *From the Hymn to Mithra (Yasht 10)*

[1]Ahura Mazdā said to Zarathustra of the Spitāmas: "When I, O Spitāma-son, set forth Mithra who provides wide pastures, then I made him as great and deserving of sacrifices, as great and deserving of hymns as myself, Ahura Mazdā.

The contract and the consequences of breaking or keeping contracts

[2]"He destroys the entire land, the contract-belying villain, O Spitāma-son. He strikes the man sustaining Order as much as a hundred magicians.

"Do not break the contract, O Spitāma-son, be it one you conclude with one possessed by the Lie or one you conclude with a sustainer of Order who follows your own Tradition. For the contract applies equally to the one possessed by the Lie and the one sustaining Order."

[3]Mithra who provides wide pastures gives speed to the horses of those who do not belie the contract. The fire of Ahura Mazdā gives them the straightest path. The good strong life-giving pre-souls of the sustainers of Order give them progeny of their own.

[4]For his wealth and fortune I shall sacrifice to him with audible sacrifice.

We sacrifice with libations to Mithra who provides wide pastures, who ensures good dwellings, peaceful dwellings for the Aryan lands.

The Aryan lands and the seven continents

[12]We sacrifice to Mithra who provides wide pastures, whose speech is well-spoken and true, who is well-fashioned, lofty, and rich in life-giving strength, who has a thousand ears and ten thousand eyes, whose sight reaches far and wide, who never sleeps but always wakes.

[13]As the first of beings in the world of thought worthy of sacrifice, he rises beyond Mount Harā in front of the immortal sun with speedy horses and is the first to seize the gold-adorned, beautiful heights.

From there, he, the one most rich in life-giving strength, looks out upon the the Aryan settlements, ¹⁴in which brave rulers lay out in straight lines their many palisades, in which tall mountains with plenty of grass and water further the pastures for the cow, in which deep bays stand with surging waters, in which flooding waters rush, broad, with a swell to Ishkata and Pouruta, to Margu, Haraēwa, and Gawa, to Sugda and Khwārizem, ¹⁵toward the seven continents of Arzahi and Sawahi, Fradadafshu and Widadafshu, Wourubarshti and Wourujarshti, and this continent, radiant Khwaniratha.

Mithra watches over the social order

¹⁷Nobody can deceive him: not the house-lord of the house, not the town-lord of the town, not the tribe-lord of the tribe, not the land-lord of the land.

¹⁸But if someone deceives him: a house-lord of the house, a town-lord of the town, a tribe-lord of the tribe, a land-lord of the land— then Mithra comes forth angered and enraged and breaks up the house and the town, the tribe and the land, the house-lords of the houses, the town-lords of the towns, the tribe-lords of the tribes, and the land-lords of the land, as well as all the foremost ones of the lands. ¹⁹Angered and enraged, he will come upon the one false to the contract from where he is paying the least attention.

²⁰The horses that belong to the one false to the contract become rebellious: running they do not arrive, carrying a rider they have no forward thrust, carrying a load they have no endurance.

Backward flies the arrow which the anti-Mithra shoots, because of all his evil spells. ²¹Even when he shoots it well and it reaches the body, even then it does not harm his target, because of all his evil spells, and the wind carries away his arrow.

Mithra's companions and chariot

⁶⁶Accompanied by good Ashi and Abundance on her fast chariot, the strong Manly Courage and the strong Fortune of the Poets, the strong Speedy One who has his own law (= the firmament) and the strong one

in the likeness of the Web-keeper, and the strong pre-souls of the sustainers of Order . . ., [67]he flies in a high-wheeled wagon, fashioned in the world of thought, from the continent of Arzahi to this continent, radiant Khwaniratha, accompanied by the Fortune and Obstruction-smashing Strength (Werthragna) set in place by Ahura Mazdā.

[68]Ashi the tall takes hold of his wagon, and the Mazdayasnian Daēnā levels its path for easy going. Coursers from the world of thought, white, bright, and brilliant, life-giving, knowing, shadowless, whose place is in the world of thought, convey it, when the One in the likeness of the Web-keeper again and again clears it well (for easy going)!

The evil gods in the world of thought and the demons of Greed possessed by the Lie all fear this: [69]"May we not here come up against the blow of the lord when angered!" he whose one thousand blows go against the opponent, he the one rich in life-giving strength, who has ten thousand watchers and knows all, deceived by none.

[70]In front of him flies the Obstruction-smashing Strength in the form of an enraged sharp-fanged, sharp-tusked boar, with legs, sinews, tail, and jaws of iron, firm, virile, and aggressive, who kills with one, unavoidable blow.

[71]When he runs forward to face the opponent, with one thought in his mind, accompanied by Manly Courage, with one swipe he strikes down the opponents. He does not think about striking, he does not realize he is striking until he crushes the marrow of the column of life and the source of the life breath. All at once, he cuts to the quick the men who break the contract, mingling all over the ground their bones, hair, brains, and blood.

Mithra battles the powers of the Lie

[95]He goes the width of the earth after sunset, touching both sides of this wide round earth with distant borders, surveying all between heaven and earth.

[96]With his golden hundred-bossed, sharp-edged cudgel, cast in gilded bronze, forceful in the attack, the most forceful of weapons, the

strongest obstruction-smasher among weapons, it fells a man in its forward thrust.

⁹⁷The destructive Evil Spirit fears it. Wrath, giver of evil gifts, whose body is forfeit, fears it. Sloth with long hands fears it. All the evil gods in the world of thought fear it, as well as the demons of Greed possessed by the Lie, thinking:

⁹⁸"May we not here come up against your thrust when you are angered, O Mithra who provide wide pastures! Do not get angry and reject us when you stand forth upon this earth, you, the strongest and firmest, the speediest and fastest among those worthy of sacrifice and the greatest obstruction-smasher!"

The sacrifice to Mithra

¹¹⁹"Sacrifice to Mithra, O Spitāma-son! Tell your students! May the Mazdayasnians sacrifice for you with sheep and cattle, with small birds and big birds, all those who fly forth with wings!"

¹²¹Zarathustra asked in turn: "How, O Ahura Mazdā, shall the man sustaining Order consume the purified libation? How may he satisfy and appease with his sacrifices Mithra who provides wide pastures?"

¹²²Then Ahura Mazdā said: "For three days and nights they should wash their bodies, they should make penance with thirty whiplashes for the sacrifice and hymn to Mithra who provides wide pastures. Then, for two days and nights, they should wash their bodies, they should make penance with twenty whiplashes for the sacrifice and hymn to Mithra who provides wide pastures."

(Mithra:) "Let no one consume these libations of mine who is not well-versed in all the models of the *Sacrifice and Texts of Praise*!"

Mithra's chariot and weapons

¹²⁴On his firm, beautiful, and well-balanced wagon all of gold, Mithra who provides wide pastures flies forth from the luminous House of Song with raised arms to battle destruction.

¹²⁵Alongside his wagon there fly four white, immortal coursers, all of the same color, who graze in the world of thought. With gold-shod

front hooves, but silver-shod hind hooves, they are all yoked with yoke, yoke pin, and yoke strap, firmly fastened with a well-made hook of Well-deserved Command (= metal).

^{126}On his right flies straightest Rashnu, most rich in life-giving strength, the most defensive. But on his left flies straightest Cistā, sustainer of Order, bearing libations. White herself, she wears white garments, in the likeness of the Mazdayasnian Daēnā.

^{127}The firm one in the likeness of the Web-keeper came flying in the form of an enraged sharp-fanged, sharp-tusked boar . . . [= par. 70].

Hot on his heals flew the blazing Fire and the strong Fortune of the Poets.

$^{128-132}$There stand in that wagon of Mithra who provides wide pastures a thousand well-made bows, some with strings from sinews of gazelles; a thousand well-made arrows with vulture feathers, some with stems made of bone; a thousand well-made spears, some with blades that cut; a thousand well-made double-edged steel axes; a thousand well-made double-edged knives; a thousand well-made bronze clubs; and a beautiful golden hundred-bossed, sharp-edged cudgel . . . [= par. 96]. Flying through the spaces of the world of thought, they all fall through the spaces of the world of thought down upon the heads of the evil gods.

^{134}Ever and again the destructive Evil Spirit fears him. . . . ^{135}"May we not here come up against his thrust when angered. . . ." [= par. 97–98]

13 From the Hymn to Ashi (Yasht 17)

^{2}Being the daughter of Ahura Mazdā, the sister of the Life-giving Immortals, she conducts forward her coursers by the perfect guiding thought of all the Revitalizers [cf. 45:3]. Upon him who invokes her from near or from afar she bestows inborn guiding thought at will and comes to his help.

He who sacrifices to Ashi with libations, he also sacrifices to Mithra with libations.

^{16}Ahura Mazdā, the greatest and best of those worthy of sacrifice, is your father. Your mother is Life-giving Humility. Your brothers are good Sraosha with the rewards, tall, forceful Rashnu, and Mithra who provides wide pastures, who has ten thousand spies, a thousand ears. Your sister is the Mazdayasnian Daēnā.

14 From the Hymn to Tishtriya (Yasht 8)

Tishtriya and the heavenly waters

[1]Ahura Mazā said to Zarathustra of the Spitāmas: "(. . .) I shall sacrifice with libations to the star Tishtriya who distributes (the waters) to the settlement."

[4]We sacrifice to the lofty and powerful star Tishtriya, wealthy and munificent, repository of the seeds of water, rich in life-giving strength, with far-reaching eyesight, whose work is above, from whose lofty place comes good fame. From the Scion of the Waters is its brightness.

[5]We sacrifice to the star Tishtriya, wealthy and munificent, whom sheep and cattle recall when faced with violent men and lying magicians, thinking: "When will Tishtriya, wealthy and munificent, rise for us? When will new springs of water flow deeper than the height of a horse?"

[8]Ever and again he comes in the form of a horse, sustainer of Order, to a bay of the Wourukasha Sea, powerful and well-shaped, deep with surging waters. He makes those waters swell, and the winds blow over it like chariots with yoked horses.

[9]Then, when Satawaēsa comes among the coverings, beautiful, pushing those waters forward over the earth with its seven continents, he stands ensuring peace and good seasons for the lands, where men wonder: "When shall the Aryan lands have good seasons?"

Tishtriya asks Ahura Mazdā for sacrifices

[10]We sacrifice to the star Tishtriya, wealthy and munificent, who spoke to Ahura Mazdā, saying: "O Ahura Mazdā, most Life-giving Spirit, creator of living beings with bones, sustainer of Order!

[11]If people were to sacrifice to me with a sacrifice in which my name is spoken as they do to others worthy of sacrifice, then I would have gone forth to the men sustaining Order for a bounded time span. I would have come for one night or two or fifty or a hundred nights of my own unbounded time, of my own sunny, immortal life."

The battle between Tishtriya and Apaosha

[13]The first ten nights, Tishtriya, wealthy and munificent, flying through the lights, blends with the form of a radiant, shiny-eyed man of fifteen, tall, overpowering, powerful, of heroic talent, [14]at that time of life when a man first ties the girdle, when a man first becomes powerful, when a man first comes of age.

[15]Here he deliberates, wondering: "Who will now sacrifice to me with libations full of *haoma* and milk? To whom should I grant his desire for men, a flock of men, and purification for his own soul? It is now that I should receive sacrifices and hymns according to best Order from the existence with bones."

[16]The second ten nights, Tishtriya . . . blends with the form of a bull with golden hooves.

[17]Here he deliberates . . .: "To whom should I grant his desire for cattle, a herd of cattle, and purification for his own soul? . . ."

[18]The third ten days, Tishtriya . . . blends with the form of of a beautiful white horse with golden ears and golden bridle.

[19]Here he deliberates, wondering "To whom should I grant his desire for horses, a herd of horses, and purification for his own soul? . . ."

[20]Then, in response, Tishtriya comes down, wealthy and munificent, to the Wourukasha Sea in the form of a beautiful white horse with golden ears and golden bridle.

[21]Then there rushes down against him the evil god Apaosha, in the form of a mangy and hairless black horse with hairless ears, mane, and tail, bridled with fright.

[22]Their forelegs clash, O Zarathustra of the Spitāmas! Tishtriya, wealthy and munificent, and the evil god Apaosha fight for three days

and nights. Then, Apaosha gains the upper hand and overcomes Tishtriya, wealthy and munificent. [23]He chases him away from the Wourukasha Sea the distance of a league.

Tishtriya, wealthy and munificent, complains: "Miserable me, O Ahura Mazdā! What misfortune, O waters and plants, what evil fate, O Mazdayasnian Daēnā! People are clearly not sacrificing with sacrifices in which my name is spoken as they do to others worthy of sacrifices. [24]If people were to offer me sacrifices in which my name is spoken as they do others worthy of sacrifices, then, surely, they would have conferred upon me the strength of ten horses, ten camels, ten bulls, ten mountains, and ten rivers in spate.

[25](Ahura Mazdā:) "I, Ahura Mazdā, shall sacrifice to Tishtriya, wealthy and munificent, with a sacrifice in which his name is spoken! I shall bring him the strength of ten horses, ten camels, ten bulls, ten mountains, and ten rivers in spate!"

[26]Then in response, Tishtriya, wealthy and munificent, comes down to the Wourukasha Sea in the form of a beautiful white horse, with golden ears and golden bridle.

[27]Then there rushes down against him the evil god Apaosha ... bridled with fright.

[28]Their forelegs clash, O Zarathustra of the Spitāmas! Then, at noon, he gains the upper hand, Tishtriya, wealthy and munificent, and overcomes the evil god Apaosha. [29]He chases him away from the Wourukasha Sea, the distance of a league.

Tishtriya, wealthy and munificent, exults: "Success for me, O Ahura Mazdā! Success for you, O waters and plants, success for you, O Mazdayasnian Daēnā! Success there shall be for you, O lands! Henceforth your grains shall come up unimpeded as pasture for living beings with bones, both big-seeded barley and small-seeded grasss."

Release of the waters

[30]Then in response, Tishtriya, wealthy and munificent, comes down to the Wourukasha Sea, in the form of a beautiful white horse, with golden ears and golden bridle.

He makes the sea swell hither and to the sides. [31]He makes the sea surge hither and to the sides. He makes the sea rush hither and to the sides. All the shores of the Wourukasha Sea surge. The entire interior swells.

[32]Then in response, Tishtriya, wealthy and munificent, stands up from the Wourukasha Sea.

Satawaēsa too, wealthy and munificent, rises from there, stands up from the Wourukasha Sea.

Then clouds assemble there on Mount Us-hendawa, which stands in the middle of the Wourukasha Sea.

[33]He pushes the fog-making clouds, sustainers of Order. He, in front, conveys the wind forth along the paths where ruddy Haoma comes, furtherer of living beings. Behind him blows the impetuous wind set in place by Ahura Mazdā, bringing rain, fog, and hail to the places, the settlements, and the seven continents.

[34]Those waters the Scion of the Waters, O Zarathustra of the Spitāmas, distributes by settlement to the existence with bones, as do the impetuous wind, the Fortune placed in the water, and the pre-souls of the sustainers of Order.

[35]Then Tishtriya flies forth from there, from the radiant Dawn, on a road turning in the distance, along the route assigned by the Distributor, along the course cut out for him for the pleasure of Ahura Mazdā, of the Life-giving Immortals.

[41]The waters recall Tishtriya, those that stand still and those that flow forth, those in wells and those in rivers, those in canals and those in bays, thinking: [42]"When will he rise for us, Tishtriya, wealthy and munificent? When will springs of water come rushing, deeper than the height of a horse, toward the beautiful places and settlements and come flowing toward the pastures, to the roots of plants? Will they grow with growth rich in life-giving strength?"

[46]Then Tishtriya, powerful and well-shaped, comes to all the bays of the deep Wourukasha Sea with surging waters and to all the beautiful inlets and outlets in the form of a beautiful white horse, with golden ears and golden bridle.

⁴⁷Then the waters rain down, O Zarathustra of the Spitāmas, from the Wourukasha Sea, falling delicate and healing. He, the richest in life-giving strength, distributes them there to these lands, if only he is sacrificed to, satisfied, befriended, and recognized.

15 From the Hymn to Ardwī Sūrā Anāhitā (Yasht 5)

Ahura Mazdā introduces the goddess to Zarathustra

¹Ahura Mazdā said to Zarathustra of the Spitāmas: "Sacrifice to Ardwī Sūrā Anāhitā for me, O Zarathustra of the Spitāmas! Her front is broad, she provides healing. She said no to the evil gods and took Ahura Mazdā as her guide. She is worthy of sacrifices and hymns from the existence with bones.

"A sustainer of Order, she furthers the grains, the flocks, and the herds, the settlements and the lands.

²"She purifies the semen of all males and the wombs of all females for birth. She gives easy delivery to all females and brings down their milk in due time and measure.

³"She is audible from afar when, forceful, she flows forth from Mount Hukarya to the Wourukasha Sea, Ardwī Sūrā Anāhitā, as large as all these waters that flow forth upon the earth. ⁴She has a thousand bays and inlets, and each of these bays and inlets is a forty days' ride for a man riding a good horse.

"All the shores of the Wourukasha Sea surge, the entire interior swells, when she flows forth into them, when she rushes into them. ⁵And now the flow of this single water of mine shall go out to all the seven continents and shall come down in the same way in summer and in winter.

"She purifies my waters, the semen of the males, the wombs of the females, and the milk of the females.

⁶"And I, Ahura Mazdā, carry her up again by the impetus of my tongue, for the furthering of the house, the town, the tribe, and the land, to protect, guard, and watch over them."

The goddess asks for sacrifices

[7]And so, O Zarathustra, Ardwī Sūrā Anāhitā went forth from Mazdā, who set her in her place. Beautiful, indeed, were her arms, white and thicker than the thighs of a horse. Two beautiful armlets were clasped around her delicate arms.

Thus she ponders: [8]"Who will praise me? Who will sacrifice to me with libations full of *haoma* and milk, purified and filtered?"

[9]For her wealth and munificence I will sacrifice to her with audible sacrifice. I will sacrifice to her with well-performed sacrifice, Ardwī Sūrā Anāhitā, sustainer of Order, with libations.

Thereby may you command when invoked, O Ardwī Sūrā Anāhitā, and partake of a better sacrifice, one with *haoma* mixed with milk, and with *barsom*, performed with the skill of my tongue and my poetic thought, with speech, action, libations and with words correctly spoken!

[11]Driving on her wagon, she recalls the man driving in front on his wagon holding the reins and ponders: "Who will praise me? . . ."

[13]Four tall white horses convey her, all of the same color and breed. They overcome the hostilities of all evil gods and men, sorcerers and witches, false teachers, poetasters, and mumblers.

[15]Forceful and radiant, she stands tall and well-shaped, when, forceful, she flows forth, her falling waters raining down by day and night as much as all these waters that flow forth over the earth.

Ahura Mazdā's sacrifice

[17]Ahura Mazdā, who has set all in its place, sacrificed to her in the Aryan Expanse of the Good Lawful River, with *haoma* mixed with milk and with *barsom* . . . with words correctly spoken. [= par. 10]

[18]Thus he asked her: "Will you give me that prize, O good, Ardwī Sūrā Anāhitā, you most rich in life-giving strength, that I shall induce Zarathustra, sustainer of Order, Pourushāspa's son, to help my vision-soul along with his thoughts, words, and actions?"

[19]She gave him that prize, Ardwī Sūrā Anāhitā, who gives prizes to the expert poet-sacrificer who, carrying *barsom* and libations, sacrifices to her and asks her for favors.

The goddess comes down from the stars

⁸⁵Ahura Mazdā the artisan invited her: "Come down, O Ardwī Sūrā Anāhitā, from yonder stars to the earth set in place by Ahura Mazdā! The speedy rulers will sacrifice to you, the lords of the lands and the sons of lords of the lands.

⁸⁶The firm men will ask you for speed for their horses and the superior gifts of Fortune. The memorizing priests will ask you for learning and life-giving knowledge, for the Obstruction-smashing Strength set in place by Ahura Mazdā and for the Victorious Superiority.

⁸⁷Nubile young women shall ask you for command of good housework and a firm houselord. Women in labor shall ask you for easy birth. You shall confer those things on them, having the power to do so, O Ardwī Sūrā Anāhitā."

⁸⁸And so she went forth, O Zarathustra, Ardwī Sūrā Anāhitā, from yonder stars to the earth set in place by Ahura Mazdā.

Thus she spoke, Ardwī Sūrā Anāhitā: ⁸⁹"O upright Spitāma-son, sustainer of Order! Ahura Mazdā set you in your place as model of every living being with bones. Ahura Mazdā set me in my place to protect the entire existence living by Order.

By my wealth and munificence, sheep and cattle roam over the earth, as do men on two feet. And so I shall protect all those good things set in place by Ahura Mazdā whose brilliance is from Order, like a shepherd his sheep.

Zarathustra and the goddess

⁹⁰Zarathustra asked her in turn: "With what sacrifice shall I sacrifice to you, O Ardwī Sūrā Anāhitā, and send you forth by my sacrifice to the course Ahura Mazdā made for you in the space in between, above the radiant sun, where they shall not bother you with snakes, spiders, and wasps, with spinners and poisons from spinners?"

⁹¹Thus she spoke, Ardwī Sūrā Anāhitā: "O upright Spitāma-son, sustainer of Order! With a sacrifice from sunrise till sunset you may sacrifice to me and send me forth by your sacrifice. Then you may drink of this my libation, with speech as asked by a priest, with

words asked in return, attentive, talented, and spinning the poetic thought.

[92]But let no one drink of this my libation who has a fever, a fat person, someone with pimples, or a woman or a skilled man who does not perform the *Gāthās*, or a leper whose body has been secluded! [93]I do not accept those libations of which females drink for my sake who are blind or deaf … or carrying the mark of one who, while not possessing much skill, launches all kinds of (unskilled) poetic thoughts."

[94]Zarathustra asked her in turn: "What happens here to those libations of yours, O Ardwī Sūrā Anāhitā, that they offer as yours, the ones possessed by the Lie and who sacrifice to evil gods after sunset?"

[95]Thus she spoke, Ardwī Sūrā Anāhitā: "O upright Spitāma-son, sustainer of Order, they are to be rejected with words of woe, to be ground under the heels, to be laughed back, to be booed back, these libations that fly after me by six-hundreds and a thousand, which are not accepted even at the sacrifice to the evil gods!"

Description of the goddess

[101]She has a thousand bays and inlets … a forty days' ride for a man riding a good horse. In each and every inlet, there stands a well-made home, radiant with a hundred windows, well made with a thousand columns, with ten thousand supporting beams, rich in life-giving strength. [102]Also, in each and every home, they lie on well-scented couches with pillows.

When Ardwī Sūrā Anāhitā, forceful, flows forth and hither, O Zarathustra, a thousand men in depth, she commands as much Fortune as all these waters that flow forth over the earth.

[126]Displayed in the shape of a beautiful young woman, Ardwī Sūrā Anāhitā stands most powerful and high-born, well-shaped and girded high, upright and splendid in her brilliance, wearing a coat with long sleeves, with rich designs, embroidered with gold.

[127]Ever and again, carrying *barsom* in her hands, wearing square earrings, high- and noble-born Ardwī Sūrā Anāhitā would wear a

golden brooch upon her beautiful neck and tighten her waistband to enhance her breasts.

¹²⁸On her head she bound a golden crown with a hundred stars, eight crenelations, and rings like wheels and with inimitable, beautiful, well-made droplets.

¹²⁹Garments of beaver fur she wore from three hundred beavers about to give birth for the fourth time, because the female beaver is most beautiful when she is adorned most colorful. For, when the female beaver lives in water for as long as she should, then her furs shine in the eyes of the beholder all silver and gold.

The poet asks the goddess for his reward

¹³⁰Then, here I ask for that prize, O you most rich in life-giving strength, O good Ardwī Sūrā Anāhitā, that I, well-invited as your friend, with large command, may win for myself snorting horses, singing wheels, swishing whips, copious well-cooked and aromatic shares of food, and plentiful stored meat. In my pantries I shall put away as much as I desire, providing everything needed for good living. For when one dies the command leaves!

¹³¹Here I ask for two coursers, one two-legged and one four-legged: the one to pull my chariot, fast when mounted, turning well the wagons in the battles, the other to turn both flanks of the broad battle line, the left and the right, the right and the left.

¹³²In return for this sacrifice and hymn, come down, O Ardwī Sūrā Anāhitā, from yonder stars to this earth set in place by Ahura Mazdā, to the sacrificing priest, you who give prizes to the expert sacrificer carrying the *barsom*, whose hands are full and overflowing with libations, who sacrifices to you and asks you for favors! Assist him now, so that all those speedy coursers may come back having won, as did those of Kawi Wishtāspa!

16 From the Hymn to the Sun (Yasht 6)

¹We sacrifice to the immortal, resplendent, radiant Sun with speedy horses, for, when He makes the sun shine in the light, when He makes

it shine with light, then those worthy of sacrifice in the world of thought stand a hundred and a thousand. They bring together that Fortune, convey it down, and apportion it over the earth set in place by Ahura Mazdā. It furthers the living beings of Order, furthers them for the body of Order.

²Then, when the sun rises, the earth set in place by Ahura Mazdā is purified, the flowing water is purified, that of the wells and that of the seas is purified, the standing water is purified, all living beings, sustainers of Order, are purified, those of the Life-giving Spirit.

³For if the sun does not rise, then the evil gods destroy all living beings in the seven continents, and those worthy of sacrifice in the world of thought or in the existence with bones will have no retreat and find no refuge.

⁴He who sacrifices to the immortal, resplendent sun with speedy horses to resist the darkness, to resist the evil gods' spawns of darkness, to resist thieves and robbers, sorcerers and witches, to resist danger, he sacrifices to Ahura Mazdā and the Life-giving Immortals and for his own soul. He who sacrifices to the immortal, resplendent sun with speedy horses wins the favor of all those worthy of sacrifice in the world of thought and in the world of the living.

17 From the Hymn to the Frawashis (Yasht 13)

Ahura Mazdā and the pre-souls

¹Ahura Mazdā said to Zarathustra of the Spitāmas:

So, I shall proclaim to you, O upright Zarathustra, the endurance and strength, the munificence, help, and support of the strong, unshakeable pre-souls of the sustainers of Order, how they helped and supported me, the strong pre-souls of the sustainers of Order.

²By their wealth and munificence, I stretched and held out, O Zarathustra, yonder sky above, luminous and visible afar, which covers and surrounds this earth like a bird its egg, which stands in the world of thought, firmly held together, with distant borders, in the form of shining bronze, shining over the three (spheres?) [cf. 70:5].

³Ahura Mazdā dons it as his robe, star-adorned, fashioned in the world of thought, when accompanied by Mithra, Rashnu, and Life-giving Humility. Nobody can see its two surrounding borders.

⁴By their wealth and munificence, I stretched and held out, O Zarathustra, Ardwī Sūrā Anāhitā. Her front is broad . . . and the milk of the females. [=15:1–5]

⁹By their wealth and munificence I stretched and held out, O Zarathustra, the wide earth, large and broad, set in place here by Ahura Mazdā, the carrier of much that is beautiful, which carries the entire existence with bones, both living and dead, and the high mountains and their waterways providing much pasture [cf. 70:5].¹⁰ Upon it the waters flow in spate with powerful thrust. All the many kinds of plants grow up all over the earth for the protection of beasts and men, the Aryan lands, and the animals of five kinds and to aid the men sustaining Order.

¹¹By their wealth and munificence I stretched and held out, O Zarathustra, the sons in the wombs, enclosed and not dying beforehand. Until the destined delivery, I assembled in the coverings in right order the bones and the hairs, the muscles and the intestines, the sinews and the limbs. [Cf. 70:5]

¹²For, if the strong pre-souls of the sustainers of Order had not supported me, then beasts and men here, the best of species, would not have been mine. The strength and command would have been the Lie's, the existence with bones would have been the Lie's.

¹³Of the two Spirits, the Lying one would have won and been sitting between heaven and earth. Thereafter, as conqueror, he would no longer be surrendered with the conquered, the Evil Spirit to the Life-giving Spirit!

¹⁴By their wealth and munificence, the waters flow forth in their courses from inexhaustible sources; the plants grow up all over the earth from inexhaustible sources; the winds blow floating with the clouds from inexhaustible sources.

¹⁵By their wealth and munificence, the females enfold the sons and give birth in easy births when they are blessed with many sons. ¹⁶(. . .)

By their wealth and munificence, the sun, moon, and stars go along yonder paths.

[28]Ahura Mazdā invoked them for the help of yonder sky, when he stretched and held it out, of the water and the earth and of the plant; when the Life-giving Spirit stretched and held out the sky, and the water and the earth, and the cow and the plant; when he stretched and held out the sons in the wombs ... and the limbs.

[29]The Life-giving Spirit stretched and held them out, the strong pre-souls. Sitting silent, with good and invigorating eyes, listening, long at peace, lofty, girded high, with good, wide roads, floating fleetly, fulfilling their obligations (to the sacrificer), and widely famed, they held up the sky.

[43]They release Satawaēsa between heaven and earth, who fills the waters when hearing the invocation, who makes the waters fall, who makes the plants grow for the protection of beasts and men, of the Aryan lands, of the animals of five kinds, and for the help of men sustaining Order.

[44]Satawaēsa will go about far and wide between heaven and earth, he who fills the waters ... for the help of men sustaining Order.

Their pre-souls' martial nature

[45]We sacrifice to the ... pre-souls of the sustainers of Order, who wear bronze helmets, bronze weapons, and bronze breastplates as they fight in victorious battles on horses with shining saddle-gear, carrying drawn, lead-pointed arrows (?) for the striking of a thousand evil gods.

The pre-souls' request for sacrifice

[49]We sacrifice to the ... pre-souls of the sustainers of Order, who fly hither throughout the town at the temporal node of the vernal equinox. For ten nights they move about here, wondering whether they will receive the aid they desire:

[50]Who will praise us? Who will sacrifice to us and weave us into hymns? Who will befriend us and recognize us with milk in the hands

and with garments, with a homage by which one reaches Order? Whose name among us will here be sent forth in song? Whose soul will be sent forth by our sacrifice?

To whom among us will that donation be given which will be for him imperishable savory food for ever and ever?

[51]But the man who does send forth to them a sacrifice with milk in the hands and with garments, with homage by which one reaches Order, him they befriend, the strong pre-souls of the sustainers of Order, when pleased, unoffended, and unantagonized.

[52]May this house have herds of cattle and men! May it have a speedy horse and a solid wagon!

May there be a man, stalwart and well-spoken, who will sacrifice to us with milk in the hands . . .!

The pre-souls set the creations in motion

[53]We sacrifice to the . . . pre-souls of the sustainers of Order, who show to the waters set in place by Ahura Mazdā beautiful paths. Before this, once brought forth, but not yet flowing forth, they stood in one and the same place for a very long time. [54]But now they flow forth along the path laid out by Ahura Mazdā, along the way assigned by the Distributor, along the course cut out for them for the pleasure of Ahura Mazdā and the Life-giving Immortals.

[55]We sacrifice to the . . . pre-souls of the sustainers of Order, who show the plants beautiful growths. Before this, once brought forth, but not yet growing forth, they stood in one and the same place for a very long time. [56]But now those grow forth along the path laid out by Ahura Mazdā. . . .

[57]We sacrifice to the . . . pre-souls of the sustainers of Order, who, sustaining Order, showed paths to the moon and the sun and to the Endless Lights with their own law, which before this stood without forward motion in one and the same place for a long time, before the hostility of the old gods. [58]But those now fly forth, reaching the turn of the road that turns in the distance, that of the good Perfectioning.

The pre-souls distribute the rain-waters

⁶⁵When the waters are carried up from the Wourukasha Sea, O Zarathustra of the Spitāmas, as well as the Fortune placed there by Ahura Mazdā, then the strong life-giving pre-souls of the sustainers of Order move forth by hundreds, by thousands, by ten thousands, ⁶⁶each seeking water for her own family, for her own town, tribe, and land, saying: "Is our land to be needy and to dry out?"

⁶⁷They fight in battles over their own places and settlements, according as each has a place or habitation for settling, just like a firm man standing in a chariot girded with his quiver-belt would strike back (enemies) from a well-assembled treasure.

⁶⁸Then those who are victorious lead away the water, each for her own family, for her own town, tribe, and land, saying: Our land shall prosper and grow!

Victory over the Evil Spirit

⁷⁶For they had the upper hand at the creations of the two Spirits, the good life-giving pre-souls of the sustainers of Order, rich in life-giving strength, they who then stood tall and straight when the two Spirits set in place the creations: the Life-giving Spirit and the Evil one.

⁷⁷When the Evil Spirit was about to pass through the foundation of the good Order, Good Thought and the Fire came down between, keeping him at bay.

⁷⁸They overcame the hostilities of the Evil Spirit possessed by the Lie so that he did not prevent the waters from flowing, nor the plants from growing. All at once, the waters flowed forth, rich in life-giving strength, and the plants grew up, those of Ahura Mazdā, rich in life-giving strength, who set them in place and commands them.

Sacrifices to the pre-souls

⁸⁰Of all these ancient pre-souls we sacrifice to yonder pre-soul, that of Ahura Mazdā, the greatest, best, and most beautiful, the most solid, the most endowed with wisdom, the most well-shaped, ⁸¹whose

breath-soul is the Life-giving Word, dawn-colored, bright, visible from afar. And (we sacrifice) to the beautiful forms with which it blends, those of the Life-giving Immortals.

[82]We sacrifice to the pre-souls of the sustainers of Order, those of the radiant Life-giving Immortals, whose eyes are in heavenly vigor, lofty, lordly, firm, and overpowering.

They present no threats, they sustain Order, [83]the seven who have one and the same thought, speech, and action, who think, speak, and perform the same thoughts, words, and deeds, who have one and the same father and ordainer: Ahura Mazdā, who set everything in place.

[84]They look at one another's breath-soul as it winds its way (?) through thoughts well thought, words well spoken, and deeds well performed to the House of Song [cf. 88:9–12]. Their paths are bright as they come flying down to the libations. They are the ones who fashioned, adorned, and set in place these living beings of Ahura Mazdā's, who oversee, protect, and guard them. They are those who will make the existence Perfect in exchange value and make it incorruptible, indestructible, undecaying, and unrotting. [Cf. 45:19; 64:11]

[85]We sacrifice to the pre-soul of the most invigorating fire, life-giving and eloquent (?).

We sacrifice to the pre-soul of the firm, lordly Sraosha with the rewards, with the defiant mace, who stretches the Life-giving Word, to that of Nairya Sangha, [86]to that of straightest Rashnu, to that of Mithra who provides wide pastures, and to that of the Life-giving Word.

[87]We sacrifice to the pre-souls of the sky, water, earth, and plant, and to that of the Bull and Gaya Martān. (...)

We sacrifice to the pre-soul of Gaya Martān, sustainer of Order, who was the first to listen to the thought and commandments of Ahura Mazdā, from whom He fashioned forth the umbilical cords of the Aryan lands, the seed of the Aryan lands.

[145]We sacrifice to the pre-souls of men sustaining Order in all the lands and of the women in all the lands, sustainers of Order.

We sacrifice to all the good life-giving pre-souls of the sustainers of Order, rich in life-giving strength, those from Gaya Martān to the obstruction-smashing Revitalizer.

[148]And among all these pre-souls of women and men sustaining Order, here we sacrifice to the pre-soul of those whose souls are worthy of being sacrificed to and whose pre-souls are worthy of being invoked.

And among all these women and men, sustainers of Order, here we sacrifice to the pre-soul of the sustainers of Order, for whose sacrifice Ahura Mazdā, sustainer of Order, knows the best reward, and, among all these, to Zarathustra, whose Guidance—the first and best, as we have always heard—was from Ahura Mazdā.

[153]And we sacrifice to this earth, to yonder sky, and to the good things in between, which are worthy of sacrifice and hymns, to which a man sustaining Order should offer sacrifices.

[154]We sacrifice to the breath-souls of the undomesticated animals, if harmless, and we sacrifice to the breath-souls of the sustainers of Order, wherever they were born, men and women, whose good vision-souls are winning, shall win, or have already won.

Prayers

[156]Satisfied may the unshakable pre-souls of the sustainers of Order, strong and rich in obstruction-smashing strength, the pre-souls of the First Guides and those of our closest relatives come to this home! Satisfied may they move about in this home! [157]Satisfied may they invite good, bountiful Ashi hither to this house as a friend! May they leave this house satisfied! May they carry with them our praises and truthful utterance for Ahura Mazdā, who has set everything in place, and for the Life-giving Immortals.

May they not leave this house of ours complaining, we who sacrifice to Ahura Mazdā.

18 *King Yima's enclosure (Videvdad 2)*

[1]Zarathustra asked Ahura Mazdā:

Ahura Mazdā, most Life-giving Spirit, who set in place all things in the world of the living with bones, sustainer of Order, with whom among men did you first converse, you, Ahura Mazdā, other than me, Zarathustra? To whom did you display the Tradition, that of Ahura Mazdā and Zarathustra?

²Then Ahura Mazdā said:

Beautiful Yima with good herds, O Zarathustra, sustainer of Order, was the first among men with whom I conversed other than you, Zarathustra. To him I displayed the Tradition, that of Ahura Mazdā and Zarathustra.

³Then I, Ahura Mazdā, said to him:

O beautiful Yima, son of Wiwanghwant! Accept to be the reciter and upholder of the Tradition!

Then beautiful Yima answered me:

It is not my place nor assignment to be the reciter and upholder of the Tradition!

The golden age

⁴Then I, Ahura Mazdā, said to him:

If you, O Yima, do not accept to be the reciter and upholder of the Tradition, then further my herds and make them grow! Accept to be the protector, guardian, and overseer of my herds!

⁵Then beautiful Yima answered me:

I shall accept to be the protector, guardian, and overseer of your herds. Under my command there shall be no cold or heat, no illness or destruction!

⁶Then I gave him two tools: a golden pick and a gilded goad. ⁷Thus Yima possessed two commands.

⁸When three hundred winters under Yima's command were complete, this earth became full of animals, small and large, of men, dogs, and birds, and of red and blazing fires, and they found no place here.

⁹Then I informed Yima:

O beautiful Yima son of Wiwanghwant! So many animals ... fires have accumulated here that this earth is full and they find no place here.

¹⁰Then, at noon, Yima went forth toward the lights on the path of the sun. He pushed this earth with the golden pick. He goaded it with the goad, saying:

O lovable Life-giving Humility, go forth, bend far and wide, O carrier of animals, small and large, and of men!

¹¹Thus Yima made this earth expand by one third of what it had been before. Here animals, small and large, and men went forth, all according to wish and pleasure.

¹²When six hundred winters of Yima's command were complete, this earth. . . .

¹⁵Thus Yima made this earth expand by two thirds of what it had been before. . . .

¹⁶When nine hundred winters of Yima's command were complete, this earth. . . .

¹⁹Thus Yima made this earth expand by three thirds of what it had been before. . . .

²⁰Ahura Mazdā, who set everything in place, convoked a meeting with those worthy of sacrifice in the world of thought, famed in the Aryan Expanse of the Good Lawful River.

Radiant Yima with good herds convoked a meeting with the best humans, famed in the Aryan Expanse of the Good Lawful River.

²¹Ahura Mazdā came to that meeting with those worthy of sacrifice. . . .

Yima with good herds came to that meeting radiant with the best humans. . . .

Yima makes the bunker

²²Then Ahura Mazdā said to Yima:

O beautiful Yima, son of Wiwanghwant, bad winters will come over the world of the living with bones, one particularly harsh, horrible winter, in which much snow will snow in drives on the tallest mountains and in the deepest river valleys.

²³And threefold cattle will perish here, O Yima, that in the most fearful of places, on the high mountains and that which is in the deep river valleys, as well as that in the most solid houses.

²⁴Before this winter, after the snow melt, pasture and water were plentiful in the land, but, now, it will seem wondrous to the existence with bones, O Yima, if the footprint of a sheep should be seen here!

²⁵"So, make an enclosure the length of a race-course on each of its four sides. Bring together there the seeds of animals, small and large, of men, dogs, and birds, and of red and blazing fires!

And make that enclosure the length of a race-course on each of its four sides as a dwelling for men, the length of a race-course on each of its four sides as a keep for cattle!

²⁶Make water flow together there the length of a league! Place evergreen meadows there, with savory, inexhaustible (pasture). Place houses there with roof and an awning, a porch and a fence!

²⁷Bring together there seeds from all the greatest, best, and most beautiful men and women on this earth; of the greatest, best, and most beautiful cattle species on this earth; ²⁸of the tallest and most sweet-smelling plants on this earth; and of the sweetest and most fragrant foods on this earth!

Make those into pairs to remain imperishable as long as these men are in the enclosures!

²⁹But include no one carrying the marks that the Evil Spirit put on man: humps in front or in the back, impotence, drivel, pustules, crooked walk, irregular teeth and no one with blotches, whose body has been secluded!

³⁰In the first section of the land make nine passages, in the middle six, and in the last three! In the first passage bring a thousand seeds of men and women, in the middle six hundred, in the last four hundred!

With the golden pick stroke the enclosure from behind to make a door admitting light, self-shining from inside!

³¹Yima reflected:

How shall I make this enclosure the way you, Ahura Mazdā, told me?

Then Ahura Mazdā said to Yima:

O beautiful Yima, son of Wiwanghwant, tread apart this earth with your heels, kneed it apart with your hands, just like people now, too, step about in wet earth!

³²And Yima did exactly what Ahura Mazdā wished him to. He trod apart this earth with his heels, he kneeded it apart with his hands, just like people now, too, step about in wet earth.

³³Then Yima made that enclosure the length of a race-course on each of its four sides. He brought together there the seeds of animals. . . .

And Yima made that enclosure the length of a race-course on each of its four sides as a dwelling for men. . . .

³⁴He made water flow forth there the length of a league. He placed meadows there. . . . He placed homes there. . . .

³⁵⁻³⁶He brought together there the seeds of the greatest, best, and most beautiful men and women. . . .

He made those into pairs. . . .

³⁷He excluded anyone carrying the marks that the Evil Spirit put on man. . . .

³⁸In the first section of the land he made nine passages, in the middle six, and in the last four. In the first passage he brought a thousand seeds of men and women, the middle six hundred, the last four hundred.

With the golden pick he stroked the enclosure from behind to make a door admitting light, self-shining from inside.

³⁹O you who set in place the world of the living with bones, sustainer of Order! What were these lights that shine hither in these enclosures that Yima made?

⁴⁰Then Ahura Mazdā said:

Those were lights set in place by themselves and for the temporal existence. Once extinguished, the stars, moon, and sun are seen to appear (?).

⁴¹And those (in the enclosure) think a year is but a day. In forty years, two humans, man and woman, are born from two humans, thus also the cattle species. And they live the most beautiful life in these enclosures that Yima made.

⁴²O you who set in place the world of the living with bones, sustainer of Order, who brought the Mazdayasnian Tradition far and wide in these enclosures that Yima made?

Then Ahura Mazdā said:

The Karshipta bird, O Zarathustra, sustainer of Order.

[43]O you who set in place the world of the living with bones, sustainer of Order, who is their Archetype (*ahu*) and Model (*ratu*)?

Then Ahura Mazdā said:

Urwatadnara and you, Zarathustra.

From the Pahlavi Texts

19 *What is said about the daily homage to Ohrmazd the creator (Dēnkard III, 81)*

[1]A Zoroastrian who has performed the sacrifice within the daily period, as is well-known, should perform the homage to Ohrmazd, the creator, addressing it to the sun in Avestan.

A common Zoroastrian, whether he usually performs the sacrifice or not, until he has completed the sacrifice, while performing the homage to Ohrmazd, the creator, should be addressing to the sun the text written below.

He who knowingly and thinkingly and in his action has spoken the Praise of Righteousness (the *Ashem Vohū*) three times at the end of the text, he should, at the end of each line, do deep homage and then give it again. Sometimes a priest utters the good Tradition:

[2]Praise of the names of him who always was, always is, and will always be: God, Spirit of Increase, who is one among the many in the other world and is in himself One, whose name is Lord Ohrmazd, the greatest knowledgeable one, who nurtures and protects, who is beneficent and pure, whose deeds are good, who forgives, whose judgements are good, who has all powers, and whose worship is great and enduring!

[3]He created by his own unmatched power and knowledge, above all, the six Amahrspands and the miracle of the many gods, the light paradise, Garōdmān, the orb of the sky, the warming sun, the shining moon, the stars containing many seeds, wind and atmosphere, fire, water, earth, plants, and beasts, metals, and mankind.

⁴We offer our sacrifice and homage to him, the lord of good deeds, who, of all the creatures in this world, made man the greatest in ability to speak, in artistry, as prince of the age, and organizer of the creatures for fighting the demons in battle.

⁵Homage to the all-aware and beneficent one, who sent Zarathustra of the Spitāmas as messenger to give the creatures knowledge and belief in the Tradition, the inborn wisdom and the wisdom-acquired-through-hearing [cf. p. 32], familiarity with the battle, the ability to organize all those who are, have been, and will be, and the skill above all skills, enabling the soul (*ruwān*) to escape the punishments in hell and pass on to the bright, fragrant Best Existence of the righteous, which is all comfort.

⁶By your command, O beneficent one, I receive, think, speak, and perform the pure Tradition, and I assign myself with praise to every good deed, and I regret my many evil deeds.

⁷I keep my selfness pure, as well as all my noble actions and abstentions and the six powers (*zōr*) of the soul (*gyān*): action, speech, thought, perception (*wīr*), intelligence (*ōsh*), and wisdom (*khrad*).

⁸At your wish, you whose deeds are good, I perform to the extent I am able, my worship of you, by good thoughts, words, and deeds, so that you may keep me on the bright road, so that the severe fright of hell may not come upon me, so that I may pass the Ford of Lamentations and arrive in that fragrant and all-adorned house of paradise, which is all comfort!

⁹Praise to him, the lord who forgives, who rewards our wishes and good deeds when we act according to his command, and who, in the end, delivers even the wicked from hell and redresses the whole creation in purity!

20 On demons (Bundahishn 27)

⁵Akōman's task is to make the creatures think the worst thoughts and take peace away from them.

⁶The demon Indar's task is to make the creatures' thought turn from good bahavior and to freeze it so it is like frozen ice. He also throws it into people's minds that they need not wear the sacred shirt and belt.

⁷The demon Sāwul is the chief of the demons and his job is to produce evil rule, violence, lawlessness, and oppression.

⁸The demon Nānghaith's task is to make the creatures unsatisfied.

⁹For, as they say, he pleases Indar, Sāwul, and Nānghaith who gives something to people who abide by the law that one need not wear the sacred shirt and belt.

¹⁰The demon Tawrij is the one who mingles poison into the plants.

¹¹As they say: Tawrij is the one who suppresses (*tarw-*) and Zairij is the one who makes poison (*zahr*).

¹²The others are the helpers and collaborators of those six (animal?-)headed demons.

¹⁸As they say: Wrath established seven powers with which to destroy the creatures.

¹⁹And the Kays and the other heroes, in their respective ages, are struck by six of those powers, leaving one. Where the demon False Speech comes, Envy abides and Wrath strikes camp. Where Wrath is camped, he causes a lot of destruction and lays all things waste.

²⁰And it was Wrath who made most of the evil that befell the creatures of Ohrmazd, and it was mostly because of Wrath's misdoings that the Kays and the other heroes were annihilated.

²²The demon Drag-off is the one who struggles with the souls of the dead during the three nights they remain in this world and brings fear and blows upon them. He sits at the door to hell.

²³And the demon Ōdag is the one who tells people when they sit on the toilet or are eating: "Just talk!" And then they talk while eating or defecating and urinating to such an extent that they will never come to paradise.

²⁴Aktash is the demon of negligence, who makes the creatures negligent of good behavior. ²⁵As they say: He who gives something to a person who keeps people negligent of good bahavior pleases the demon Aktash. He who gives something to a person who abides by the rule that one needs no teacher to guide one pleases the demon Wrath. He who gives something to a person who abides by the

rule that one needs no snake-beater pleases Ahrimen and all the other demons. ²⁶About him they say that he strikes no evil animals when he sees them. ²⁷The snake-beater is a piece of wood with a piece of pelt attached to the end, and it is manifest that every good Zoroastrian should have one for striking evil animals and evil-doers. Killing them (in this way) is to be considered one of one's greater good deeds.

³⁰The demon Greed is the one who performs evil intercourse. ³¹ As they say: Greed is the one who leads where one should not go.

³⁹The demon Slander is he who brings and takes away words, and there is none like him. He speaks and insinuates in such a way that people strike and destroy one another.

⁴¹The demon Evil-eye is the lie-demon with salty eyes, who strikes people with the eyes.

⁴²The demon Bud ("idol") is the one they worship in India. And his word resides in those idols (*bud*), because they worshiped Būdāsf (the bodhisattva).

21 How the Spirit who makes Increase governs (Dēnkard III, 84)

The way the Spirit who makes Increase governs (*rāyēn-*) the Foul Spirit lies in the name itself of the Spirit who makes Increase, which is explained as "increase in being knowledgeable." And Foul is explained as "the most egregious bad awareness."

As witness one may adduce the fact that the more powerful (*nērōg*) the knowledge is, the more its governance results in increase. And the more bad awareness prevails, the more its governing results in neediness.

There are innumerable examples among humans, as well, that those who govern with knowledge stand above those who govern with bad awareness, and the ones with bad awareness need to be governed by those with knowledge.

According to the Tradition, the selfness of that Spirit is this: nothing is exempt from being governed by the Spirit who makes Increase. It is well known that it is typical of everything that comes from the Foul Spirit that the Spirit who makes Increase brings it all under his own governance.

The Foul Spirit's selfness has many reasons. One is connected with the diminished power of the Foul Spirit's selfness with regard to causing damage and harm to the creatures of the Spirit who makes Increase.

The victory over the Foul Spirit by the selfness of his self is even more manifest at the Perfectioning, when the Foul Spirit's selfness is completely anihilated by that governance.

22 About what this world is and as what it was established
   (Dēnkard III, 123)

About its function, borders, seed (tōhmag), shape (dēsag), kind (ēwēnag), form (kerb), and the strength (zōr) of its coming into existence.

About the reason for its growth, by what it came into existence, by what it was set in place.

To what (end) the things will come that have been disturbed, and whether they will be reorganized (ārāy-) or not. If they are reorganized, whether they will be reorganized in the appearance (chihr) they have taken on now or in a different one.

Whether there is some of the other world in this world, and what need there would be for that.

Where the other world borders on this world.

How the other world has power (nērōg) over growth, appearance, and what is of the other world, and how they combine and are complemented by one another.

Whether both gods and demons are of the other world. If both are of the other world, in what way they differ from one another.

About the creations of this world. What was established before the others and what after the others. How can they be seen and explained?

About the best of the creations of this world, the essence (gōhr) of the creatures and how it was contaminated. Where the world of the living will be purified of contamination and the one who purifies it.

About the power by which the world of the living was ordered and its beginning and end.

From what is told in the Tradition.

This world is a (temporal) being (*stī*), endowed with a body, visible and tangible. It was established to push back the oppression of the struggle, the oppressor being precisely the one who opposed its establishment. Connected with it is its eternal state of goodness.

As for the *function* assigned to it, this too will be manifest when the creatures of this world will have no function divested of pushing back the oppression.

The *borders* of this world are (defined by) what can be seen and touched: all that can be seen by the eyes of the body and touched by the hands of the body is this world.

The *seed* of this world is what had come into being by the creator's creation, established by means of the skill of his strength (*ōz*). Its name in the Tradition is "becoming," and the original of the creatures in this world is also known, notably, as "the warm-and-moist" and as "matter" (*mādī*).

Its *first shape* is that which had come into being from "becoming" by the creator's measured activity. Its name in the Tradition is "the process of becoming." Wind, fire, water, clay, the origin of the appearance of those in this world—these are the four that explicitly give it birth.

And its *second shape* is that which had come into being from "the process of becoming" by the creator's prudent (*frazānag*) activity. Its name is "state of becoming." It has, notably, four modes (*ristag*) from being mingled with (the four kinds of?) living beings.

Its *third shape* is from the creator's "watering" activity: the pre-soul and the breath-soul, temporal beings that unite the combined modes. They are, notably, humans, animals, and the other good living beings.

Since they were the last to receive a shape, they have been distributed in various forms and in so many single *powers* that are in them and have also come into other, different ones, but with the same essence.

23 On the Creation (Pahlavi Rivayat 46)

How and from what the sky was made

[2]The tool was something like a cinder of fire of pure light, which was fashioned from the Endless Light. [3]He made all the creations and creatures from it, and when he had made it, then he brought it into his body. He kept it for 3000 years in the body, making it grow and making it better. Then he kept fashioning (things) from his own body.

[4]First he fashioned the sky from the head. Its essence is of white crystal. It is as wide as it is high, and the depth to its foundation is as much as the depth of empty space. It is held up and out by the Righteous Man and the Expert Invitation, but it is held up by nothing in the world of the living. Ohrmazd sits inside it with his creations and creatures.

[5]Then he fashioned the earth from the feet. It is held up and out by the mountains. He filled it with Fortune as essence (gōhr), and from that essence the mountains grew for eighteen years both upward and downward. Then they stopped growing downward and only grew upward for another eight hundred years, until they reached the sky. The sky lies around the whole earth, like an egg with a chick in it. The earth is held up by nothing in the world of the living.

The world of the living

[9]There are seven continents. After Ahrimen attacked the world of the living, only Zarathustra had seen them all. Inside the sky is Mount Hariburz (surrounding the earth). It consists of 2244 mountains. [10]The Wourukasha Sea makes up one-third of this earth.

[11]Then he fashioned the water from the tears and placed some of it inside the earth, some on the earth, and some up in the air, and all of it began moving. [12]The water that contains more libations than polluted water, goes back to the Wourukasha Sea in three years; that which has as much of the one as the other, goes back in six years; and that which contains more polluted water than libations, goes back in nine years.

[13]Then he fashioned the plants from the hair. The first one was as tall as the width of a hand and two fingers, and it contained all plants

except one. This plant he placed in Ērānwēz. [14]Then birds, water, and men carried the plants from place to place.

The Bull and Gayōmard

[15]Then he fashioned the Bull from the right hand and placed it in the Aryan Expanse. It was as high and wide as five men. When Ahrimen attacked, it died right away, but its semen fell on the ground, and Ohrmazd made all the animal species from it. First he made a male and female of every species, and their lineage went forth. They rejoice when they get water and fodder both summer and winter, but suffer when men kill and treat them without law and order and give them no water and fodder and do not protect them from enemies, thieves, and wolves. Such thirst and hunger came upon the Bull that it lost the strength of its body (ōz), its endurance (zōr), its power (nērōg), and ability to see and hear.

[28]Then he fashioned the fire from its "core" (wārom), and he fashioned its brilliance (brāh) from the Endless Lights.

[36]Then he made mankind from the clay from which Gayōmard was made. This clay had been deposited in Spandarmad (the earth) in the form of semen, and Gayōmard was then fashioned and born from Spandarmad. He remained immobile for 3000 years, and when Ahrimen rushed in, it took thirty years before he moved. He was killed the day of Ohrmazd, month of Frawardīn (at spring-equinox, first day of the year). His semen fell on the earth and lay in the earth for forty years.

[37]Then Mahlī and Mahliyānī grew up from the earth in the form of a rhubarb, straight up with their hands in the back. Then they were turned into human form and bore six sons and six daughters. Some of them lived, and some died, and from them all of humanity is descended.

24 On the Creation (Bundahishn 1)

About Ohrmazd and the Foul Spirit

[0]That awareness from the Zand concerning what Ohrmazd set in place in the beginning and the Opposition of the Foul Spirit. Next,

about how everything was set in place, from the beginning to the end, as it is manifest in the Mazdayasnian Tradition . . .:

¹Ohrmazd was in the highest place in omniscience and goodness for an unlimited time in the light. ²That light is the throne and place of Ohrmazd. Some say the "Endless Lights." That omniscience and goodness was there for an unbounded time, that is, there were Ohrmazd, his goodness, the Tradition, and the Time of Ohrmazd.

³Ahrimen was in darkness in the depths with backward knowledge and desire to kill. ⁴His desire to kill is his nature (*khēm*) and that darkness his place. Some say "Endless Darkness."

⁵⁻⁶Between them there was the Emptiness—some (say) "Wāy"— in which what is bounded and what is unbounded mingle.

⁷When it says "highest," it means the "endless lights," that is, they have no "head" (= end). And the depth is the "endless darkness," and that is something unbounded.

⁸And at the border they are both bounded, for between them is emptiness, so they are not connected with one another. Any other being in the world of thought is also bounded in its body.

⁹As for the "all-awareness" of Ohrmazd: everything that is in the knowledge of Ohrmazd is bounded, because he knows the measure of the two Spirits.

¹⁰The total rule of the creation of Ohrmazd at the Final Body is for ever and ever, and that is something unbounded. ¹¹At that time, the creation of Ahrimen will be cut off, so that the Final Body may come into being, which is also something bounded.

¹²Ohrmazd in his all-awareness knew: "The Foul Spirit exists. He is plotting in his envy how to mingle with my Creation from the beginning to the end!" and also with what and how many tools. So he brought forth that creation as the tool *he* needed for that.

¹³For 3000 years—which are over— the creation remained in the world of thought, unthinking, unmoving, and untouchable.

¹⁴The Foul Spirit, because of his backward knowledge, was unaware of the existence of Ohrmazd. Then he rose up from those depths and came to the border where he could see the lights.

¹⁵When he saw that light of Ohrmazd, untouchable and blazing (*payrōg*) forth, because his desire is to kill and his essence (*gōhr*) is envy, he attacked it in order to destroy it.

¹⁶But when he saw valor and superiority greater than his own, he rushed down to the darkness and fashioned forth, inexpertly, many demons and lie-demons, a destructive creation suited for the battle.

¹⁷Ohrmazd saw the creation of the Foul Spirit, and it pleased him not. They were terrifying, rotten creatures of evil desire, and he did not honor them.

¹⁸Then the Foul Spirit saw Ohrmazd's creation, and it pleased him. It was a great creation, profound, victorious, all-informed, and he honored it.

¹⁹Then Ohrmazd, although he knew how the creation would be in the end, offered the Foul Spirit peace, saying: "Bring my creation aid, and praise it! As reward, you will not die or grow old, you will not deteriorate or be impaired."

²⁰The meaning is that, if he were not to provoke the battle, then he would not himself become undone, and profit would accrue to both Spirits from it.

²¹The Foul Spirit howled: "I shall not bring your creation aid, I shall not praise it! Rather, I shall destroy you *and* your creation for ever and ever! I shall incite all your creations to unfriendliness to you but friendliness to me!"

²²And the explanation for it is this: he thought that Ohrmazd could do nothing against him, therefore he was offering peace, so he refused and even threatened.

²³And Ohrmazd said: "You cannot do everything, Foul Spirit," i.e., you cannot destroy my creation, and you can also not cause my creation *not* to come back into my possession.

²⁴Then Ohrmazd in his all-awareness knew: "If I do not set a time for the battle with him, then he can do to my creation as he threatened, and there will be struggle and mixture forever from it. He can sit down in the Mixture of the creation and make it his own, in the way

that there are many people now in the Mixture who do more evil than good things, so that they always do the will of the Foul Spirit.

²⁵And Ohrmazd said to the Foul Spirit: "Pick a date for the battle. By this pact we will delay it to 9000 years from now!" For he knew that by setting the date he would undo the Foul Spirit.

²⁶Then the Foul Spirit, who could not see what the end would be, agreed to the extent of the delay, in the same way that two men set the time for a duel: "Let us do battle on such and such a day until night-fall!"

²⁷Ohrmazd knew this too in his all-awareness that, during these 9000 years, 3000 years would go all according to the will of Ohrmazd, the 3000 years of the Mixture would go according to the will of both Ohrmazd and Ahrimen, and in the final battle it would be possible to undo the Foul Spirit and keep Opposition away from the creation.

²⁸Then Ohrmazd uttered the twenty-one words of the *Ahuna Wairiya*, showing the Foul Spirit his own final victory, the undoing of the Foul Spirit, the annihilation of the demons, the resurrection and the Final Body, and the freedom from Opposition for the creation for ever and ever.

²⁹When the Foul Spirit saw his own undoing together with the annihilation of the demons, he was stunned and lost consciousness. He fell back to the darkness.

³⁰As it is said in the Tradition: "When one-third was spoken, the Foul Spirit blanked out for fear; when two-thirds were spoken the Foul Spirit fell to his knees; when it was all spoken, the Foul Spirit became undone."

³¹Unable to harm Ohrmazd's creation, the Foul Spirit lay in a stupor for 3000 years.

The world of thought

³³First I shall discuss how the creations were set in place in the world of thought, then in the world of the living.

³⁴Before his creations were set in place, Ohrmazd was not Lord, but afterward he became "Lord, profit-seeker, wise, harm-discarding,

apparent, all-arranging, increasing, and all-observing." [These are Pahlavi renderings of Avestan terms.]

³⁴His first creation was self-established Well-being, that entity in the world of thought by which he made his body better when he *thought* the Creation. For his being "lord" is from setting in place the creation.

³⁵By his clear-sight, he saw that the Foul Spirit would never turn away from bringing Opposition; that the Opposition would not be undone other than by setting in place the creation; that the creation would not come into motion other than through time; and that, when he fashioned time, the creation of Ahrimen would also be set in motion.

³⁶But, having no other way out (*chārag*), he fashioned Time in order to undo the Opposition.

³⁷The meaning of this is: the Foul Spirit can only be undone through battle. The meaning of "battle" (*kār-chār*) is this: an action (*kār*) must be performed by a means (*chār*) and according to one's means.

³⁸After unbounded time, he created Time-of-long-rule. Some call it bounded time. From Time-of-long-rule he created "Non-passing-away," so that nothing made by Ohrmazd would pass away.

From Non-passing-away "Lack of comfort" appeared, so that the demons should have no comfort.

³⁹Ahrimen was in his evil creation, knowing nothing and obeying no laws.

⁴⁰Its meaning and explanation is: when Ahrimen fights with Ohrmazd, the lordly prudence, naming, excellence, and non-passing-away of Ohrmazd and the inefficiency of his self-loving and non-excellence of the backward knowledge of the Foul Spirit appeared when he set in place the creation.

⁴¹For Time of long rule was also the first creation Ohrmazd fashioned. For time was bounded before Ohrmazd's eternity was affected by the Mixture. He now fashioned bounded time from the unbounded time. That is, from the first creation, when he set in place the creations, to the end, when the Foul Spirit becomes undone, there is a

measure of 12,000 years, which is bounded. Then it returns to being unbounded. That is, the creation of Ohrmazd will then be with Ohrmazd forever in a state of purity.

[43]From his own selfness, from the existing (*stī*) light, Ohrmazd fashioned forth the form of his own creatures, in the form of fire, white, round, visible from afar.

[44]From the living form of the entity in the world of thought that is capable of removing the Opposition in both creations, that is Time— he fashioned the form of Good Wāy, since Wāy was needed. Some say it was Wāy-of-long-rule.

[45]He fashioned the creation with the help of Wāy-of-long-rule. For when he set in place the creation, Wāy was also one of the tools he needed.

[46]The Foul Spirit fashioned, inexpertly, from essential darkness, his own creation in a black form the color of ashes, "worthy of darkness," lying, like the most sinful evil animal.

[47]From existing self-love he fashioned Greed (Waran) in the form of the worst Dēn; for Greed was needed.

[48]First he set in place "evil going" as the selfness of the demons, the entity in the world of thought from which foulness came to the creatures of Ohrmazd. For he set in place a creation by which he made his body worse, so that he will become undone.

From existing darkness, the Endless Darkness, he set in place Lying Speech; it appeared from the evilness of that Foul Spirit. From Endless Darkness he fashioned that form, and he placed his creation inside that form, and he will be undone from the creation he himself created.

[49]From existing light Ohrmazd set in place Truthful Speech. And from Truthful Speech the creator's ability to increase appeared, which he fashioned from the Endless Light. And the creation too was set in place inside an endless form, separate from the passing of time.

From this form the *Ahuna Wairiya* appeared in the world of thought, from which the creation and the end of the creatures was manifest. That is the Tradition, as the Tradition was set in place when the creation was set in place.

From the *Ahuna Wairiya* the year in the world of thought came about, which now in the Mixture is half light and half dark, 365 days-and-nights, which is the division of Time-of-long-rule.

[50]And in the struggle both creations were set in motion by it.

[52](. . .) And Ohrmazd maintained the world of thought in the world of thought.

He set in place the world of the living in the world of thought, and then he passed it on to the world of the living.

Of the creation in the world of thought, first he set in place the Amahrspands, first six, then the others. The seventh was Ohrmazd himself.

Of the creation of the world of the living in the world of thought, first six, the seventh was he himself. For both the world of thought and the world of the living in the world of thought are Ohrmazd('s). First, the world of the living is from the Amahrspands, then from Time-of-long-rule.

First of them he fashioned Wahman, from whom the creatures of Ohrmazd were set in motion.

The Foul Spirit first fashioned Akōman by uttering a false statement.

Of the creation of the world of the living, first there was the sky.

And first he fashioned Wahman from the goodness of the exisiting light, together with whom was the good Mazdayasnian Tradition. This implies that he knew what was going to befall the creation until the Perfectioning.

Next came Ardwahisht, Shahrewar, Spandarmad, Hordad, Amurdad, and the seventh was Ohrmazd himself.

The eighth was Truthful Speech, the ninth Srōsh-ahlaw, the tenth the Divine Word, the eleventh Nēryōsang, the twelfth the Exalted Model, the thirteenth Rashn the Straight, the fourteenth Mihr Frākh-gōyōd, the fifteenth good Arshishwang, the sixteenth Pārand, the seventeenth sleep, the eighteenth the wind, the nineteenth lawfulness, the twentieth debate, prosecution and defense, peace, and ability to grow.

The world of the living in the world of thought

[53]Of the world of the living first the sky, second the water, third the earth, fourth the plants, fifth the cattle, sixth mankind, seventh Ohrmazd himself.

And he fashioned the creation with the help of Wāy-of-long-rule.(. . .)

[54]As Opponents, the Foul Spirit fashioned first Akōman, then Indar, Sāwul, Nānghaith, Tarōmad, Tawrij and Zairij, the other demons, and seventh the Foul Spirit himself.

[55]Never does he think, say, or do anything good. He has no use for the goodness of Ohrmazd's creation, and Ohrmazd has no use for the "goodness" of the Foul Spirit's creation.

[56]Ohrmazd does not think something that he cannot do. The Foul Spirit thinks what he cannot do and even threatens to do it.

Gestation of the world of the living in the world of thought

[57]Ohrmazd nurtured his creation in the world of thought in such a way that it was in moisture, unthinking, unseizable, unmoving, like semen.

After the state of moisture, there was a mixture like semen and blood; after the mixture there was a rolled-up lump, like a . . ., then protrusions, like hands and feet, then cavities, like eyes and mouth, then motion, when it came into the light. Still, in the world of the living, they are formed in the mother's womb and born and nurtured in that way.

[58]And by setting in place the creation Ohrmazd is its father and mother. For when he nurtured the creation in the world of thought, that was being its mother, when he transferred it into the world of the living, that was being its father.

25 *Creation of the world of the living in the world of the living*
   (*Bundahishn 1a*)

[1]When the Foul Spirit was undone and lying unconscious, as I wrote above, he lay stunned for 3000 years.

²During that inactivity of the Foul Spirit, Ohrmazd fashioned the creation into the world of the living.

From the Endless Light he fashioned fire, from fire wind, from wind water, and from water the earth with all things with bones.

³As it says in the Tradition: The first creation was a drop of all waters, that is, everything was from water, except the semen of men and animals, for that semen is from fire.

³First he set in place the sky to keep back—some say *it* was the first; second the water, to strike the lie-demon of thirst; third the earth with all things with bones; fourth the plants, to help the beneficent cow; fifth the Bull/cow, to help the Righteous Man (i.e., Gayōmard); sixth he set in place the Righteous Man, to strike and undo the Foul Spirit together with the demons.

⁴Next he set in place the fire as ember (*khwarg*) and attached to it the brilliance (*brāh*) of the Endless Light. Thus it has a good form, as is the fire's wish.

Next he set in place the wind in the form of a fifteen-year-old youth, to carry and hold up the water and plants, the Bull/cow and the Righteous Man, and everything else.

⁵And I shall say how they are.

⁶First he set in place the sky, light, visible, very far and in the shape of an egg, made of shining metal, that is, its essence was steel and male, and connected its top to the Endless Light [cf. 17:2]. He set in place the entire creation inside the sky, like a fortified camp, in which all the tools needed for the battle have been placed, or like a house in which everything is stored.

The foundation of the sky is as thick as it is long, as long as it is high, as high as it is deep, with uniform measure, like the helmet of a mace-bearing (soldier). It was endowed with thought, speech, and action and was aware, causing increase, and discriminating. Thus was the sky in the world of thought.

It received a firm fortification against the Foul Spirit in order not to let him run back. Like a heroic soldier dressed in armor so that he is saved from the battle without fear, thus the sky in the world of thought holds up the sky (in this world).

To help the sky he established bliss, for by means of it he established bliss, for even now in the Mixture the creation is *in* bliss.

⁷Second, from the essence of the sky he fashioned water, which flowed as deep as when a man puts his hands on the earth and walks on hands and feet and the water reaches him to the stomach. To help it he gave it the wind, the rain, fog, mist, and snow.

⁸Third, from the water he created the earth, round, with its passages reaching far into the distance, without depressions or elevations, even, its length equal to its width, its width equal to its depth. He set it up in the middle of the sky.

. . .

¹¹Fourth he created the plants. First, one grew up above the earth as high as a stride, without branches, bark, or thorns, moist and sweet. And it contained the power of all the plant species in its seed. To help the plant he gave it water and fire, for every single species of plants has a drop of water at the end and a fire four fingers long before it. By that power it kept growing.

¹²Fifth, in Ērānwēz in the middle of the world on the shore of the good River Dāitī, where the middle of the world is, he fashioned the Bull placed alone: white, luminous, like a moon that measures three spears in height. To help it he gave it water and plants, for during the Mixture it receives strength and growth from them.

¹³Sixth he fashioned Gayōmard, luminous like the sun—he measured four spears in height, his width equal to his height—on the shore of the River Dāitī, where the middle of the world is, Gayōmard on the left, the Bull on the right. And the distance between them and the distance from the water of the Dāitī was as much as their respective heights. He possessed eyes, ears, a tongue, and a mark. The "mark" of Gayōmard is the following: mankind is born from his seed in that manner.

To help him he gave him sleep, the relaxation of the creator. For Ohrmazd fashioned forth that sleep in the shape of a luminous tall young man of fifteen. And he fashioned Gayōmard together with the Bull from the earth. And from the light and turquoise color of the sky he fashioned the semen of humans and cattle, as these two semens are seed from fire, not from water. He placed them in the bodies of Gayōmard and the Bull so that it would produce plenitude of men and cattle.

26 Preparations for the battle (Bundahishn 3)

[2]When the Foul Spirit came against Ohrmazd, he fashioned Time-of-long-rule in the form of a fifteen-year-old man, luminous, white-eyed, tall, strong, with his strength from skill, not from theft and violence.

[3]He donned a white garment and held the office of High Priest. For all knowledge is with the high priests, who then teach people, and everybody learns from them. [4]Ohrmazd's proper function was setting in place the creation, and the creation can be set in place by knowledge. Therefore he donned the office of knowledgeable men, that is, that of High Priest.

[5]Good Wāy donned a gold and silver, diamond-studded garment, variegated, multicolored, and held the office of Warriorhood. For he was to go after the enemies to smash the Opposition and protect the creation. [6]As it is said: Wāy's proper function is removing the Opposition in both creations, the ones the Life-giving and Foul Spirits set in place, so that, when they start the battle, then Ohrmazd's creation will be increasing, while that of the Foul Spirit will be cut off.

[7]From Time, he fashioned the firmament, the body of Zurwān-of-long-rule, the good assignment of fates. He donned a dark-blue garment and held the office of Husbandry. For his proper function is like that of husbandmen to cultivate herds appropriately.

[8]Ohrmazd set in place the world of thought and the world of the living in the same manner in groups of seven.

In the world of thought, there were Ohrmazd and the six Amahrspands.

Likewise, the sky has seven levels: the cloud level; the sphere with the stars; the unmingled stars; paradise, where the moon is; Garōdmān, also called the light without beginning, where the sun is; the throne of the Amahrsapands; and the Endless Light, the throne of Ohrmazd.

[9]In the same way, he fashioned seven creations in the world of the living: the sky, the water, the earth, the plant, the cattle, man, and the fire, whose brilliance is from the Endless Light, the throne of Ohrmazd.

[10]Then he filled fire into each creation that he fashioned, like a house-master who goes into the house and puts his clothes down neatly in the house.

[11]He ordered the Fire to serve men during the Assault, to make food, and strike away pain. (...)

[12]And he appointed and positioned all the Amahrspands so as to take part in the battle of the creatures, so that when the Assault comes, each takes on his own opponent to fight, that is, no new command is needed. I shall say how they are below.

Creation of the seven Life-giving Immortals and their corresponding helpers and their charges in the world of the living

[14]The first of beings in the world of thought is Ohrmazd. He took mankind as his own, as the first of beings in the world of the living. And he gave them as helpers the three "Creators": the Throne (*gāh*), the Tradition (*dēn*), and Time (*zamān*), all having the name "Creator" (*day*), from which the entire creation in the world of thought comes.

[15]He set in place mankind in five parts: body, breath-soul (*gyān*), soul (*ruwān*), frame (*ēwēnag*), and pre-soul (*frawahr*). That is, the body is what is living. The breath-soul is what is connected with the wind, inhaling and exhaling (?). The soul is that which, in the body together with the consciousness (*bōy*), hears, sees, talks, and knows. The frame is what is on the sun level. The pre-soul is what is before the Lord Ohrmazd. They were fashioned in order that, when men die during the period of the Assault, the body is connected with the earth, the breath-soul with the wind, the frame with the sun, and the soul with the pre-soul, so that it will be impossible for the demons to destroy the soul.

[16]Second of beings in the world of thought is Wahman. Of beings in the world of the living, he received the cattle species as his own. And to help him he gave him the Moon, Gōsh (Avestan "cow"), the Lord Firmament, boundless Time, and Time-of-long-rule.

[17]He brought forth cattle in five parts: body, breath-soul, soul, frame, and spirit (*mēnōy*), so that, during the period of the Assault, Gōshurūn would receive the seed of cattle from the moon level and, with the help of good Rām (= Wāy), would send it forth among the living. When they die, the body is attached to Gōshurūn, the soul to Rām, the frame to the moon, and the "spirit" to Wahman, so that it will be impossible for the demons to destroy them.

[18]Third of beings in the world of thought is Ardwahisht. Of beings in the world of the living, he received the fire as his own. To help him he gave him Ādur (the Fire), Srōsh, Warahrān, and Nēryōsang, so that, during the period of the Assault, Warahrān would provide a stronghold for the fire that is seated and arrayed in the house, and Srōsh would protect it. When it goes out, it goes from Warahrān to Srōsh, from Srōsh to Ādur, and from Ādur it is again attached to Ardwahisht, so that it will be impossible for the demons to destroy it.

[19]Fourth of beings in the world of thought is Shahrewar. Of beings in the world of the living he took the metals as his own. To help him he gave him the Sun, Mihr, the Sky, Anagrān (Avestan: the Light without beginning), the good Sōg (Glow?), Ardwīsūr, the divine Hōm, the Exalted divine one (Burz-yazd), and Dahmān Āfrīn. For the solidity of metals is from the sky. The primary essence of the sky is . . . (?) metal. And it is arrayed from Anagrān, in which there is a luminous house of gold, studded with precious stones, and it is connected upward to the throne of the Amahrspands, so that, in the period of the Assault, it will be impossible for the demons to destroy it.

[20]Fifth of beings in the world of thought is Spandarmad. Of beings in the world of the living, she received the earth as her own. To help her he gave her Ābān (the Waters), Dēn, Ard, Mahr-spand, Arshishwang, and Ardwīsūr Anāhīd. As for Arshishwang, she is the one in the world of thought who purifies the earth and the seed of the

waters. And before her is Mahr-spand or Mānsr-spand, the speech of Ohrmazd. And Ard and Dēn are in the Fortune of the house. From Arshishwang, one says, comes the Fortune of paradise, one-ness with Order. Ardwīsūr Anāhīd is father and mother of the waters. In the period of the Assault, Spandarmad is set up with these assistants, who help her safeguard the Fortune in the world of thought.

[21] Sixth of beings in the world of thought is Hordad. Of beings in the world of the living he received the water as his own. To help him, he gave him Tīr or Tishtar, the Wind, and Frawardīn (the pre-souls), so that, in the period of the Assault, with the help of Frawardīn, some say the pre-souls (frawahr) of the Righteous, he may take that water and deliver it in the world of thought to the wind. The Wind drives those waters briskly to the various continents and makes them pass (from one to the next), and, together with its helpers, rains it down by means of the clouds.

[22] Seventh of beings in the world of thought is Amurdad. Of beings in the world of the living he received the plant as his own. To help him he gave him Rashn, Ashtād (Rectitude), and Zamyād (the Fortune placed in the earth), the three Fortunes who are there at the Chinwad bridge and, in the period of the Assault, bring the souls of men to account for their good and bad deeds.

Ohrmazd's sacrifice and the pre-souls

[26] At Midday, Ohrmazd with the Amahrspands prepared the sacrifice in the world of thought. During the performance of the sacrifice, the entire creation was set in place. With him were the pre-souls of mankind, who brought all-aware, thoughtful wisdom to mankind.

He said: "Which seems more profitable to you: that I fashion you forth to the world of the living so that you will fight in bodily form with the Lie until you cut it off and I will redress you immortal in the end and again give you to the world of the living where you will forever be deathless, ageless, without Opponents, or that you should eternally protect (the world of thought) against the Assault?"

²⁷The pre-souls of mankind saw by their all-aware wisdom the evil from the Lie and Ahrimen that would befall them in the world of the living, but, because the opposition from the Adversary would disappear in the end and they would again become sound and immortal in the Final Body for ever and ever, they agreed to go (to the world of the living).

27 The Assault (Bundahishn 4)

The Foul Spirit is roused

¹It says in the Tradition that, when the Foul Spirit saw that both he and the demons would be undone by the Righteous Man, he had been stunned. For 3000 years he lay stunned.

²During that stupor, the (animal-?)headed demons one by one lied: "Rise up, our father, for we will fight such a battle that Ohrmazd and the Amahrspands will be in dire straits!"

³One by one they enumerated their evil deeds in detail.

⁴It did not pacify the wicked Foul Spirit, and he did not rise from his stupor for fear of the Righteous Man until the wicked Whore came at the completion of the 3000 years and lied: "Rise up, our father, for in that battle I shall let loose so much harm upon the Righteous Man and the toiling Bull that their lives will not be worth living. I shall steal their Fortune, I shall harm the water, the earth, the fire, the plant, and the entire creation established by Ohrmazd!"

⁵She enumerated her evil-doings in such detail that the Foul Spirit was pacified. He jumped out of his stupor and placed a kiss on the Whore's head. The pollution now called "menses" appeared on the Whore then.

⁶The Foul Spirit lied to the Whore: "Ask for whatever you want, and I will give it to you!"

⁷Then Ohrmazd knew in his omniscience that, at that time, the Foul Spirit was able to give the Whore what she wanted and that she would acquire much profit thereby.

The Foul Spirit's body was like a frog to look at, but he showed a man like a fifteen-year-old youth to the Whore and bound the Whore's mind to him.

⁸The Whore lied to the Foul Spirit: "Give me the desire for man, so that I can sit down as his ward in his house!"

⁹The Foul Spirit lied to her: "I shall not tell you to ask for anything again, for you only know how to ask for profitless, bad things." But the time had passed, and if she had asked for it, he would not have been able to give it to her.

The assault on the sky

¹⁰Then the Foul Spirit rose up together with mighty demons to oppose the lights. He saw that sky which they had shown him when in the world of thought, at a time when it had not yet been set in place with bones (= in this world), and in his envious desire he attacked it.

The sky stood on the star level, but he dragged it down into the empty space—which, as I wrote at the start, was between the original light and darkness—so that one-third of it stood above the star level. Like a snake, the sky jumped below this earth, where it was thrashed and broken.

He rushed in at Midday on the day of Ohrmazd in the month of Frawardīn, and the sky feared him like a sheep fears the wolf.

[The assaults on the water, earth, and plant]

The assault on the Bull, Gayōmard, and the Fire

¹⁹He let loose upon the Bull and Gayōmard Lust (Āz) and Need, Danger, Pain and Disease, Greed and Procrastination.

²⁰Before he came to the Bull, Ohrmazd fed it healing henbane and smeared it before its eyes so that the evil, damage, and discomfort from their blows might be less. It immediately became weak and sick, its milk (= semen) came out, and it passed away.

²¹And the Bull said: "Excellent work and labor should be ordered for the cattle creation!" [from Yasna 35.4]

²²Before he came to Gayōmard, Ohrmazd brought sleep, fashioned in the form of a luminous, tall fifteen-year-old man, upon Gayōmard for as long as it takes to utter one strophe of the *Gāthās*.

²³When Gayōmard came out of his sleep, he saw that the entire world of the living was dark as night. The earth appeared scorched and teamed with evil animals. The firmament was turning, the sun and the moon were moving, the world of the living was resounding with the thundering of the giant demons fighting with the stars.

²⁴The Foul Spirit thought: "I have undone all the creations of Ohrmazd except Gayōmard." So he let loose upon Gayōmard the Bone-untier with a thousand death-making demons, but, because his time was appointed, they found no means to kill him.

²⁵As it says: At the first creation, when the Foul Spirit came to oppose it, the time for Gayōmard to live and rule was fashioned to be thirty years. That is, after the coming of the Opposition he lived for thirty years.

²⁶Gayōmard said: "Now that the Assault has come, mankind will be from my seed. One good thing will come from it: that they will perform good deeds."

²⁷Next he came to the fire, and he mixed smoke and murkiness into it.

First victory of the gods

The seven planets with numerous demons to help them were mingled into the firmament for the battle with the stars. He sullied the entire creation as when a fire rages and smoke rises everywhere, and they fought to reach the throne of those whose actions are above in order to mingle with them too.

For ninety days and nights (i.e., until midsummer?), the gods in the world of thought were fighting with the Foul Spirit and the demons, until they overcame them and threw them back into hell. The sky was made into a stronghold, so that the Opposition was unable to mingle with them.

²⁸Hell is the center of the earth, where the Foul Spirit pierced the earth and rushed through.

28 The complaint of the soul of the Bull (Bundahishn 4a)

¹It also says that, when the Bull placed alone passed away, *he* fell to the right, and, after Gayōmard passed away, *he* fell to the left.

²Gōshurūn, that is, the soul of the Bull placed alone, came out of the body of the Bull, stood before the Bull, and, with a voice as when a thousand men cry together, complained to Ohrmazd: "To whom have you entrusted the guardianship of the creation, since the earth is lying trembling, the plant is dry, the water fouled? Where is that man of yours whom you said you would give so that he would utter care (for cattle)?"

³Ohrmazd said: "You are sick, Gōshurūn, with the Foul Spirit's sickness and the malice the demons have brought upon you. If it were possible to set in place that man at this time, then the Foul Spirit would not possess this power to do violence."

⁴Gōshurūn went forth to the star, moon, and sun levels, complaining in the same manner.

⁵Then they showed it the pre-soul of Zarathustra, saying: "We shall set this one in place in the world of the living to utter care."

⁶Gōshurūn was contented and accepted: "I shall nurture the creation," that is, it agreed to cattle being placed in the world of the living.

29 The battles of the creations

The Sky (Bundahishn 6a)

¹It says in the Tradition: As the Foul Spirit rushed in and saw the purpose for which the creations had been set in place—the supremacy of the deities, and his own impotence—he wished to rush back.

²But the sky in the world of thought, that is, that brave warrior who wears the steel armor that is the very sky that was set up against the Foul Spirit, presented a threat to him until Ohrmazd had made a stronghold harder than the sky around the sky.

³He appointed the warrior pre-souls of the sustainers of Order, with valiant horses and spears in the hands, around that stronghold, numerous as hairs on the heads of (the soldiers) who mount the guard

of a stronghold. That stronghold, which the Righteous are in, they call Awareness-of-the-Righteous.

[4]When the Foul Spirit found no passage to rush back through, he saw how the demons would be cut off and he himself undone as clearly as Ohrmazd did his future victory and the Perfectioning for ever and ever.

[5]This was the first battle, which the sky in the world of thought fought with the Foul Spirit.

[*The battles of the water, earth, and plant*]

The Bull (Bundahishn 6e)

[1]When it passed away, because it contained the seed (*chihr*) of the plants, from the limbs of the Bull placed alone there grew out of the earth fifty-five species of grain and twelve species of healing plants.

[2]They transferred the light and the strength (*zōr*) that was in the seed (*tōhm*) of the Bull to the moon.

[3]That seed was purified by the light of the moon, was arranged in various colors, and a soul (*gyān*) was inserted in it.

[4]From there one pair of kine, one male, one female, appeared on the earth; then from each species two, that is 282, in the same way that two miles (*frasang*) are said in the Tradition to be eighteen leagues (*hāsr*).

[5]The cattle took their abodes on the earth, the birds in the air, and the fish swam in the water, from which there was enough to nourish the creatures abundantly.

[6]This was the first battle the Bull fought with the Foul Spirit.

Gayōmard (Bundahishn 6f)

[1]It was manifest in the firmament about Gayōmard that he would live for thirty years after the Assault, during the struggle between the stars and the planets.

[2]As it has been said about the time before the Assault: "Brave Gayōmard's life and rule had been set to thirty winters." (. . .)

[7]As Gayōmard passed away, his seed went into the earth, in the same way that now, too, all men pour out their seed at their passing.

⁸Because the body of Gayōmard was made of metal, seven metals appeared from the body of Gayōmard.

⁹As for the seed that went into the earth, after forty years, Mashī and Mashiyānī grew up from it, from whose coupling (*khwēdōdah*) the world of the living was filled up, the demons cut off, and the Foul Spirit undone.

[*The battles of the fire and the stars against the planets, and the gods in the world of thought*]

The unmingled stars (Bundahishn 6j)

⁰The tenth battle the unmingled stars fought to prevent darkness and sinfulness being mingled in with those whose work is above.

¹As it says: "The Fortune of the good Mazdayasnian Tradition was held around the sky like the Girdle, that is the *kusti*, star-adorned, fashioned in the world of thought, with three folds, and four knots."

²Those stars were in battle with him until the end, as already written.

30 About the creation and the Assault (Dādestān ī dēnīg 36)

¹⁵He divided the well-made sky into three thirds, one above, connected to the Endless Light, in which is the Treasure containing eternal profit; one below, attached to the Darkness in the Depth, in which dwells the Lie full of evil: one below and above the two other thirds.

¹⁶Then he made the uppermost third, called Garōdmān, into a stronghold in purity, all light and happiness, so that the Lie cannot reach them.

¹⁷He equipped that third so that the pure Amahrspands might be invoked without fear of the Adversary by the righteous ones who performed service to the gods, who, like noble heroes set against an unprepared opponent, fight with all they have in the battle and overcome the opponent. Having extricated their kin (*gōhrag*), they proceed to rest in the company of the Amahrspands and the Fortune of the Creator. And again they seek a means to achieve freedom from fear, to strike down the demons, and to help the creations, like

someone who, he too, as long as he has no fear of arrows or being hit, unreachable, shoots an arrow down from a stronghold, but is mindful of his friends.

¹⁸With his divine wonder-power (*warz*) and Fortune, he separated out the opposite matter and contamination and placed it in the lower-most third, so that the lie-demon of un-goodness might come and fill that third with darkness and demons and make it horrible. In that hard-ship, when the Millennium comes about, it will be a prison providing a way (*ristag*) for the demons to do penitence, as well as for the wicked whom the demons deceived and who fled from the fighting, in which they will be made responsible for their sins. Patiently, they will let no lie-demon in through the enclosure (*parwastār*) of the lights until the appointed time, when the punishment of the demons and the remorse of the wicked are completed.

¹⁹Then he fashioned the creation of this world and placed it in the middle third to be the front line (*radag*) of this world and that world. Among those creatures, he set in place man, who can organize, as the master of the creatures; discerning wisdom as a tool for mankind; and the true Tradition of those who possess the best knowledge.

²⁰He built the world of the living as the place where the battle would be fought between the two with opposite essences.

²¹On the summit of this third, he placed the bright sun, the shiny moon, and the stars endowed with Fortune. ²²He equipped them so that they should fly and turn around about the creations. Their light, whose radiance reaches far and wide over the earth, and their copious good rain, as well as the many good gods, will strike down and overcome the sorcerers and witches who rush up beneath them to soil the creations. And they fight fiercely to withstand that stench and terror.

²³And so, by their revolution, the creations will ascend and descend, increase and decrease, the oceans will flow and ebb, vegetation will grow, and the creatures will prosper. ²⁴By their revolution, the appointed amount and number of days, nights, months, years, and eras containing all time will be measured.

²⁵He fashioned in the dress of the fathers (?), which is nothing but the garment of existence (*stī*), the courageous and brave pre-souls of the sustainers of Order.

²⁶He also equipped that flock of Aryans, as many as were needed for the work of that era, so that, from time to time, they would stand forth in their own essence and come into the garment they wore in this world and be born among their kin:

those with many children, like Frawāg [cf. 31:33];
those set in place before any others, like Hōshang;
the smashers of demons, like Tahmōred;
those endowed with Fortune, like Jam;
those endowed with healing power, like Frēdōn;
those with both kinds of wisdom, like the righteous Manushchihr;
those full of strength, like Garishāsp;
those from the seed of Fortune, like Kay Kawād;
those full of wisdom, like Ōshnar;
the noble ones, like Siyāwakhsh;
those whose work was above, like Kay Husrōy;
the exalted ones, like Kay Wishtāsp;
those full of good things, like the Righteous Zarathustra;
those who redress the world of the living, like Pishyōtan;
those of the Life-giving Word, like Ushēdar;
those of the law, like Ushēdarmāh;
and those of the *Gāthās*, who will be at the end, like Sōshāns.

Between them, there were many bringers of the Tradition who performed wonderful deeds, deeds of Fortune, and arranged good things, and who strove to overcome the Lie and performed the will of the Creator.(…)

²⁸In particular, he made the thoughts of the contaminated living beings content by a vicarious (*guharīg*) way of getting away from evil, namely, to be content about death. For they know their limited (*sāmān*) term will be cut off (*brīn*) and end, but also that evil in this

world will be cut off. What they are not content about would be for their term to have no limit and not be cut off so that evil in this world will last eternally with pain.

²⁹By a great and marvelous mystery, he gave living beings a vicarious immortality, the very best while living with the Adversary. For eternal life with the Adversary is pain, but he who has obtained a lineage (*paywand*) of offspring has a fierce strength. He will be forever young through his good lineage, family, and generations to come, while still living with the Adversary. His life will be eternal, in the sense that, through their own children and generations, their lives will be connected (*paywand-*) forever. In this way, all will obtain old age, and every one will again be renewed from illness and decrepitude in the form of a youth through one's own children and kin (*gōhrag*), as long as they are plentiful. Not a single one who fights in this struggle to overcome his opponent in the battle will be lost, but, because his sins weigh lightly, will go forth to paradise.

³⁰For, also the Righteous Zarathustra of the Spitāmas, supreme among the righteous, the greatest among messengers, the most Fortunate of those born, and model for those in this world, luck came upon him from Ohrmazd the Creator in the form of the all-aware wisdom. He saw one who was immortal and childless and one who was mortal but had children. Then he found terrifying the one with eternal life but without children, but praiseworthy him whose lineage went forth while mortal himself. For he much rather wished and desired to have a child born from his loins come to him—namely Ushēdar, Ushēdar-māh, and Sōshāns—and mortality rather than eternal life for himself.

³¹When he who is all goodness and all-aware had arranged the tools he needed to set against the Lie as a shield, that Lie with its deceiving kin came rushing against them, foul, its desire evil, fighting in front together with Akōman, Wrath, Decrepitude, Procrastination, Dearth that creates Need, the demon Bud, the evil Wāy, Greed, the Bone-untier, the demon Drag-off, together with innumerable giant

demons and lie-demons, poison and venom, and all kinds of corruption in the lower third.

³²The one of evil knowledge flew up toward the middle third, in which the good creation of Ohrmazd had been set in place. ³³He struck down the Bull and made Gayōmard mortal. He made the earth tremble and broke through the earth. ³⁴The creation became dark. The demons rushed about in areas below and above. They hurried up to the upper third, as well, to the pure Garōdmān in the upper sky, which is between the two thirds.

³⁵There it is clasped, blazing in the world of thought, that fastness of bonds guarding all bonds, which is nothing but the great Fortune guarding all bonds, the pure, doubt-dispelling Tradition, which shone brightly and lit up in the distance, like a Girdle, star-adorned and fashioned in the world of thought, the good Mazdayasnian Tradition [cf. p. 19]. Thus, too, the lights full of Fortune shone. ³⁶As it was not within the capacity of any evil god or lie-demon, not even of the most giant one, the greatest demon among demons, by any warrior-like feat, to run up past that border, they fell down again [cf. p. 9].

⁴¹In order to make people wicked and their souls go to hell, Deception became their leader, the one that is called False Speech in the word of the Tradition. For it is said in the Tradition that there is as much evil from speaking False Speech as in all the demons together, including Akōman, the most evil among demons, the companion of the Foul Spirit.

⁴²So, by teaching a tradition that is all deception, he caused the creatures to be reached by deceiving Slander, self-indulgent Greed, Hate and Envy, foolhardy Shamefulness, indecent Desire for fame, Indolence in seeking wisdom, Indebtedness incurred by uneducated showing off, and a hundred blows to the righteous, as well as the other numerous powers that lead astray and demons leading astray. These he made the helpers for the tradition that is all lies and deceives the creatures.

⁴³He also fashioned, inexpertly, against the other various creatures numerous demons as Opponents.

⁴⁴To help those doing battle, he placed, one by one, many witches whose essence was darkness, but who entered the paths of the lights

so that they could rush, fall, and turn about everywhere beneath the lights that flew in their own paths in order to waylay them and to hide the many small ones in this and the other world. They rob them of their light and Fortune and their ability to distribute the Fortune over the earth. [16:1]. They blow from their own sicknesses onto the creatures nothing but pain and death together with the evil that is the home of those demons.

⁴⁷For beings in this world can recognize in this world the work and ways (*ristag*) of those in the other world by examining straight with their wisdom, when, by the straight analogy of the strength of wisdom, they examine, recognize, and expose what is not visible from what is visible and what used to be from what has come down to us. In the same way, the end of the struggle between the two sides is certain by the witness of knowledge, being clearly to be seen by the visible marks and evident signs that came to the wisdom of those who were before. Even if the knowledge of this supreme chapter is in many ways hidden, the demons who hide it from the grasp of those in this world and from reaching those in this world can themselves be grasped.

⁴⁸But the various parts that the foreknowledgeable teachers before us knew and transmitted to those who came after and so were tied (*paywand-*) to this era were so through people who took things away, transmitted falsely, and added deceit. From era to era, among what was yoked to my knowledge, the greater part remained in my memory. The endeavor to write it down, at the command given by the discerning mind of those in this world, from the endless Tradition that is my memory, is a good work I cannot refuse.

⁴⁹So, it is clear as the day that the power of that lie-demon among us is inferior and that the road prepared by the Creator will lead it to destruction and impotence. In the same way, it is clear for all to see that the army of the gods is all-powerful and that the Creator of what is good will certainly be victorious in the end. In his omnipotence, he will bring to fruition the fruit of his entire creation by its completely good progress for the duration of the world of those he has set in place. Many marks and signs of this are clearly to be seen.

⁵⁰One is this, that the Creator's dwelling was set in place by the Distributor and the way the lie-demon, while trying to get up above, rushed in to prevent the creation.

⁵¹Another is that Ohrmazd's creation is both in the other world and in this world, while that of the lie-demon is not in this world, but he can yoke the evil in the other world to this world. For the superiority of the good beings in the other world and in this world over the evil ones in the other world is perfectly clear.

⁵²Yet another is that he will be struck down in the end, as is evident from the fact that he struggled and was already struck down earlier.

⁶⁵The most frightening Opposition planned by the lie-demon for the creatures in this world was causing the living to die, which he did by crooked command and in the hope that it would be his greatest victory. But this proved very damaging to himself, for, when he causes death to a wicked person, who is precisely the one who does what he wishes, he becomes unable to accomplish his wish to perform sinful deeds. The soul of that wicked one, whose sin is in the other world, goes to where that person will be made sorry for having let himself be thus deceived.

⁶⁶But the righteous person, whose body in this world is in captivity and suffers pain, will be far removed from that captivity and pain. He will then go to paradise, which is the most fortified of castles, where he will fight fearlessly against the lie-demon, ⁶⁷just as Jamshēd's pre-soul is recorded for keeping terror and fright away, Frēdōn's pre-soul for keeping back by means of healers those who cause sickness, and the other pre-souls for having struck down many demons.

⁶⁸Another is that the most grievous fabrication of his, above and beyond making the creatures prone to death, was the terrifying demon Bone-untier with his many giant (animal-)headed demons.

He despised the Creator, who causes growth, to the extent that he destroyed the one body called Gayōmard. But there came back to this world a man and woman, Mahlī and Mahliyānī, who, by uniting as brother and sister in *khwēdōdah*, organized the lineages and tied them together.

31 The origin of mankind (Bundahišn 14)

Gayōmard

¹It says in the Tradition: "I fashioned forth mankind in ten species, first that luminous, white-eyed one, Gayōmard, and so forth to the tenth." The tenth was the monkey, whom one calls the lowest of mankind.

²When illness befell Gayōmard, he fell on the left side.

³Then lead appeared from his head, tin from his blood, silver from his brain, iron from his feet, copper from his bones, crystal from his fat, steel from his arms, and gold from his soul (gyān) as it went forth. (…)

⁴Through his left side mortality entered Gayōmard's body. Mortality thus came upon all creatures to last until the Perfectioning.

⁵When Gayōmard gave up his seed at death, it was purified by the light of the sun. One half was preserved by Nēryōsang; Spandarmad received the other half. It was placed in the earth for forty years.

Mašī and Mašiyānī/Mahlī and Mahliyānī

⁶At the completion of forty years, Mahlī and Mahliyānī grew up from the earth as a plant in the shape of a rhubarb with one stem and fifteen leaves. Their hands were in the back (or: at their ears), and they were attached (paywand-) to one another. They were of the same height and same appearance. ⁷Between them Fortune came up. They were of the same height, so that it was not apparent which was the male and which was the female. That Ohrmazd-given Fortune that was with them is the Fortune placed in mankind.

⁸As it says: Which was made first: the Fortune or the body? And Ohrmazd said: "The Fortune was made first, then the body was made for it, placed in the body," that is, once one's "duties" had been fashioned, the body was made for performing one's duties [cf. p. 18]. ⁹And the explanation is that the soul (ruwān) was made first, then the body. The soul inside the body guides one's duties.

¹⁰Then they both changed from rhubarb-form to people-form. And that Fortune went into them from the world of thought, that is the soul.

Similarly, now, too, a tree grows, whose fruits are the ten kinds of humans.

¹¹Ohrmazd said to Mashī and Mashiyānī: "You are humans. You are the parents of the world of the living. You were the first creations of my Complete Thought (= Ārmaiti), so you must perform work and law with complete thought! Think good thoughts, speak good speech, perform good action! And do not sacrifice to the demons!"

¹²Then the first thought the two of them thought was when they thought about each other: "That is a human."

¹³And the first deed they did was to go and pee.

The first humans learn to lie and basic survival techniques

¹⁴And the first speech they spoke was: "Ohrmazd set in place the water, the earth, the plants, the cattle, the stars, the moon, the sun, and all prosperity whose appearance is from righteousness." That is everything in a nutshell.

¹⁵Then the Opponent rushed into their thoughts, making their thought sinful, and they howled: "The Foul Spirit set in place the water, the earth, the plants, and the other things."

¹⁶That was the first lying speech of theirs, which went astray, uttered to satisfy the demons. This was the first bliss the Foul Spirit took from them to be his own. By that lying speech they both became possessed by the Lie, and their souls (*ruwān*) will be in hell until the Final Body.

¹⁷And for thirty days they had to go without food, and they wore grass as garments.

¹⁸After thirty days, in the wilderness, they came upon a white-haired goat. With their mouths they sucked the milk of her udder. ¹⁹When they had drunk the milk, Mashiyānī said: "My peace of mind at the time when I had not yet drunk that semen—milk—was greater than it is now when I have drunk it and my body feels bad."

²⁰That was the second lying speech from which the demons received strength. They stole the taste of the food so that only one-hundredth remained.

They perform their first sacrifices

²¹After another thirty days and nights, they came upon a sheep with dark wool and white cheeks, which they killed. Using lote (?) and box tree, guided by those in the other world, they built a fire, for those two trees make the best fire. They kindled the fire again using their mouths, and as the first firewood they burnt wood from frankincense and (other various trees). They roasted that goat on a spit, leaving a piece of meat the size of three fists in the fire. They said: "It is the fire's share." And one piece of it was shot up to heaven. They said: "This is the gods' share."

A vulture dove for it and carried it off from them, for this was the first meat dogs ate.

²²The first garments they wore were from skins. Then, in the wilderness, they wove . . . (?). The woven cloth they made into clothes and put them on.

²³They dug a kiln in the ground, smelted iron, struck it with stones, made a blade out of it, cut trees with it, and prepared wooden bowls from it.

²⁴For these pious actions the demons caused them much oppression, ²⁵and they began envying one another. They set upon one another, striking, tearing, and pulling out hairs. ²⁶Then the demons bellowed from the darkness: "You are humans! Sacrifice to the demons, so that your envy may subside!"

²⁷Mashiyānī jumped up, milked a cow, and poured the milk toward the north. ²⁸By that sacrifice, the demons became strong. They made both of them so dry-assed (= impotent) that for fifty years they had no desire to get together. Even when they did get together, no children were born.

After fifty years, they thought about getting children, first Mashī, then Mashiyānī. Mashī said to Mashiyānī: "When I look at your belly, this thing of mine grows and rises up." Then Mashiyānī said: "Brother, when I see that member of yours, my belly flutters." ²⁹Then they desired each other, and as they were performing their desire they thought: "We should have been doing this for fifty years already!"

[30]After nine months, a pair of twins were born, a girl and a boy, but because they were so sweet, the mother devoured one, the father the other. Then Ohrmazd removed the sweetness of the children from their thoughts and left only enough for the parents to bring up.

[31]Six pair of twins were then born from them, male and female, and all the brothers married their sisters.

[32]Each couple bore a child after fifty years, and they themselves died at the age of a hundred.

[33]Of those six pairs of twins, one was Siyāmak, a boy, and Washāg, a girl. From them, one pair was born, a boy, Frawāg, and a girl, Frawāgī.

[34]From them fifteen pairs of twins were born, each of whom was one species. Their descendants filled the world.

[35]From every fifteen species, nine species were transferred on the back of the bull Srisōg across the Frākh-kerd Sea to the other six continents and settled there.

Six species remained in Khwanirah, among whom there was a couple called Tāz and Tāzag, who settled in the Arab (Tāzīg) desert. Another couple was Hōshang and Gūzag, from whom the Iranians are descended.

32 Mashī and Mashiyānī (Dēnkard VII.1)

[9]When Gayōmard passed away, the second time the speech of Ohrmazd appeared to the creatures in this world, it was to Mashī and Mashiyānī, Gayōmard's first offspring. When he had created them, he said to them: "You are men. I created you as the parents of the entire world with bones, so do not worship the demons. For I made keeping my Complete Thought the best thing for you to do, so that you may see to your work and law with complete thought."

[10]And they praised Ohrmazd's work of creation and went about their duties. They did the will of the Creator and laid the foundation of much activity that was to benefit the world, especially *khwēdōdah*, the most pious of deeds for giving birth, for establishing lineages (*paywand-*), and for the creatures of the world to go forth in large numbers.

[11]The Creator showed them how to sow barley, saying: "This, Mashī, is your ox, and this is your barley, and these are your other tools, which from now on you should know well!"

[12]And this too is manifest in the good Tradition that Ohrmazd said to Hadish (genius of the homestead), Worthy in Righteousness—one of the gods—: "Hadish Worthy in Righteousness, go to Mashī and Mashyānī, and ask from Mashī and Mashiyānī that bread made of barley. Bless that bread of theirs: 'May this barley go out from you! As it came to you from Ohrmazd and the Amahrspands, so may this barley go out from you to your descendants, to keep off the Adversity coming from the demons. In order for demons and the Lie to stay away two *Ahunwars* should be recited!'"

[13]Hadish, Worthy in Righteousness, went to Mashī and Mashiyānī and asked from them that bread made of barley. He blessed that bread of theirs: "May this barley go out from you! As it came to you from Ohrmazd and the Amahrspands, so may this barley go out from you to your descendants, to keep off the Adversity coming from the demons." In order for demons and the Lie to stay away he recited two *Ahunwars*.

[14]Taught by the gods, Mashī and Mashiyānī began making clothes, herding animals, and working iron and wood, which together with agriculture and husbandry, were their foremost crafts. (...)

[15]After that the transmission of the Word came to their son Siyāmak and those of the same lineage, telling them to move to the various continents and districts, as far as the Creator had chosen for that continent and district. People went to each continent and district, spread out there, and filled them.

✦

CHAPTER THREE

TEXTS ON MYTHICAL HISTORY

Hero-Sacrificers of the First Ages in the Young Avesta

33 Yima (Yasht 9)

[8]Radiant Yima with good herds sacrificed to Druwāspā from high Mount Hukarya a hundred stallions, a thousand bulls, ten thousand rams, and also bringing a libation, saying:

"Give me that prize, O good, strongest Druwāspā, that I may bring flocks of sheep and herds of cattle to Ahura Mazdā's creatures and bring them non-destruction; that I may remove hunger and thirst, old age and death, heat and cold from Ahura Mazdā's creatures for a thousand autumns!"

34 Yima (Yasht 19)

[31]The Fortune followed splendid Yima with good herds for quite a long time thereafter, so that he ruled on the sevenfold earth over evil gods ... and mumblers [cf. 15:13].[32] He deprived the evil gods of sheep and herds, satisfaction and glorification, and all their wishes and burning desires. Under his command, beasts and men never died, waters and plants never dried out, and there was no lack of savory foods. [33]There was no cold or heat, no old age or death. Envy made by the evil gods there was not.

That was before, when he had not yet lied, before this one insidiously brought him the word Deception, for him to understand (the world?) as it not really was. [34]After that, the Fortune, now visible, ran away from him in the form of a bird. No longer seeing the Fortune and seeking it in vain, radiant Yima with good herds roamed unhappy and despondent. Senseless he blundered about on the earth.

35 Thraētaona (Yasht 5)

[33]Thraētaona of Āthviya's house, rich in life-giving strength, sacrificed to Ardwī Sūrā Anāhitā by four-cornered Varna a hundred stallions, a thousand bulls, ten thousand rams, [34]asking her:

"Give me that prize, O good, Ardwī Sūrā Anāhitā, you most rich in life-giving strength, that I may overcome the Giant Dragon with three mouths, three heads, six eyes, a thousand tricks, the mighty strong, deceiving Lie, this evil possessed by the Lie and afflicting living beings, which the Evil Spirit fashioned, inexpertly, upon the world of the living with bones for the destruction of the living beings of Order.

May I also carry off his two beloved women Sanghawācī and Arnawācī, who have the most beautiful, the most wonderful bodies to be won in the world of the living!"

36 The Kawis (Yasht 19)

[70]We sacrifice to the strong Fortune of the Kawis ... [71]which followed Kawi Kawāta, Kawi Aipiwohu, and Kawi Usadhan, as well as Kawi Arshna, Kawi Pisina, Kawi Biyarshan, and Kawi Siyāwarshan, so that they all became brave, firm, and skilled, endowed with wondrous powers, performing daring deeds.

37 Kawi Haosrawah (Yasht 5)

[49]Haosrawah, the virile hero of the Aryan lands, sacrificed to Ardwī Sūrā Anāhitā on the shore of deep Lake Chaēchasta with surging waters a hundred stallions, a thousand bulls, ten thousand rams, [50]asking her:

"Give me that prize, O good, Ardwī Sūrā Anāhitā, you most rich in life-giving strength, that I may become possessed of the highest command over all the lands, over evil gods and men ... and mumblers, and that, of all chariots pulled by two horses, I may be the one to drive the foremost one along that long race-course!"

38 Haoma (Yasht 9)

[17]Ruddy, beautiful Haoma, healing, commanding, tawny-eyed, sacrificed to Druwāspā on the highest peak on high Haraitī, [18]asking her:

"Give me that prize, O good Druwāspā, you most rich in life-giving strength, that I may bind the Turian villain Frangrasyān and that I may lead and bring him bound before Kawi Haosrawah, so that he may kill him on the shore of the deep Lake Chaēchasta with wide waters, by way of revenge for Siyāwarshan, his son, the hero killed through deceit.

39 Frangrasyān (Yasht 19)

[56]The Turian villain Frangrasyān sought the strong unseizable Fortune from the Wourukasha Sea. Throwing off his clothes, naked, he sought that Fortune which belongs to the Aryan lands, to the born and unborn, and to Zarathustra, sustainer of Order. But that Fortune rushed forth, ran away, and evaded him.

Then that stream came into being, flowing out of the Wourukasha Sea, the lake called Haosrawah.

[57]Then Frangrasyān flew up, the greatly skilled Turanian, O Zarathustra of the Spitāmas, from the Wourukasha Sea, speaking evil deception:

"Blast it! I could not grab that Fortune which belongs to . . . and to Zarathustra. [58]So I shall mingle with (and pollute) all things thirsty and wet, all things great, good, and beautiful. Ahura Mazdā will be upset when he sees again the creations he set in place!"

[59]Then Frangrasyān flew down, the greatly skilled Turanian, O Zarathustra of the Spitāmas, to the Wourukasha Sea. For the second time throwing off his clothes. . . . But that Fortune rushed forth. . . .

Then that stream came into being, flowing out of the Wourukasha Sea, the lake called Wahyaz-dā (= giver of the better [reward]).

[60]Then Frangrasyān flew up . . . speaking evil deception:

"Dash it! Blast him! Darn it all! I could not grab that Fortune . . . all things great, good, and beautiful. Ahura Mazdā will be upset. . . ."

[61]Then Frangrasyān flew down . . . to the Wourukasha Sea.

⁶²For the third time, throwing off his clothes. . . . But that Fortune rushed forth. . . .

Then that stream came into being, flowing out of the Wourukasha Sea, the water called Avzh-dānwā (= stream of water).

⁶³Then Frangrasyān flew up . . . speaking evil deception:

"Dash it! Blast him! Darn it all and woe to him! I could not grab that Fortune . . . all things great, good, and beautiful.

He did not grab that Fortune which belongs to the Aryan lands, to the born and the unborn, and to Zarathustra, sustainer of Order.

Hero-Sacrificers of the First Ages in the Pahlavi Texts

40 On the harm that befell Iran in each millennium (Bundahishn 33)

¹When the Foul Spirit rushed in, at the beginning of the first millennium in the Mixture, there were the Bull and Gayōmard.

Mashī and Mashiyānī performed their good service (to the gods) for fifty years, but had no children.

In the same millennium, for seventy years, Hōshang and Tahmūraf both killed demons. At the end of the millennium, the demons cut Jam in half [cf. 62.8].

²At the beginning of the second millennium, Azhidahāg took up his evil rule and ruled for a hundred years. At the end of the millennium, Frēdōn seized and bound him.

³At the beginning of the third millennium, Salm and Tūz shared Frēdōn's land. Then they killed Ērij and destroyed his children and family.

⁴In the same millennium, Mānushchihr was born and sought vengeance for Ērij.

Frāsiyāb and the Kays

⁵Than Frāsiyāb came and pushed Mānushchihr and the Iranians back to Mount Padishkhwār and destroyed them with much damage and destruction. He killed Mānushchihr's sons Frīy and Nōdar, until Iran was taken from Frāsiyāb by another lineage.

⁶When Mānushchihr had departed, Frāsiyāb once more came and caused much disturbance and devastation in Iran. He kept rain back from Iran until Uzaw, son of Tahmāsp, came and pushed Frāsiyāb back and made the rain that they called "new rain."

⁷After Uzaw, Frāsiyāb once more caused severe evil to Iran, until Kawād sat upon the throne.

⁸During the kingship of Kay-Us (Kāyus) in the same millennium, the demons were very violent, and Ōshnar came to strike them down. But Kay-Us's mind became unhinged, and he went to do battle with the sky. He fell down, and the Fortune was taken from him. Then he devastated the world of the living with horses and men, and, by deceit, they bound him and the notables of the realm in the land of Shambarān.

⁹There was one called Zēnīgāw, who had poison in his eyes. He had come from the Arabs to be king over Iran. Whomever he looked at with his evil eye was killed. ¹⁰The Iranians went to seek out Frāsiyāb, who killed Zēnīgāw and ruled over Iran. He carried many people off from Iran and settled them in Turkestān. He laid Iran waste and brought confusion, until Rōstam raised an army from Sagestān and seized the Shambarānians. He released Kay-Us and the other Iranians from their imprisonment.

By the river Hurīy, which they also call Spāhān, he fought a battle with Frāsiyāb, who was defeated and fled. He fought many other battles with him, until he pushed him back to Turkestān, and Iran was again made prosperous.

¹¹Frāsiyāb made another attempt, and Kay Siyāwakhsh came to do battle.

Because Kay Kāyus's wife, Sūdābī, accused him wrongly of misdoings (by trying to seduce him), ¹²Siyāwakhsh did not return to Iran to Kay Kāyus, but went to Turkestan. There, he stayed with Frāsiyāb, who had granted him protection, and married one of Frāsiyāb's daughters, from whom Kay Husrōy was born. ¹³Siyāwakhsh was killed there.

¹⁴In the same millennium, Kay Husrōy killed Frāsiyāb, then went to Kang castle, passing the kingship on to Luhrāsp.

[15]When Luhrāsp's son King Wishtāsp had ruled for thirty years, the millennium came to an end.

Zarathustra and Wishtāsp

[16]Then the fourth millennium began, [17]in which Zarathustra received the Tradition from Ohrmazd and brought it to Iran. King Wishtāsp received it and made it go forth, but fought a fierce battle with Arzāsp, in which Iranians and non-Iranians were greatly decimated.

[18]In the same millennium, Wahman, son of Spandyād (son of Wishtāsp), became king. There was internal struggle, in which Iranians decimated one another. There was no man left of the royal lineage who could become king, and so they made Wahman's daughter Humā queen.

Dārā, Alexander, and the Sasanians

[19]Then, during the rule of Dārā son of Dārā, Alexander Kēsar rushed into Iran from Rome. He killed King Dārā and annihilated the entire royal family, the Magu's, and the notables of Iran.

He extinguished numerous fires, took the Mazdayasnian Tradition and the *Zand* and sent it to Rome, and the *Avesta* was burned. Iran was divided among ninety petty kings.

[20]In the same millennium, Ardakhshahr (Ardashīr), son of Pābag, appeared. He killed the petty kings, redressed the kingdom, sent forth the Mazdayasnian Tradition, and organized many customs, which continued in his lineage.

[21]During the rule of Shābuhr (II), son of Ohrmazd, the Arabs came and seized and held the Hurīy river for many years of marauding and plundering while Shābuhr was king. He pushed them back, took their cities, destroyed many of their kings, and killed them in large numbers.

[22]During the rule of Pērōz, son of Yazdegerd (II), for six years there was no rain, and people experienced severe evil and hardship. [23]Then Hashnawāz (?), king of the Hephthalites, came, killed Pērōz, and carried off (his son) Kawād, his sister, and a fire as hostages to the Hephthalites.

²⁴During the reign of Kawād, Mazdak, son of Bāmdād, appeared and laid down the law of Mazdakism. Kawād was deceived and led astray. He ordered that wife, children, and property should be held in common and be shared. He discontinued the Mazdayasnian Tradition until the blessed Husrōy (Khusraw), son of Kawād, came of age, killed Mazdak, re-established the Mazdayasnian Tradition, and pushed back the Khiyonians (Chionites), who were making incursions into Iran, closed the passes, and made Iran free from fear.

²⁵Then, when Yazdegerd (III) had ruled for twenty years, the Arabs rushed upon Iran in large numbers. Yazdegerd could not withstand them in battle, but went to Khorāsān and Turkestān, where he called horses and men to help, but was killed there.

²⁶Yazdegerd's son brought a large army to India, but, before he reached Khorāsān, he passed away, the large army was thrown into confusion, and Iran remained in the hands of the Arabs. They sent forth their own law and evil tradition, and threw into confusion many customs of old. The Mazdayasnian Tradition was weakened, and it became customary to wash, bury, and eat corpses.

41 The coming of the Tradition (Denkard VII.1)

Hōshang and Tahmūraf

¹⁶In that era the Word came to Waēgird and Hōshang Pēshdād telling them to organize in the world the law of land-holding for cultivating the world and land-lordship for protecting the world.

¹⁷By their collaboration, the law of their Tradition, and the power of their hymns (*wahm*), land-lordship for cultivating the world was organized for the lineages of Ohrmazd's creatures in order to organize and send forth the Tradition and law of Ohrmazd.

¹⁸By that Fortune, Hōshang smashed two-thirds of the giant demons and the seven minions spawned by Wrath.

¹⁹After that it came to Tahmūraf with the Weapon, who conquered demons and evil men, sorcerers, and witches. He abolished sacrifices to idols and sent forth among the creations homage and sacrifices to

the Creator. The Dark Spirit turned himself into the form of a horse and carried him for thirty winters.

Jamshēd

²⁰Then it came to Jamshēd, son of Wiwangh, telling him to converse with Ohrmazd. Of the four branches of the Tradition—priests, warriors, husbandmen, and artisans—he received all four. This enabled him to expand, increase, and make grow the world and, by the strength ($\bar{o}z$) of moderation, to establish among the creatures absence of death, old age, corrosion and rot, making them blessed with Fortune and completely confident.

²¹It is known from the good Tradition that the Creator Ohrmazd said to Jam: "Further my world!"—i.e., make it more numerous—"Make my world prosper!"—i.e., make it more prosperous—"And accept to protect, nurture, guard, and maintain my world so that nobody will be able to harm or damage another!" [18:4–5]

²²Jam agreed and did as Ohrmazd had commanded. By the same Fortune, he expanded the earth by two-thirds its original size.

²³During his kingship, he made animals and men deathless, water and plants indesiccable, and eating of foods uninterrupted.

²⁴This too is known from the Tradition, that he made the world as pleasant as paradise. From him who set all things in place he received the order to protect the creatures from the destruction of the winter of Malkūs and so constructed the fortress "Made by Jam," as well as many other wondrous things as is known from the Tradition. [18:22–38]

Frēdōn

²⁵In another age, when Jam's Fortune was divided, by order of the Creator Ohrmazd, husbandry, the second branch of the Tradition, came to Frēdōn of the Āspiyāns as his share while still in his mother's womb.

²⁶He was thereby made victorious and became able to respond to Dahāg from within the womb, hurting and stunning him, that mighty Lie! When he was nine years old he went forth to smash him, and,

by his victoriousness, overcame Dahāg and delivered the creatures from him and made them breathe easily. He overcame the Mazandaranians and pushed back their harm and damage from the continent of Khwanirah. He divided Khwanirah between his three sons.

²⁷By husbandry, he revealed the diseases that plague the body and showed people the art of healing. He also performed many other wondrous deeds benefiting the world.

²⁸During Frēdōn's lifetime, the transmission of the same Word came from the Creator to his son Ērij, who spread and cultivated the law of the Iranians. This he chose as his best request from his father Frēdōn and received it from the Creator by the blessing of Frēdōn.

Karisāsp/Garshāsp

³²At another time, when Jam's Fortune was divided, warriordom, the second branch of the Tradition, came to Karisāsp, son of Sām, as his share. With it he smashed the horned, horse-swallowing, man-swallowing dragon, as well as the demon Gandarw and many other demons and the Lie that was opposing and destroying the creatures.

The Kays

³⁷Then it came to Kay-Us and placed him in command. During his kingship, he became the ruler of the seven continents. He discovered and taught the very useful art of telling boundaries. The non-Iranians were overcome by his responses, and the Iranian lands were instructed by his most well-informed instructions.

³⁸It then came to splendid Kay Siyāwakhsh, who with it built the miraculous Kang castle in order to keep within it for protection the many marvels, the Fortune, and the mysteries of the Tradition, from which the age was redressed, the rule of the Iranians re-ordered, and strength and victoriousness again tied to the Tradition of Ohrmazd.

³⁹It came to Kay Husrōy, son of Siyāwakhsh, enabling him to conquer Frangrasyā, the Turanian sorcerer, and many of the same brood, who destroyed the world of the living. He attacked the

idol-temple on the shore of Lake Chēchast, breaking and smashing that terrible Liedom.

⁴⁰Because he was needed as a tool for the Perfectioning, he was secluded by a spell to a secret place for his body to be kept there immortal until the Perfectioning, as willed by the Creator.

Zarathustra

⁴¹After that, Zarathustra of the Spitāmas came to converse with the all-aware Creator Ohrmazd and received from him, altogether complete and detailed, awareness about the knowledge and practice of priesthood, warriordom, husbandry, and artisanship, all the parts making up the Tradition. At the Creator's command, he brought it to King Kay Wishtāsp and, with it, greatly enlightened the wise men in the country of that supreme ruler of the world. The king sent it forth in the seven continents, so that it could no more be separated from its union with the creation until the Perfectioning.

Zarathustra and the Gathic Characters in the Gāthās

42 From Yasna 28

¹With hands upstretched in homage to *him*, my support, I ask you all first for the spirit/inspiration, O All-knowing one, that will be life-giving by my Order, by my action, and on account of which you may listen favorably to both the guiding wisdom (*khratu*) of my good thought and the cow's breath-soul (*urwan*),—

²I who want to circumambulate you all, O All-knowing Lord, with my good thought for you to give to *me* the spoils of both worlds, that which has bones and that of thought, in accordance with Order—spoils by which one may also place one's supporters in comfort.

³With my Order and a new good (poetic) thought, I shall now weave you all together with the All-knowing Lord into my poetic web. Humility shall then increase for all of you the royal command so that it will not diminish. So, come to my calls and support me!

⁴I, the knowing one of the All-knowing Lord, am now, with my good thought composed, paying heed to my breath-soul for my song and to the rewards for my actions. To the best of my ability, I shall try to achieve Order.

⁵Shall I see you through Order [cf. p. 14], I wonder, finding both good thought for myself and, as the route for the Lord with greatest life-giving strength, my readiness to listen (*sraosha*) offered to the All-knowing one, which is greatest by that poetic thought of yours! May we ward off evil beings by our tongue!

⁶Come now with your good thought! Give me now on account of my Order the gift of a long lifespan! On account of his capacious utterances, you gave, O All-knowing one, support with strength to Zarathustra. Give to us, too, O Lord, support by which we shall over-come the hostilities of the one hostile to us.

⁷Now give on account of my Order *that* reward: the spoils of my good thought! Give, you, O Humility, the invigorant to Wishtāspa! To *me*, too, *you* have now given it, O All-knowing one. Command, too, O All-knowing one, for us your generous gifts, which we wish to hear about in *your* poetic thought, O All-knowing one, and that of those like you.

⁸You, the best, who have the same pleasure as the best Order, I ask for the best things, you whom, as the Lord, I as the winner am here and now asking for them to be given to the hero Frasha-ushtra and to me and to those from whom you shall receive them for the whole lifespan of their good thought.

⁹May we not, O All-knowing one, anger you all with those requests to you, as well as Order and *your* Thought, the best, we who have taken our places to fulfill our obligations with praises. *You* are the fastest invig-orants, and yours is the command over the life-giving strengths.

¹⁰Thus, those whom you know to be, from the point of view of Order and good thought, following the established rules, and so are according to the models—I shall fill for them, O All-knowing one, O Lord, with attainments their wish. Thus, I know for *you* all songs bringing fame full of life-giving power for *you* and having their own chariot horses and victorious.

¹¹*You*, who with the help of these (songs/men) are guarding Order and good thought for the duration of a lifespan, teach *you me*, O All-knowing one, O Lord, to speak in accordance with *your* inspiration, by your mouth, the words by which the first existence will be here again (every time).

43 *From Yasna 29*

¹To you gods the breath-soul of the cow complains: "For whom have you carved me? Who has fashioned me? Wrath, violence, and restraint keep me bound, as well as fetter and oppression. I have no pastor other than you gods, so appear to me with a good forager!" [cf. 28]

²Then the fashioner of the cow asks Order: "How was your model for the cow, when you gods who are in command established her together with her pasture as 'cow-nourishing diligence'? Whom do you all wish to be a Lord for her, someone who may push back Wrath together with those possessed by the Lie?"

⁶Thus he has said, the All-knowing Lord, who knows the webs by their texture (?): "Neither has a model been found during this one period of existence nor one just in accordance with Order. For the carpenter fashioned you for the cattle-tender and the forager."

⁷The Lord, who has the same pleasure as Order, fashioned that poetic thought for the cow to be that of the fat dripping, as well as the milk, he, the All-knowing one. He is vitalizing for the meager ones by his ordinance. "Whom do you have, (O fashioner of the cow?), who by his good thought shall bring them down to the mortals?"

⁸"This one here is the one found by me who alone listens to our ordinances, Zarathustra of the Spitāmas. He wishes, O All-knowing one, to make poems of praise heard for us and for Order, if only I am tied (as) the good control of his speech organ (?)."

⁹Thus promised, the breath-soul of the cow lamented: "Am I one who would direct a forceless voice at the pleasing (of the heavenly arbiters?), the voice of a man without life-giving power? He whom I wish here and now to have command through this invigorant, when will he ever be there who will give him help with his hands?"

44 From Yasna 43

⁵Thus, I now think of you as life-giving, O All-knowing Lord, when I now see you at the rebirth of the new existence, as when you established, for the first time, actions as fee-earning, as well as the words that are to be uttered, and established a bad reward for the bad and a good one for the good—by your artistry—at the final turn about the *dāmi*.

⁶The turn at which you come with *your* life-giving spirit/inspiration, O All-knowing one, and your command, at that turn *he* is on account of his good thought, he by whose actions the herds are furthered with Order. For *these* actions Humility is announcing the models of *your* guiding wisdom, which no one can cause to lie.

⁷Thus, I now think of *you* as life-giving, O All-knowing Lord. When one surrounds *me* with good thought and asks *me* "Who are you? Whose are you? How would you submit your daily earning tallies for questioning regarding *your* herds and men?"—

⁸then I declare myself to him first as the *real* Zarathustra; second, that I wish to command hostilities for the one possessed by the Lie, but for the sustainer of Order I wish to be support and strength, for I would like to receive the adornments of one who commands at will; and, third, that, to the extent that I can, I am praising you, O All-knowing one, and weaving you (into hymns).

¹⁶Thus, Zarathustra, O Ahura, prefers your spirit/inspiration, whichever, O All-knowing one, is most life-giving for you. May Order have bones through my/his life breath and be strong! May Humility be in your command and in full sight of the sun! May she by her works give me my reward for my good thought!

45 From Yasna 46

¹To what earth/ground am I bending? Where shall I go to (find) a grass land? They do not recognize me as a member of the family and community. The household which I want to pursue has not favored me with its generosity nor the rulers of the land, who are possessed by the Lie. How shall I win your favor, O All-knowing Lord?

²I know why I am weak, O All-knowing one. It is because of my lack of cattle and because I have few men. I am complaining to you: look at it, O Lord. Consider the support that a friend, having offered it, may give to his friend! You now look hither down through Order at what my good thought offers up to you in sacrifice.

³When, O All-knowing one, will those who are the bulls of the days move forth for the upholding of the new existence of Order by our announcements now grown more powerful, namely, the guiding thoughts of the Revitalizers [cf. 13:2]? To whom will he come for support for what is to be woven (?) with good thought? I, O Lord, am now choosing *you* to come to announce it to *me* (for me) to announce it (to others ?).

⁴But the one possessed by the Lie will keep those conveyors of Order, the bulls, from moving forth, being the bad invoker of the settlement or the land and repugnant by his own actions. Whoever removes him from his command, O All-knowing one, or his livelihood, *he* will put those bulls before the flight of his good understanding.

⁶Thus, the man who shall come to him (at the judgement?) without being capable, that one will find himself in the net of the web of the Lie. For, when you, O Lord, set in place the first vision-souls, you said: That one is possessed by the Lie who is best for the one possessed by the Lie, and that one is a sustainer of Order who has a sustainer of Order as friend.

⁷Whom, I wonder, O All-knowing one, do you assign to one like me as protector—when the one possessed by the Lie ogles me with sinful intent—other than *your* fire and thought, through the actions of which you assembled Order, O Lord? Proclaim, now, that skill to my vision-soul!

⁸Or he who is taking those herds that are mine to hand over to sin: may misfortune not reach *me* by *his* actions; rather, may it return with that same hostility upon his body so that one may keep him from good living, but not from evil living, O All-knowing one, by any hostility whatever.

⁹Who will he be, the one first in line, a heavenly arbiter who will point *me* out, for (?) how we invigorate (?) *you* (O Fire?), the speediest one, in our action, you the life-giving Lord, a sustainer of Order. "Those things which are by the Order of your ritual are those which are for our Order," the fashioner of the cow tells me. They (= the arbiters?) wish to come to *me* on account of *that* good thought of mine.

¹⁰In return for the Order of my ritual and the command conferred by my good thought, let a noble man or noble woman give to me as reward all those things of this existence which *you*, O All-knowing Lord, know are the best! Let them also give their rewards to all those (gods, heroes) whom I shall lead into my poetic web! Then, with all those I shall cross the Ford of the Accountant.

¹¹By their bad commands, the "poetasters" (*kawis*) and "mumblers" (*karpans*) have harnessed mortal man to evil actions in order for the present existence to keep being destroyed, they whom *their own* breath-soul and *their own* vision-soul will cause to shudder in anger when they have come to the Ford of the Accountant and become, for their entire lifespan, guests in the house of the Lie.

¹²But when the winner has come up through Order among the great-grandchildren and grandchildren to be declared as those of Tura son of Friia, you, O All-knowing Lord, further his herds with the diligence of Humility. Thus, the All-knowing Lord has mustered (?) them on account of their good thought for these our men for their support in order for them to announce it to others.

¹³He who once favored Zarathustra of the Spitāmas with his generosity among mortals, that man is in accordance with the divine models and ready to be renowned by my song. Thus, for *him* the All-knowing Lord establishes the new existence, for *him* he furthers his herds on account of his good thought. We now think of him as a good companion of Order.

¹⁴O Zarathushtra, which sustainer of Order abiding by the deals is for *you* for the great gift exchange? Or, who wishes to be renowned in song? Well, there is Kawi Wishtāspa at the audition. In fact, all of those whom you, O All-knowing Lord, sustain in one and the same

house as yourself, those I want to invoke with the utterances of my good thought.

^{15}O Haēchad-aspas, O Spitāmas, I shall tell you all so that you can distinguish those who are according to the rules from those who are not. By the established rules, first *you* shall establish for yourselves by your actions what is Order, the (rules) by which the Order of the Lord was established.

^{16}You, O Frasha-ushtra, go there with the heavenly arbiters, you of the Huwagwas, go with those whom we two (the breath-souls of the cow and the poet?) here and now wish to be in *their* wish, where Humility is now with Order, where in the ritual of (someone of) good thought there is command, where the All-knowing Lord is now dwelling in increase,—

^{17}where I shall announce to you all metrical verses, O Jāmāspa of the Huwagwas, not unmetrical ones, and, together with that readiness of yours to listen, hymns for a generous gift. He who distinguishes what is according to the rules from what is not, by his masterly intent (?), by his Order, he, the Lord, is the All-knowing one.

^{18}He who assigns to *me* the best things of a full lifespan, to *him*, as the best parts of *my* ritual, I have now assigned by my good thought even my bones, but miseries to *him* who would receive us in order to give us over to misery, O All-knowing one and you others, seeking, by the Order of my ritual, to win the favor of *your* approval. That is the discrimination of *my* guiding wisdom and thought.

^{19}He who shall now produce for me the *true* new existence in accordance with Order, for Zarathustra, one which is the most Juicy in exchange value, for this one who earns it as his fee, an existence of the highest order: a bull and a cow together with all things to be found in one's thought. *You,* O All-knowing one, appear to me as the one who finds the most often just those things for me.

46 From Yasna 49

^{4}Those who by their evil guiding wisdom and by the utterances of their tongues will only increase Wrath and Obstruction, they who

tend no cattle among those who do and not one of whom has overcome bad deeds by good deeds, they will define the old gods as the
vision-soul of the one possessed by the Lie.

⁵But, he there, O All-knowing one, is milk libation and fat dripping
for you, who has now united his vision-soul with good thought,
whoever by his Order is of the good lineage of Humility, and on
account of all those things is in *your* command, O Lord.

⁶I am now sending my vision-soul forth to you, O All-knowing one,
as well as to Order, for her to speak the words that are being sent to
you, for them to be judged there by a thought inspired by *your* guiding
wisdom, with respect to how we may make them heard correctly—
that vision-soul, which belongs to one like you all, O Lord.

⁷And let her hear that, O All-knowing one, on account of her good
thought! Let her hear on account of her Order!—And you too listen,
O Lord!— namely: Which shall be the community, who shall he
be, who by the Laws of family shall give our household a good
reputation?

⁸You made for Frasha-ushtra the most blissful union with Order.
That I am now asking *you* for, O All-knowing Lord, for me too: that
union which is there in *your* command in the race for a good reward.
Let us be your dearest friends for an entire lifespan!

⁹Let him too hear the ordinances, the curry-groomer (?) who was
fashioned for revitalizing. He who does not utter the words correctly
is someone about to tie a union with the one possessed by the Lie
when their vision-souls harness their coursers in the race for the best
fee, O Jāmāspa, at the harnessing of the Order of his poems at the
audition.

¹⁰And *that* you are now guarding there in *your* abode, O All-knowing
one: the good thought and the breath-souls of the sustainers of Order,
and the homage on account of which Humility is present, as well as
the milk libation, which bestows command. With the fat offering, set
yonder (sky?) in motion!

¹¹But those whose command, actions, speech, vision-souls, and
thoughts are all bad, the wicked ones, their breath-souls are at this

very moment coming toward them with bad foods. On account of their true state they shall be guests in the house of the Lie.

¹²What help did you have for him when he invoked you with Order, for Zarathustra? What help do you have for me who with good thought shall make you all my friends with my praises to you, O All-knowing one, O Lord, asking for yonder reward which is the best you all have at the sending off (of my offerings)?

Zarathustra and the Gathic Characters in the Young Avesta

47 The first haoma sacrificers (Yasna 9)

¹At the proper time, at the Haoma-pressing Hour, Haoma went up to Zarathustra as he was ritually cleansing the fire and chanting the *Gāthās*.

Zarathustra asked him: "Who are you, the most beautiful I have ever seen in the entire existence with bones, whose life is sunny and immortal?"

²The death-averting Haoma, sustainer of Order, answered me: "I, O Zarathustra, am the death-averting Haoma, sustainer of Order. Ask me hither, Spitāma-son! Press me forth to drink! Praise me for strength, as the future Revitalizers too will praise me!"

Yima's father

³Zarathustra said: "Homage to Haoma! Who was the first man, O Haoma, to press you for the world of the living with bones? What reward was sent to him? What prize came to him?"

⁴The death-averting Haoma, sustainer of Order, answered me: "Wiwanghwant was the first man to press me for the world of the living with bones. That reward was sent to him, that prize came to him that a son was born to him: radiant Yima with good herds, the most Fortunate among those born, like the sun to look at among men. ⁵Under his command, beasts and men never died, waters and plants never dried out, and there was no lack of savory foods. There was no cold or heat, no old age or death. Envy made by the evil gods there was

not. Father and son went forth as fifteen-year-olds for as long as Yima with good herds ruled, Wiwanghwant's son."

⁶"Who was the second man, O Haoma . . .?"

⁷The death-averting Haoma, sustainer of Order, answered me: Āthviya was the second to press me for the world of the living with bones. That reward was sent to him, that prize came to him that a son was born to him: Thraētaona of the house rich in life-giving strength. ⁸He smashed the Giant Dragon . . . [= 35:33].

Kersāspa's father

⁹"Who was the third man, O Haoma . . .?"

¹⁰The death-averting Haoma, sustainer of Order, answered me: "Thrita of the Sāmas, most rich in life-giving strength, was the third man to press me for the world of the living with bones. That reward was sent to him, that prize came to him, that two sons were born to him: Urwākhshaya and Kersāspa, one a guide regulating the law, but the other's work was above, the curly-headed, mace-bearing youth. ¹¹He smashed the horse-devouring, man-devouring horned dragon, over whom the yellow venom rose up to the height of a spear. Kersāspa cooked his meal on its back in an iron pot at noon time, but the villain got hot and began to sweat. He shot out from under the pot, scattering the boiling water. Frightened, the heroic-minded Kersāspa ran off and away!"

Pourushāspa, Zarathustra's father

¹²"Who was the fourth man, O Haoma . . .?"

¹³The death-averting Haoma, sustainer of Order, answered me: "Pourushāspa was the third man to press me for the world of the living with bones. That reward was sent to him, that prize came to him that you were born to him, you, O upright Zarathustra, of the house of Pourushāspa, you who said no to the evil gods and took Ahura Mazdā as your guide. ¹⁴Renowned in the Aryan Expanse, you were the first, O Zarathustra, to chant the *Ahuna Wairiya* with pauses and fourfold repetitions, the last time with stronger enunciation. ¹⁵You made all the

evil gods hide in the ground, who before that went about on this earth in the shape of men, you the strongest and firmest, the speediest and fastest, and the greatest obstruction-smasher among the Creations of the two Spirits.

48 Zarathustra's birth (Yasht 13)

[87]We sacrifice to the reward and pre-soul (*ashi* and *frawashi*) of Zarathustra of the Spitāmas, sustainer of Order, [88]who was the first to think good thoughts, speak good words, and perform good acts; who was the first priest, charioteer, and husbandman; and who was the first to make known to others and to himself, the first to have gained for himself and for others the cow, the Order, the word to be spoken, as well as his readiness to listen to Ahura Mazdā's utterance and command, and all good things whose seed (*chithra*) is from Order, which Ahura Mazdā set in place.

[89]He was the first priest, charioteer, and husbandman. He was the first to turn his seed away from evil gods and men and their brood. In the existence with bones, he was the first to praise Order and scorn the old gods. He chose to sacrifice to Ahura Mazdā in the manner of Zarathustra; he said no to the evil gods and took Ahura Mazdā as his guide.

[90]In the existence with bones, he was the first to utter and pronounce the word by which he said no to the old gods and took Ahura Mazdā as his guide. In the existence with bones, he was the first to have always declared the evil gods as a whole to be unworthy of sacrifices or hymns, he who himself was rich in life-giving strength, providing all good life, and the first guide among the lands.

[93]When he was born and grew up, waters and plants prospered, waters and plants grew, and all the creations set in place by the Life-giving Spirit called down blessing:

[94]"Blessed are we! A priest is born, Zarathustra of the Spitāmas. He will spread out the barsom and send forth our sacrifice with libations. Here, hereafter, the good Mazdayasnian Tradition will go far and wide to the seven continents.

[95]Here, hereafter, Mithra who provides wide pastures will further all the foremost ones of the lands. He will pacify those that are in commotion. The Scion of the Waters, rich in life-giving strength, will keep a firm hold on those that are in commotion.

49 Ashi and Zarathustra (Yasht 17)

[17]Praised among those worthy of sacrifice, not to be moved away from the straightest paths, she stood on the chariot, good Ashi the tall, thus speaking with words: "Who are you who invoke me whose voice resounds in my ear as the most beautiful, more so than all others?"

[18]Zarathustra of the Spitāmas drove forth from there on his chariot, he, the first to praise Order, the best, to sacrifice to Ahura Mazdā and the Life-giving Immortals. When he was born and grew up, the waters and plants prospered, the waters and plants grew.

[19]When he was born and grew up, the Evil Spirit ran away from the wide, round earth with distant borders. Thus he spoke, the Evil Spirit full of destruction, the giver of evil gifts: "All those worthy of sacrifice could not catch up with me against my will, but Zarathustra, all alone, reaches me against my will! [20]He smashes me with the *Ahuna Wairiya*, as with a stone the size of a house. He heats me with the *Ashem Wohū*, just like metal. He, Zarathustra of the Spitāmas, chases me from this good earth, coming against me all alone!" [Cf. 60:41]

[21]Then Ashi drove forth from there on her chariot, good Ashi the tall, speaking thus: "Stand closer to me, O upright Spitāma-son, sustainer of Order, lean against my wagon!"

He stood closer to her, Zarathustra of the Spitāmas, he leaned against her wagon.

[22]Standing above, she stroked him all around with her left hand and her right, with her right hand and her left, speaking thus with words: "You are beautiful, O Zarathustra, you are well-made, O Spitāma-son. You have good legs and long arms. Fortune is in your body and long well-being for your soul, just as I told you."

50 Zarathustra and the Fortune of the Kawis (Yasht 19)

[78]We sacrifice to the strong Fortune of the Kawis . . . set beyond other living beings, [79]which followed Zarathustra, sustainer of Order, making him help the vision-soul along with his thoughts, words, and acts. In the entire existence with bones, in Order he was the greatest sustainer of Order, in command the one with best command, in wealth the wealthiest, in Fortune the most Fortunate, in valor the most valor-smashing.

[80]Before that, the evil gods would run about and indulge their pleasures in full view. In full view they would drag off the women from the humans and forcefully debase them, weeping and complaining.

[81]Then a single *Ahuna Wairiya* of yours, which you, Zarathustra, sustainer of Order, chanted, with partitions spoken four times, the last with stronger enunciation, drove all the evil gods under ground, depriving them of sacrifice and hymn. [Cf. 60:46]

51 Zarathustra and Wishtāspa's sacrifices (Yasht 5)

[104]Zarathustra, sustainer of Order, sacrificed to her . . . [= 15:9], [105]asking her: "Give me that prize, O good, Ardwī Sūrā Anāhitā, you most rich in life-giving strength, that I shall make the son of Arwad-aspa, the firm Kawi Wishtāspa, help my vision-soul along with his thoughts, words, and acts!"

[108]Kawi Wishtāspa, who saw on high, sacrificed to her, Ardwī Sūrā Anāhitā, at the heel of the river Frazdānu, a hundred stallions, a thousand bulls, ten thousand rams, asking her: "Give me that prize, O good, Ardwī Sūrā Anāhitā, you most rich in life-giving strength, that I may overcome in battles in this world Man of Darkness, whose vision-soul is evil; Man of War, who sacrifices to evil gods; and Arjad-aspa possessed by the Lie!"

52 Zarathustra and Wishtāspa's sacrifices (Yasht 9)

[25]Zarathustra, sustainer of Order, sacrificed to her . . . [26]asking her:

"Give me that prize, O good Druwāspā, you most rich in life-giving strength, that I shall make the good noble Hutaosā help my vision-soul along with her thoughts, words, and acts, she who has believed in and is informed about my vision-soul, which is also that of those who sacrifice to Ahura Mazdā, she who has given good glorification to my clan!"

[29]Kawi Wishtāspa, who saw on high, sacrificed to her on the shore of the Good Lawful river a hundred stallions, a thousand bulls, ten thousand rams and also bringing a libation (saying:) [30]"Give me that prize, O good Druwāspā, most rich in life-giving strength, that I may conduct battles ... with the Khiyonian villain Arjad-aspa; with Daredevil, who sacrifices to evil gods; [31]and that I may strike down Man of Darkness, whose vison-soul is evil, and Spinjarushka, who sacrifices to evil gods!

[32]May I also bring back home Humāyā and Vardkanā from the Khiyonian lands, and may I strike down of the Khiyonian lands fifty times and a hundred, a hundred times and a thousand, a thousand times and ten thousand, and uncountable times more than that!"

53 Zarathustra and Hwōwī's sacrifices (Yasht 16)

[5]We sacrifice to Chistā the straightest, sustainer of Order, set in place by Ahura Mazdā, [6]to whom Zarathustra sacrificed, for well-thought thought, well-spoken speech, well-performed acts, and for yonder boon, [7]that she, Chistā the straightest, sustainer of Order, set in place by Ahura Mazdā, should give strength to his feet and arms, hearing to his ears, health and fattiness to his entire body, and that clear-sight which the Kara fish in the sea has, who can see the distant turn as narrow as a hair of the river Ranghā with distant shores, deep as the height of a thousand men.

[14]We sacrifice to Chistā, sustainer of Order ..., the good vision-soul of those who sacrifice to Ahura Mazdā, [15]to whom Hwōwī, sustainer of Order, sacrificed, knowledgeable, seeking the good dispenser, Zarathustra, sustainer of Order, to help his vision-soul along with her thoughts, words, and acts.

54 Kawi Wishtāspa and the Fortune of the Kawis (Yasht 13)

[99]We sacrifice to the strong Fortune of the Kawis ... which followed Kawi Wishtāspa, making him help the vision-soul along with his

thoughts, words, and acts, so that he chose to praise this vision-soul, chasing the enemy, sending the evil gods on their way.

He sought free space for Order in tree and stone. He found free space for Order in tree and stone. He served as arm and support of this vision-soul, that of Ahura Mazdā and Zarathustra. [100]When she was exhausted and bound, he extracted her from her bonds. He set her down in the middle, making straight lines on high, without running forth (ahead of her companions?), sustaining Order, to be satisfied with cattle and grass, to be made friendly with cattle and grass.

55 Hutaosā's sacrifice (Yasht 15)

[35]Hutaosā of many brothers sacrificed to him on the golden throne in the town of the Naotaras.(. . .)

[36]She asked him: "Give me that prize, O Wāyu, whose work is above, that I may be dear, beloved, and recognized in the home of Kawi Wishtāspa!

56 Zarathustra exorcizes evil from the world (Videvdad 19)

The Evil Spirit tempts Zarathustra [cf. 60]

[1]From the northern regions the destructive Evil Spirit ran forth, the greatest of evil gods, giver of evil gifts, speaking deceptively: "O Lie, run hither, destroy Zarathustra, sustainer of Order!" The lie ran around him, the evil Butī, dangerous, destructive, and deceitful.

[2]Zarathustra chanted the *Ahuna Wairiya* and sacrificed to the good waters of the Good Lawful River, choosing as his own the vision-soul of those who sacrifice to Ahura Mazdā.

Stricken, the Lie ran away from him, the evil Butī, the destructive, deceitful Danger, [3]answering the Evil Spirit deceptively: "I see no death for Zarathustra, sustainer of Order, for he is possessed of Fortune."

Zarathustra looked around in his mind, thinking: "The evil gods, possessed by the Lie, givers of evil gifts, are plotting my death!"

[4]Zarathustra rose and went forth, undaunted by their evil thought and the harshness of their hateful plots, carrying stones in his hand

the size of houses, which he had obtained from the Creator Ahura Mazdā.

—Where in this wide, round earth with distant borders are you carrying them, there on the shore of the Drejya, in the home of Pourushāspa?—

⁵Zarathustra made the Evil Spirit a promise: "Evil Spirit, who give evil gifts, I shall smash the creation of the evil gods, I shall smash the corpse made by the evil gods, I shall smash the witch Khnanthaitī against whom the obstruction-smashing Revitalizer will be born from the Kansaoya Sea, from the southern regions."

⁶The Evil Spirit of evil creations answered him deceptively: "Do not destroy my creation, Zarathustra, sustainer of Order! You are the son of Pourushāspa, bathed in libations from the time in the womb. Praise *back* the good vision-soul of those who sacrifice to Ahura Mazdā, and you shall obtain a boon such as the one the land-lord Wadagana obtained."

⁷Zarathustra of the Spitāmas attacked him back: "I shall not praise back the good vision-soul of those who sacrifice to Ahura Mazdā, not if my bones, life breath, and consciousness were to be wrenched apart!"

⁸The Evil Spirit of evil creations answered him deceptively: "With whose word will you overcome and remove my creation and with what well-made weapon?"

⁹Zarathustra of the Spitāmas attacked him back: "With the mortar and the bowl, the *haoma*, and the word spoken by Ahura Mazdā! That is my weapon, the best. With that word I shall overcome and take it away, O Evil Spirit who give evil gifts, with that well-made weapon. The Life-giving Spirit made it for unbounded time. The Life-giving Immortals, who bestow good command and give good gifts, brought it forth."

¹⁰Zarathustra chanted the *Ahuna Wairiya*.

The Evil Spirit is defeated

⁴³He exhorted, he dissuaded, he took courage, he lost courage, the destructive Evil Spirit, the greatest of evil gods. There were the evil

gods Indra, Sāurwa, Nānghaithya, Taurwi and Zairi, Wrath with the bloody mace, Evil-fashioner, the Winter made by evil gods, dangerous, destructive Senility, Butī, Drivel, Deceit, Pustule, and others.

[44]Thus he spoke deceptively, the destructive Evil Spirit: "Let us gather, O evil gods possessed by the Lie, givers of evil gifts, on the top of Mount Arzūra.

[45]They ran thither chattering evil deception, howling evil deception: "Let us gather on the top of Mount Arzūra! [46]He is born, Zarathustra, sustainer of Order, of the house of Pourushāspa! How shall we find death for him? He opposes and strikes down the evil gods, he, the greatest of destroyers of evil gods!"

Down they tumbled, the sacrificers to evil gods, the Corpse made by evil gods, the falsely spoken Untruth. [47]They ran thither, chattering evil deception, to the bottom of the dark existence, to the frightening hell.

Zarathustra in the Pahlavi Texts

57 Birth and life of Zarathustra (Dēnkard VII.2)

Zarathustra's mother

[1]About the miracles that were revealed about him from the birth of the mother of that most Fortunate of those born.

[2]It is all manifest from the Tradition that the Creator transferred the Fortune of Zarathustra through the side of the womb to Zarathustra when Ohrmazd gave the order that his Fortune should go from the world of thought to the world of the living and to that womb.

[3]When Ohrmazd had fashioned the creature (*dahishn*) of Zarathustra, the Fortune was then before Ohrmazd. The creature of Zarathustra fell down upon the Endless Lights and, via the sun, moon, and stars, upon the fire in the house of Zōish and upon the wife of Zōish, when that girl was born who became Zarathustra's birth mother.

[4]Because that light filled the space between earth and heaven, people began to ask: "Does that fire in the house of Zōish burn all by itself?" i.e., needing no wood.

⁵They went to the soothsayer (kēd), who interpreted it for them, saying: "The fullness of Fortune of the existence with bones comes from the Fortune of that body," i.e., every duty is set in motion from this.

⁶The demons took a bad beating from that Fortune, so they brought three plagues down upon that village to make adversity for that girl: a winter, all kinds of dangers, and oppressive disrespect. And they threw into the thoughts of the villagers: "This harm has come upon the village from this girl's sorcery!" Then the villagers accused the girl of sorcery, and the parents were pressured to expel her.

⁷The girl's father had much to say about the accusation of sorcery. They were completely unjustified, he told the villagers, explaining: "When this girl was born in my house, that all-blazing fire appeared, which produced light, so that it lit up everything in the dark night. ⁸When this girl sits in the innermost room of the house, where there is no fire, and one lights a tall fire in the great hall, then, where this girl sits, it is brighter from the light that shines from her body than where they light a bonfire. One so endowed with Fortune has never been a sorcerer."

⁹Even then, goaded by the demons, the evil priests in the land were not satisfied. The father ordered the girl to go to Padērēdarāsp, the father of a family in the Spitāma village, and the girl obeyed.

¹⁰Thus, the gods, by their miraculous power, turned the tumult the demons had caused out of spite in order for the girl to be exiled into the reason why the girl became the wife of Zarathustra's father Pōrushāsp, whose father was none other than Padērēdarāsp.

¹¹As the girl was on her way to that family and she stopped on the highest place in the land of the Spitāmas and looked around, a great wonder appeared. A voice called to her, saying: "Go to that village which lies on the highest hill and is larger than all the others, for most living creatures and cattle are assembled there! A munificent distributer god fashioned that village to help you!"

¹²The future wife stood and looked: "I have to remember clearly what was said, so I have to do what my father ordered me to do."

¹³Then she washed her hands and went from those of her own village to yonder village, that of Padērēdarāsp. Then that Fortune came to Padērēdarāsp's son Pōrushāsp.

The Amahrspands fashion Zarathustra's pre-soul

¹⁴Ohrmazd the Creator then transmitted Zarathustra's pre-soul through the *hōm* to the parents of Zarathustra by a miracle.

¹⁵It was the conclusion of the third millennium, at the end of the 3000 years when the creation was in the world of thought without the Assault—after the creation was in the world of thought but before the Lie came upon it—that the Amahrspands fashioned the pre-soul of Zarathustra. It sat down among them in a man's body, speaking with mouth and tongue, ¹⁶and for three millennia Zarathustra appeared frequently to their eyes and hearing, looking just like the Amahrspands.

¹⁷When it was the conclusion of the third millennium, after Zarathustra had been fashioned, but before he was brought down to the world of the living—at the end of the 3000 years of the world of the living, being still in the world of thought without the Assault—then Ohrmazd discussed with Wahman and Ardwahisht: "Have you discovered a mother in whom we can place Zarathustra?"

¹⁸Ardwahisht answered: "You know that yourself, O Life-giving one! Let *us* make Zarathustra just as you made us, Ohrmazd! You know who we are. Tell us where, for *you* know where it is, O Life-giving Spirit!"

¹⁹Ohrmazd argued: "It is not seemly that we should send Zarathustra down to the world of the living with bones, equipped with a mouth, tongue, and speech. ²⁰If we send Zarathustra down to the world of the living in a man's body, with a mouth, tongue, and speech, it will be apparent that he is my seed (*tōhmag*). They will say about him: "It is the Righteous Man!" Therefore we shall fashion him together in water, earth, plants, and· animals, ²¹and we shall bring him to Pōrushāsp's village, so that they shall say Zarathustra is from two good seeds (*tōhm*), one from the Amahrspands, namely Nēryōsang, and one from men, namely Jam."

The Amahrspands fashion the hōm for Zarathustra's pre-soul

[22]Then the Amahrspands fashioned a stalk of *hōm*, the height of a man and of superior color and moist, brought Zarathustra's pre-soul into it, made it go forth from the Endless Light, and placed it there on Mount Asnwend. [23]They set up a wall around it, saying: "Rise up!" And water ever poured from the *hōm*, i.e., it was moist.

[24]When 330 years were left of the 3000 years of the world, the living without the Assault, Wahman and Ashwahisht made their plan. They went down to the existence (*okh*) of those with bones and came to where two birds were sitting trying to make chicks. Seven years earlier, snakes had devoured them. [25]Wahman and Ashwahisht went to their abode, where the birds were discussing: "We must go out. We must seek that *hōm*!" [26]According to the plan, the birds sought the *hōm*, and the *hōm* fell two ells. They seized it with their legs, brought it to the tree, and placed it in the nest.

[27]Then snakes climbed up, i.e., they went for the chick. Then Zarathustra's pre-soul went forth. All the snakes on that tree ran out on the branches, but Zarathustra's pre-soul smote them in their jaws, and they fell down and died. Those of them who remained in holes were necessary to maintain the semen (*shusr*) of that one species.

[28]The *hōm* connected (*paywand-*) with the tree and kept growing on the top of the tree where the nest of the birds was, ever moist and green.

Pōrushāsp finds the hōm

[29]After Zarathustra's birth mother came to marry Pōrushāsp, Wahman and Ashwahisht, according to the plan, proceded to the pastures of the Spitāmas where Pōrushāsp was, and they brought him to the *hōm* and thus bound his thoughts to it.

[30]Then Pōrushāsp went forth, according to the will of those in the world of thought, to the water of the river Dāitīy, where he caught sight of the *hōm*, which was growing in the nest on that tree.

[31]He thought: "I have to get to it, but, since I cannot reach that high, I have to cut down the tree. For you seem moister than (the

other creatures) of Ohrmazd," i.e., the goodness of something from you is better than everything else.

³²Then Pōrushāsp went forth, he washed his garments, and witnessed a great wonder, ³³about which it is said: By the time Pōrushāsp had washed the garments, the *hōm* had gone forth from the top third to the middle of the tree, which means it wished to be picked up by Pōrushāsp.

³⁴Then Pōrushāsp went forth to it with clean garments. He cut all of it off and took it with him, and, like someone who was to carry a two-year-old or a three-year-old, it seemed to him that it gave him pleasure.

³⁵Pōrushāsp carried those *hōm* twigs to his oldest wife and said: "Dugdōw, you take care of the *hōm* twigs until they are ready for work and law!"

Ohrmazd transmits Zarathustra's body essence to his parents

³⁶It is also manifest that the Creator transmitted Zarathustra's body essence (*gōhr*) via water and plants into his parents. When the order was issued that it should enter into his parents' body, a great miracle appeared to many.

³⁷As the Tradition says: Then, when Ohrmazd had fashioned the body essence of the creature of Zarathustra, the creature of Zarathustra fell from before Ohrmazd upon Hordad and Amurdad, upon a cloud.

³⁸Then the cloud released its water, again and again, drop by drop, and in equal measure and warmth. By this there was joy for beasts and men: as much semen as two plowing oxen. Thereupon plants of all species grew up, even on dry ground, at a time when other plants are wilted, and Zarathustra's essence came from that water to those plants.

³⁹It is also manifest that, in order that Zarathustra's essence should come to his parents, Pōrushāsp was induced by the Amahrspands to drive six white, yellow-eared cows to those plants.

⁴⁰Here a great wonder appeared: Among those cows there were two heifers that began to produce milk, and Zarathustra's essence went from the plant into that cow and was mingled with its milk.

⁴¹Pōrushāsp drove the cows back and said to Dugdōw: "Dugdōw, those two heifers began to produce milk, so milk those two cows, for there is Fortune from them for the world of the living!" ⁴²Dugdōw got up, took a pot, and milked the milk in those two heifers, which they gave willingly. She added water, and Zarathustra's essence was in that milk.

The Adversary tries to destroy Zarathustra

⁴³As the Adversary struggled to make that milk ineffective and disappear—as is well known from the Tradition—he, the greatest among them, assembled the demons and said: "You will be annihilated, O demons, if that food is set up," i.e., (if) it was made and placed, "and a man comes into existence in it, namely, Righteous Zarathustra. Who among you agrees to destroy him while he is but a fetus?" i.e., it would be easier to undo him.

⁴⁴The ignorant Chishmag said: "I will destroy him!" ⁴⁵and ran with 150 demons looking like himself. They tore down the town, turning it into rubble, but he could not break that great opponent who was in it, but was warded off by him.

Zarathustra's Fortune, pre-soul, and body essence are assembled

⁴⁶Afterward, Pōrushāsp asked that *hōm* back from Dugdōw, and he pounded it and mixed it with the milk that contained Zarathustra's body essence. Here, then, the pre-soul and Zarathustra's body essence came together. ⁴⁷When the *hōm* and milk were mixed and had been announced (*niwēyēn-*) to Ohrmazd, Pōrushāsp and Dugdōw drank it. Here, then, Zarathustra's Fortune, pre-soul, and body essence were completely assembled (*hangerd-*) in his parents. [Cf. p. 28]

Demons try to prevent his parents from having intercourse

⁴⁸Here, a great wonder appeared to them: They lay down for the first time trying to make a son. The demons howled at them with their voices of villains, accusing them of sinful behavior: "O Pōrushāsp, what are you doing and why?" Thereupon they became contrite, like people who are ashamed.

⁴⁹⁻⁵⁰They lay down a second and a third time. The demons howled at them with their voices of villains. Again they became contrite, like people who are ashamed.

⁵¹But they spoke to each other and got down to it. They embraced, saying: "We shall not do this kind of thing again, not if Rāg and Nōdar ("East and West") were to come together here!"

Demons try to destroy Zarathustra while a fetus

⁵²Then that man was conceived, Righteous Zarathustra, when his body essence, pre-soul, and Fortune came together in the womb of his mother.

⁵³After the conception of Zarathustra, the demons again strove hard to destroy Zarathustra in the belly of the mother, and they made her womb sick with the sharpest and most painful pain, so much so that she consulted the witch doctors about how to seek healing.

⁵⁴Again, a great wonder appeared: She heard a loud voice from high above, from Ohrmazd and the Amahrspands: "O wife! Go not where you are going! This disease cannnot be healed by the witch doctor's medicine. Wash your hand, take firewood in that hand, and bring meat and cow's fat to that child. Bring fire, heat him with the fire, and lay him on the bed, and you shall be well!"

⁵⁵Then that young woman washed her hand, and she did as she had heard, and she became well.

What happened shortly before his birth

⁵⁶Yet another thing appeared to many: When three days remained till his birth—in the manner of the rising sun, as it comes close, when its first light is spread out, then its body appears—as the Tradition says: Then in those last three nights when Zarathustra was in the womb, when three days remained, after which he would be born, Pōurushāsp's house was all lit up.

⁵⁷Then the horse- and sheep-masters of the Spitāmas said as they were running away: The house of Pōrushāsp is bound to be destroyed. There are flames licking out of every nook and cranny!

⁵⁸Then they said as they were running back together: The house of Pōrushāsp has not been destroyed; flames are not licking out of every nook and cranny! In that house a magnificent man has been born!

⁵⁹This too was one of the wonders: The renown of the wondrous birth of that man of great Fortune had also been spoken of by Jam and other miracle-workers as they brought the Word from the gods. ⁶⁰Jam said to the demons: "Here the pure Righteous Zarathustra shall be born who shall give you, O demons, that which is not your desire"—i.e., he shall render you incapable—"who shall give you inability to act!"—i.e., you cannot seek it for yourselves, and nobody will seek it for you.

⁶¹That Zarathustra would be born and bring the Word was made known not only by Jam and Frēdōn and many learned men. The gods, too, proclaimed it through the language of animals and sent it forth in the world so that it too might be witness to his bringing of the Word.

⁶⁷As for the Bull placed alone, we know that it spoke against Ahrimen's striking: "Even if you think, O Evil Spirit, that you can overcome everything by this killing, even so you cannot overcome us by this killing"—i.e., you are not able to destroy me—"so that I do not come back to life. I shall proclaim even now: At the last turn, that man shall come, Zarathustra of the Spitāmas, who shall place in a tight spot the demons, the helpers of demons, and also those on two feet possessed by the Lie."

58 Ahrimen tries to prevent Zarathustra from being born
(Selections of Zādspram 8)

⁸The night he was born, Ahrimen appointed his generals and drew up their armies. Some fought with a thousand demons, others with forty thousand demons, rushing and falling upon him. The gods' counter-attack was mainly to reveal the Fortune in the form of fire when he was born, ⁹and, because it blazed and shone far and wide, they were unable to reach him.

¹⁰Finally, Ahrimen sent Akōman upon him: "You belong more to the other world and are most inside it. Go with deception into Zarathustra's mind and turn it toward us demons!"

¹¹Ohrmazd sent Wahman against him.

¹²Akōman was just about to enter the door, ¹³but Wahman, ingeniously, opened it and said: "Go in!" ¹⁴and Akōman thought: "I should not do something Wahman tells me to do," and turned back. Then Wahman went in and mingled with Zarathustra's "core" (*wārom*). Zarathustra laughed, because Wahman is the "happy-maker" in the other world.

59 From his birth to the conversation with Ohrmazd (Dēnkard VII.3)

Zarathustra's laughter and the evil priest

²He laughed at birth. The seven nurses who were sitting around him were frightened and said: "What was this? Was it on account of greatness or disrespect that this young child laughed at his birth like a worthy man pleased with performing his duties?"

³Pōrushāsp said: "Dugdōw, take this man to a bed with soft wool. It is on account of your goodness that this man saw Fortune and well-being coming when he laughed at birth."

⁴Afterward, Pōrushāsp went to Dūrasraw, an evil priest (*karb*), the one best known in that village for his sorcery. He told him about the wonders revealed about Zarathustra after his birth and brought him home to see the child.

⁵The sorcerer was hurt by the Fortune in Zarathustra and plotted evil. Ingloriously, he wished to squeeze with his own evil hand the tender head of that Fortunate child and kill him.

⁶Here a great wonder appeared to many: That villain's hands turned backward, i.e., they withered, and never again was he able to take meat with his evil hand and chew it with his foul mouth.

⁷That evil priest also howled that the signs upon Zarathustra were marks of evil. He frightened Pōrushāsp sorely by the destruction that might come from Zarathustra and incited him to destroy the child.

⁸By this sorcery, Dūrasraw filled the mind of Pōrushāsp with fear of Zarathustra and perverted Pōrushāsp's mind so much that he sought to have him cause Zarathustra's death. ⁹He consulted Dūrasraw about how to destroy him in such a manner that he himself would not be

affected. The evil priest howled that the remedy was for him to pile up firewood and place Zarathustra in the middle of it, then light the fire and burn him. Pōrushāsp did so. ¹⁰And here a great wonder appeared to many: The fire did not fall upon the plant, and the plant did not catch fire.

At dawn that son-loving mother came running, approached him cautiously, and took him and placed him on her right arm on her sleeve.

¹¹Pōrushāsp then told Dūrasraw how the fire had not burned him and again asked him how to destroy Zarathustra. The evil priest howled that the remedy was for Pōrushāsp to put Zarathustra in a narrow passage and drive many cows through it, so that he would be trampled under their feet. Pōrushāsp did so.

¹²And here too a great wonder appeared to many: A cow went up to him, whose concern was greater than that of the others, and went in front of him, i.e., before the lead cow. It ran before him, i.e., it stood before Zarathustra, and looked after him all day, i.e., it kept the cows away from him. It was the first to arrive, the last to leave.

At dawn that son-loving mother came running. . . .

[*The same with a herd of horses*]

¹⁵Pōrushāsp told Dūrasraw how the horses had not trampled Zarathustra either and again asked him how to destroy Zarathustra. The evil priest howled that the remedy was for Pōrushāsp to throw Zarathustra into a lair with slaughtered wolflings, so that when the wolf came and saw them, in her rage, as revenge for her young, she would tear Zarathustra apart and eat him. Pōrushāsp did so.

¹⁶Here too a great wonder appeared to many: When the wolf had come within a few meters, then Zarathustra, with the help of the gods, struck the jaws of the wolf, so that its jaws hung slack and impotent. ¹⁷Then Srōsh-ahlīy and Wahman came, bringing a ewe, and she suckled him all through the night.

¹⁸At dawn that son-loving mother came running. When the ewe came out of the pen, the daughter of Zōish said: "You have eaten, and you run away satiated!" For she thought it was the wolf. "Good for that

son,"—i.e., you are good for me—"that they should see you," all bones
or blood.

[19]She approached him cautiously and took him and placed him on
her right arm on her sleeve, and said: "From now on I shall not let
them take you from me, not if both Rāg and Nōdar were to come
together here!"

Zarathustra at seven

[32/34]When Zarathustra was seven years old, Dūrasraw together with
Brādrōrēsh, another evil priest, came to the village of Pōrushāsp to see
Zarathustra. Pōrushāsp ordered food to be prepared for them, and he
made the meal and poured a bowl full of mare's milk.

[35]He said to Dūrasraw: "In our village you are the most learned in
how to sacrifice to the demons. Sacrifice this of mine!"

[36]A great wonder appeared showing Zarathustra's knowledge at
that tender age, when he said: "I shall sacrifice this, father. Let him not
sacrifice that which I ought to sacrifice."

[37]Pōrushāsp said: "You shall not sacrifice mine. Let him sacrifice
mine!"

[38]Three times those men exchanged these words. Zarathustra stood
up and said to them, breaking (the jar) with his right foot: "I sacrifice
for Righteous men and women! I sacrifice for the poor men and
women. If Pōrushāsp engages any men or women possessed by the
Lie," i.e., to perform the sacrifice, "the sacrifice will embrace the
sacrificers!"—i.e., he should sacrifice who ought to sacrifice!"

Wahman brings Zarathustra at thirty to his first Interview

[51]When Zarathustra was thirty years old, Wahman the Amahrspand
was sent by Ohrmazd and came to him as he was carrying water with
hōm from the Ēwtāg river. As the Tradition says: When he came to the
third affluent of the Good Dāitīy river, he went into it. When Zarathustra
came out of it, he saw a man come walking from the southern direction.

[52]That was Wahman, who seemed to him of outstanding body, i.e.,
in body more pleasing to the eye, and outstandingly beautiful, i.e., he

was outstanding in every thing. Wahman seemed to him as tall as three men as tall as spears. Wahman seemed to him to be carrying a branch of . . . , which he had removed from that plant without harming the plant. That was the branch of the Tradition in the world of thought. By it he indicated that one should behave according to the Tradition thus, without harming anything.

[54]When Zarathustra came to the fourth affluent of the Good Dāitīy river, the Hōshān (?) river, he took water with *hōm* from the middle of it. He lifted his right foot out of the river and put his garment over it, and, at that moment, in front of him, Wahman came toward him and joined him.

[55]He asked him: "Who are you? From whom are you (descended)?"

Zarathustra answered: "I am Zarathustra of the Spitāmas."

[56]Wahman said: "O Zarathustra of the Spitāmas, what are you laboring for? What are you striving for? And what do you make your desire?"

[57]Zarathustra answered: "I labor and strive for righteousness. I make righteousness my desire. And I think righteousness as much as I seek it."

[60]Wahman said: "O Zarathustra of the Spitāmas, give away this garment you are carrying, as we shall consult him who made you, who made me, who is the most life-giving of those in the world of thought, who is the most munificent of beings, whose speaker I am!" i.e., I am his messenger."

[61]Then Zarathustra thought: "He must be good, the creator who is better than this messenger."

[62]Then they went together, Wahman in front and Zarathustra behind.

60 Zarathustra and Wishtāsp (Dēnkard VII.4–5)

Zarathustra chases the demons from the earth, but people still sacrifice to them [cf. 56]

[36]The Foul Spirit ran forth to kill Zarathustra. As the Tradition says: From the northern direction ran forth the destructive Foul

Spirit, lying: "Demons, run upon and destroy Righteous Zarathustra!" [cf. 56:1–4]

[37]The demons rushed upon him, the demon Bud and secretive, deceptive Harmfulness.

[38]But Zarathustra recited the *Ahuna Wairiya*, at which the demons were stunned. They ran back, the demon Bud and secretive, deceptive Harmfulness.

[39]The demons lied: "You don't see straight, Foul Spirit!" i.e., you do not see things the way they are. "You order that done which cannot be done! We could not find a way to kill Zarathustra of the Spitāmas."

[40]Fully endowed with Fortune, Zarathustra saw in his mind that the demons possessed by the Lie, of evil knowledge, were plotting his death. Up rose Zarathustra. Forth went Zarathustra.

[41]Here a great wonder appeared to many: Zarathustra took a stone in his hand the size of a house, the divine *Ahuna Wairiya*, which he had received from Ohrmazd the creator. [42]Thereby, not only in Iran, but in the entire earth, as was manifest to the Iranians and to every species, the bodily frames of the demons were broken. [Cf. 49:19–20]

[46]After that, they were no longer able to appear in the world in demon-shape in order to cause harm, so they appeared to people with the character (*khēm*) of gods. But people recognized them as demons, not as gods. [Cf. 50:81]

Wishtāsp is tricked into throwing Zarathustra in jail

[64]This too: Zarathustra was aware that Wishtāsp's evil priest, that destructive brood who had turned from the Tradition to evil, as well as the other evil priests at Wishtāsp's court, all of them were plotting his death, upon which heavy damage would befall Wishtāsp. He also knew that they were inciting Wishtāsp to cause his death, so that, at Wishtāsp's command, he would have to endure horrible incarceration and punishment.

[65]He was aware, however, that he would be set free, that he had revealed wonders, and bore witness to how he had become a bringer of the Word. So, after ten years of interviews (with Ohrmazd) had

passed, on Ohrmazd's advice and at his command, he proceeded alone to Wishtāsp's court and the trial by cup and battle.

⁶⁶At Aspānwar, Wishtāsp's residence, he spoke forcefully and victoriously about himself being the one who brought the Word of Ohrmazd, and he called Wishtāsp to the Tradition. With his great wisdom, his perfect thought, and belief in the world of thought, Wishtāsp would have listened to Zarathustra's words and would have called him to prepare for bringing the Word, ⁶⁷but then, before he heard Zarathustra's words and learned about him, by the machinations of that destructive brood and the other evil priests, who knew how to slander him and turn things around, Wishtāsp turned against Zarathustra and delivered him to chains and punishment.

As Zarathustra himself said: "They attributed to me thirty-three crimes, and they bound me with thirty-three chains, those wicked villains who sacrifice to the demons. ⁶⁸That fasting weakened me and cut off the energy of my feet, the strength of my arms, the hearing of my ears, and the sight of my eyes [cf. 62:6; 74; 75]. My rib-cage joined my back," i.e., it touched my back, "by the persistence of that weakening, destructive fast."

⁶⁹And here it was made known about the stamina of Zarathustra that he endured and survived even the punishment of hunger, thirst, heavy chains, and other sufferings, the endurance of which is not laid down in the natural strength of men.

A great wonder appeared to King Wishtāsp and his courtiers, when they found his body endowed with Fortune in horror and imprisonment, but alive because he courageously withstood the long fasting.

Wahman, Ashwahisht, and the Fire visit Wishtāsp

⁷⁴In order to convince King Wishtāsp and the learned men with him of the truth of the Tradition, Ohrmazd the Creator sent Wahman, Ashwahisht, and the Life-giving Fire to Wishtāsp to convey the message that Zarathustra was the one true bringer of the Word and that Ohrmazd wished Wishtāsp would receive the Mazdayasnian Tradition and send it forth in the world.

[75]A miracle appeared to the countrymen of Wishtāsp when the Amahrspands flew down from heaven to earth and into the house of Wishtāsp. As it is said in the Tradition: Then Ohrmazd said to them, to Wahman, Ashwahisht, and the Fire of Ohrmazd: "Go forth, O Amahrspands, to the house of Wishtāsp, strong in cattle, famed afar, and make him steadfast in the Tradition, so that he abides by this Tradition and gives the right answer to Zarathustra of the Spitāmas, who has accepted their word!"

[76]The Amahrspands went to the house of Wishtāsp, strong in cattle, famed afar. Their chariot seemed to Wishtāsp in that tall dwelling to be all light. When he saw them, the exalted Kay Wishtāsp trembled in all his members before their great might and victoriousness. His entire upper body trembled, like a horse pulling a chariot.

[77]The Fire of Ohrmazd spoke with the speech of men: "Do not fear, exalted Kay Wishtāsp, for there is nothing to fear. It is not the herald of your enemy Arzāsp (king of the Khionians) who has come to your house, nor his tax-collectors, and we are certainly not an all-conquering, thrashing thief, bandit, and highway-robber. [78]We are Wahman, Ashwahisht, and the Fire of the Life-giving Lord. Be aware and know this well! [79]If clairvoyance follows you," i.e., you have the knowledge needed, "then praise the good Mazdayasnian Tradition, which spreads in pure fashion by memorization, which is that of Zarathustra of the Spitāmas. [80]Recite the *Ahuna Wairiya*, praise Best Order, deprive the demons of sacrifices! For it is Ohrmazd's wish for you, as well as that of the Amahrspands and the other gods who are munificent and sustain Order, that you stay in this Tradition.

[81]"As a favor, as a reward if you praise the pure good Tradition of Righteous Zarathustra of the Spitāmas, we shall give you long reign for your kingdom and long life for your soul," i.e., 150 years [cf. 49:22]. "We shall give you Ahrishwang and Ability to stand on the chariot to last as long as you wish and to be with you forever and never pass away. We shall give you a son, Pishishōtan by name, immortal and unaging, undeteriorating and undecaying, alive and king in both exist-

ences, both in the world of thought and in that of the living. [82]And as a favor, as a reward if you do not praise the pure good Tradition of Righteous Zarathustra of the Spitāmas, we shall make you fly up in the air, and we shall send after you *zarnumaini* vultures "thinking of old age." They shall eat your bones, and your blood shall reach the earth, but water shall not reach your body."

60a After Wishtāsp accepts the Tradition (Dēnkard VII.5)

[1]On the wonders that were revealed from the time Wishtāsp accepted the Tradition until Zarathustra's pre-soul went back to the Best Existence. When it left, it was seventy-seven years from his birth, forty-seven from the Interview, and thirty-five from when Wishtāsp accepted the Tradition.

[2]When Zarathustra recited the Tradition in the house of Wishtāsp it appeared to the eye that bliss was also disclosed to small and large animals, to the fires, and also to the entity in the world of thought protecting the dwelling and the house.

61 Zarathustra asks Ohrmazd for immortality (Pahlavi Rivāyat 36)

[1]This too is manifest in the Tradition that Zarathustra said to Ohrmazd: "When you leave and I leave, when shall we again have a body?" [2]Ohrmazd said: "In the Assembly of Isadwāstar," [3]where, according to the Tradition, the souls will come together: friends, brothers, fathers, sons, other close relatives, wives, and husbands [cf. 70:10]. [4]But if they are wicked, they will not come, in the end.

[5]When Zarathustra came before Ohrmazd, he wept and said: "Ohrmazd, make me immortal!"

[6]Ohrmazd said: "I cannot do that, for, if I do, then Ahrimen's brood, the villainous Tūr Brādrōkhsh, who was made to kill you, will become immortal, and there will be no Resurrection and the Final Body will not be made, which is what the poor hope for."

[7]Weeping, Zarathustra answered: "You made the wind, water, clay, and fire, you made everything. See if you cannot find a way for me to escape death!"

⁸Then Ohrmazd endowed Zarathustra with the all-aware wisdom, ⁹and he saw all that was, is, and will be here in this world, there in that world, and among all of humanity. ¹⁰He saw the place of him who was immortal and had no children, and it seemed to him sad and distressing. ¹¹He saw the place of him who was mortal but had children, and it seemed to him to be a thing of joy and happiness. ¹²Then he said to Ohrmazd: "It seems better to me to have to pass on than to live forever but have no children."

¹³Ohrmazd said: "It is better. You have listened and observed well, Zarathustra. He who has noble children seems to me to be better off than if he were to live forever. Take a wife and have children! For whoever commits the sin of not taking a wife will not come to paradise."

¹⁴People should learn and listen to what they see in the *Avesta* and *Zand* with their own eyes and hear it with their own ears. For they acquire knowledge from learning, and from listening they become cultured and kind. By knowledge and kindness, one becomes worthy of going to paradise and Garōdmān to see Ohrmazd and the Amahrspands.

62   Where Zarathustra was when he received the Tradition
(Pahlavi Rivāyat 47, 46)

¹At the age of thirty, Zarathustra came to converse with Ohrmazd. ²All in all, he received the Tradition seven times.

³The first time was in Ērānwēz in Azerbaijan. That time, he conversed with Ohrmazd for ten years, ⁴during which he suffered much evil, by chains and prison that the Foul Spirit had fashioned forth and brought upon him.

⁵Once, the Foul Spirit said: "Let us harm the Tradition! When he has gone out, steal another coat of Zarathustra's and place human bones in the pocket, and tell people that Zarathustra is not quite the way they have assumed. He has another coat for the divine service, for he is really an undertaker, this Zarathustra." To show them he was right, he took it and turned the pocket upside-down, shook it out on the ground, and human heads, hands, and feet fell out.

⁶Then they bound him with thirty-three chains, and, after a while, he became so hungry and thirsty that he lost all strength, as well as his sight and hearing [cf. 60:67–68].

¹⁶After that, he went to Wishtāsp and spent two years trying to make him follow the Tradition, saying to him: "Accept the Tradition! For it is the will of Ohrmazd, the Amahrspands, and the other gods that you should stand by the Tradition." ¹⁷But Wishtāsp said: "If you have come for a horse or wealth, take everything you need and leave!"

¹⁸Again, Zarathustra said: "Accept the Tradition!" Wishtāsp said: "I have committed so many sins that, even if I were to accept the Tradition, it would have no good effect on my soul. For, in my first battle, I slew six thousand, in the second five thousand, and in the third, too, five thousand. If I were to fight again, in the first I would slay a thousand, in the second ten thousand, and in the third a thousand, again." ¹⁹Zarathustra said: "There was no sin in killing those, for they were the brood of wolves. It was, in fact, good of you to kill them."

²⁰Again he said: "Accept the Tradition! For many were those who did not accept it." (...)

⁸(He said:) "For Ohrmazd tried to lead radiant Jam to the Tradition, but Jam scorned Ohrmazd, saying: "Astwihād will not come upon me!" and, because he scorned him, demons and men cut him in half [cf. 40:1].

⁹"He tried to lead Frēdōn to the Tradition, and he too scorned him. And, because he scorned him, Old Age fell upon him."

¹¹Even then Wishtāsp did not accept the Tradition.

¹²Then Ohrmazd sent Wahman, Ardwahisht, and the Burzēnmihr Fire to Wishtāsp's house, ¹³and they said to him: "Accept the Tradition! For, if you accept the Tradition, then we shall all bless you with long-lasting rule for your kingship. . . ."

¹⁴Even then Wishtāsp did not accept the Tradition.

¹⁵Then Ohrmazd sent Nēryōsang, saying: "Go to Ardwahisht and tell him to mix hemp into his wine and give it him to drink!" ¹⁶Ardwahisht did so.

¹⁷When Wishtāsp had drunk the wine, immediately he lost consciousness and they led his soul to Garōdmān and showed him the value of receiving the Tradition.

¹⁸When he came to, Wishtāsp called to his wife Hudōs and said: "Where is Zarathustra? I want to receive the Tradition!"

¹⁹But Zarathustra had heard him and had already gone forth, and so Wishtāsp received the Tradition.

²⁰All the sheep and cattle and all the burning fires rejoiced ²¹when they heard what Zarathustra said when he taught Wishtāsp the Tradition. He then appointed Zarathustra to the office of high priest, ²²which he held for thirty-five years.

²³After that, Zarathustra was killed by Tūr Brādrēsh in the shape of a wolf, ²⁴but that wicked one died on the spot from a worse death.

²⁵And Zarathustra's end came on Sunday in the month of Day.

✦

CHAPTER FOUR

TEXTS ON ESCHATOLOGY AND THE END OF THE WORLD

On the Actors of the Final Battles

63 The eschatological agents (Yasht 13)

⁶¹We sacrifice to the good strong life-giving pre-souls of the sustainers of Order, who watch over yonder body, that of Kersāspa son of Sāma, the curly-haired mace-bearer, nine and ninety thousand nine thousand nine hundred and ninety-nine [cf. 47:10].

⁶²We sacrifice to the ... pre-souls of the sustainers of Order, who watch over yonder semen, that of Righteous Zarathustra of the Spitāmas, nine and ninety ... [cf. 65:61].

⁹⁷We sacrifice to the pre-soul of Saēna, sustainer of Order, son of Ahum-stut (= he who praised the new existence), who was the first to stand forth upon this earth with a hundred students. (...)

⁹⁸We sacrifice to the pre-soul of Isad-wāstra (= seeker of pasture), sustainer of Order, son of Zarathustra [cf. 18:43].

We sacrifice to the pre-soul of Urwatad-nara (= organizer of men), sustainer of Order, son of Zarathustra.

We sacrifice to the pre-soul of the Huwar-chithra (= with the brilliance of the sun), sustainer of Order, son of Zarathustra. [Cf. 65:56]

⁹⁹We sacrifice to the pre-soul of Kawi Wishtāspa, sustainer of Order, firm and lordly, who spun out the Life-giving Word, carrying the defiant mace. (...)

¹⁰³We sacrifice to the pre-soul of Pishishyaothna (son of Wishtāspa), sustainer of Order.

[128]We sacrifice to the pre-soul of the Ukhshyad-erta and Ukhshyad-nemah, sustainers of Order.

We sacrifice to the pre-soul of the Astwad-erta, sustainer of Order, [129]who shall be called "obstruction-smashing Revitalizer" and "Astwad-erta": "Revitalizer" because he will revitalize the existence and give it bones; "Astwad-erta" because, when "possessing bones" (*astwad*) and life breath, he will seek again "bony" freedom from danger for withstanding the Lie.

64 On the Revitalizers (from the Hymn to the Divine Fortune, Yasht 19)

Cosmogonic and eschatological functions

[9]We sacrifice to the strong Fortune of the Kawis set in place by Ahura Mazdā, worthy of great honor, whose work is superior, skillful, careful, and crafty, set beyond other living beings, [10]which was Ahura Mazdā's, when, by it, he set in place the creations, many and good, beautiful and wonderful, perfect and radiant.

[11]With it *they* shall make the existence Perfect (*frasha*), incorruptible, indestructible, undecaying, unrotting, ever-living, ever-life-giving, having command at will, so that when the dead arise again *he* will come, making alive and free from destruction, and the existence will be made Perfect in exchange value [cf. 17:84; 45:19].

[12]Living beings who hold the announcements of Order will be indestructible.

The Lie will be destroyed and dispelled to the very place it had come from for the destruction of the sustainers of Order, as well as yonder seed and being. The villainess will cower in fear, and the villain will be destroyed. Thus is the model.

The Fortune of the Kawis and the Revitalizers

[21]We sacrifice to the strong Fortune of the Kawis . . . set beyond other living beings, [22]which belongs to those worthy of sacrifices both in the world of thought and in the world of the living, to the Revitalizers, who will make the existence Perfect, both those born and

those as yet unborn. ²³Those are the ones who will make the existence Perfect in exchange value, incorruptible, indestructible, undecaying, and unrotting.

⁶⁶It will follow him who shall stand forth from the Kansaoya Sea, at Mount Ushadā, around which plentiful waters come together pouring down from the mountains. (...)

⁶⁷Toward it flows together, toward it runs together the wealthy and munificent Haētumant (Helmand) river, swelling into white surfs, throwing down copious floods. (...)

⁸⁸We sacrifice to the strong Fortune of the Kawis ... ⁸⁹which will follow the obstruction-smashing Revitalizer, as well the other Companions, so that he will make the existence Perfect, incorruptible and indestructible, undecaying and unrotting, ever-living and ever-life-giving ... [cf. 70:16]. Living beings who hold the announcements of Order will be indestructible. (...)

⁹⁰The Lie will be destroyed. ... Thus is the model.

⁹²When Astwad-erta stands forth from the Kansaoya Sea, the messenger of Ahura Mazdā, the son of Wispa-taurwairī (= she who overcomes all), brandishing his obstruction-smashing weapon, which firm Thraētaona also carried when he smashed the Giant Dragon; ⁹³which the Turian Frangrasyān bore when he smashed Zainigao (= Zēnīgāw), possessed by the Lie [cf. 40:9]; which Kawi Haosrawa bore when he smashed Tura Frangrasyān; which Kawi Wishtāspa bore as he was about to gather the armies of Order: With it he will remove the Lie from the living beings of Order.

⁹⁴He will see with the eyes of the guiding wisdom. He will look out for all living beings, chasing *her*, the one of evil seed. He will see the entire existence with bones with the eyes of the milk libation. He will make firmly indestructible the entire world of the living with bones.

⁹⁵The Companions of obstruction-smashing Astwad-erta will come forth, those of good thought, speech, and deeds, of good vision-souls, who none of them have ever once spoken anything wrong with their own tongue. Wrath with the bloody mace, he of evil Fortune,

will retreat before them. With Order he shall overcome the evil Lie, the one of darkness, of evil seed.

[96]He overcomes even evil thought. His good thought overcomes it. He overcomes the wrongly spoken speech. His correctly spoken word overcomes it. Wholeness and Immortality shall overcome both hunger and thirst, evil hunger and thirst.

The Evil Spirit, who performs no deeds that are not evil, shall retreat, commanding nothing at will [cf. 107:6].

65 On Zarathustra and Wishtāsp's offspring (Bundahishn 35)

[56]From Zarathustra were born three sons and three daughters. [57]The sons were Isadwāstar, Urwatadnar, and Khwarshēd-chihr [cf. 63:98].

Isadwāstar was head priest (*āsrōn*) and High Priest (*mowbedān mowbed*); he died a hundred years after the coming of the Tradition. Urwatadnar was chief of the husbandmen in the bunker that Jam made in the earth. Khwarshēd-chihr was a warrior and a general.

Pishōtan, son of Wishtāsp, lives in Kang castle.

[61]As it is said: Three times Zarathustra approached Hwōw. Each time his seed (*tōhm*) went onto the ground. The divine Nēryōsang kept receiving the luminous strength of that seed and entrusted it to the divine Anāhīd for safe keeping. In due time she will mingle it with the mother. 99,999 pre-souls of the sustainers of Order are appointed to guard it so that the demons do not spoil it. [Cf. 63:62]

On the Evils that are Befalling and will Befall Iran

66 From Dēnkard VII, 8

[1]About the wonders that will appear after the Iranians' rule of the land of the Iranians comes to an end at the end of the millennium of Zarathustra and at the coming of Ushēdar son of Zarathustra.

[2]The awareness acquired through predictions in the *Avesta* about the ninth and tenth centuries (of the last millennium), the nature of which is now visibly exposed, will turn out to be true, such as: the rule of Iranians will come to an end (and depart) from the land of the

Iranians; law, practice, and custom will be destroyed; and the long-limbed Christians with parted hair will rule.

³The four classes will be mingled and merged; people not notable in their age, together with the lowly and insignificant, will be elevated to higher rank; and people notable in their age will be destroyed and degraded.

⁴Because of the non-Iranians, wisdom and character will decline and vanish from the Iranian towns, that is, the truth of the Tradition, as well as dignity, affection, gratitude, peace, and generosity and other good things in man based on wisdom and character.

⁵Heresy, wickedness, idolatry, calumny, coarseness, lying, ingratitude, discord, and avarice and other evil things connected with (the lack of) wisdom and character will increase and prevail. They will abandon care of fire and water, the world of the living, and the Amahrspands.

⁶The tyranny of evil Tradition, idolatry, and little culture will increase, and Lust (Āz) will rule people's bodies. Contrary judgments on sorcery will abound, and there will be much evil talk about how oppressive the gods' Tradition is.

⁷People will destroy each other's kingdoms, and places and territories will be devastated by the violence the winners and evil kings will visit upon one another. Cattle will be severely wounded, killed, and cooked. Divine peacefulness will leave the Iranian towns, replaced by weeping, crying, lamentation, and complaining. People will get no profit from their work. Their strength will be destroyed, their Fortune struck down, and their life short.

⁸Enemy armies of various kinds will abound. Heretics will be received among the evil rulers, while those with knowledge and good character will not. In quick succession, the conquerors will visit distress and plagues and other adversity and oppression and slavery upon the lands and places of the Iranians.

⁹The Tradition from the gods will be considered a "non-path," and those of good Tradition will weaken, suffer pain, and pale away. The carriers of the Tradition will be ridiculed, and their steadfastness will

be considered wickedness. The prevalence of good works in the lands of the Iranians will be destroyed.

¹⁰There will be much other evil, as well, as enumerated in the *Avesta*. Some of it has passed, some of it is still visible, and some of it is clearly still to come.

¹¹This is a bit of what the Tradition says: In that age which is mixed with iron—i.e., wherever one looks it is of iron—heretics, seeking coarseness, are born. ¹²They are said to be "coarse" because, to them, what pleases them and what is blameworthy are one and the same. They are said to "seek" because they do evil to people whenever they can. Youths will appear as old men on account of the bad times in which men are born who are unfriendly toward learned men and school teachers.

¹³Their speech is of approval, spoken gently, yet they are wicked. Their speech places people in debt, rendering that of teachers and advisers useless. They do not care if it is a lord (*ahū*) or a master (*rad*), disrespecting both rulers and teachers and, with few exceptions, treating them as evil.

¹⁴Whenever somebody says something and is regarded as the town judge, they throw them down to hell into that "foul pool," that is, they perform evil upon them until they, too, become wicked. They keep enumerating (their evil Tradition?), both the heretic with evil offspring, himself conceived by evil sodomy, and the bad, calamitous wolf.

¹⁵Here friends strike down their friend, and they take from him what he himself has made, and, whenever they can, they take his possessions and give them to whomever they make prosper with it. And they rob the poor of his possessions, and, when he complains, they taunt him: ¹⁶"There still is some, but we will not give it to you!"

Here, no friend will counsel his friend, nor a brother his brother, nor a son his father, nor a father his son: "Make me have faith!" They dwell wherever they wish and act however it pleases them, and they say it is stupid to talk about the path of truth and about the benefits of education.

[17]We know these three to be the benefits of education for us: the lesser should be held as superior, the greater as inferior, and the greater should be taught by the lesser. (...)

[19]Then, when character and wisdom decline and disappear from the towns of the Iranians, then, on account of the proximity of calamities, the demonic destitution and the demon-made winter full of snow run together—i.e., rain becomes less—as well as the secretive, deceptive Harmfulness—i.e., there is greater mortality. Then the wicked heretics will band together, [20]lying: "Eat and kill, O land-lord! You must eat and kill. Kill the fire, too, and cook food with it!" Those whose only protection are the judges, they lead away, the poor whose law is Righteous—[21]i.e., they oppress him. And they strike him and unjustly carry off his possessions.

[22]Into that age you will not wish to come, O pure Righteous Spitāma-son.... The heretics will bring your Word to perdition, the *Avesta* and the *Zand*—i.e., weaken it—and they will torture their own souls for love of their possessions.

[23]About the ninth and tenth centuries it says this, too: That age will come, O Zarathustra of the Spitāmas, when many heretics will talk about masters, teachers, and the righteous, and few about the wicked, yet they will dry out the waters and the plants and destroy all prosperity, all that is manifest as being from righteousness.

67 From Bundahishn 33

The end of Zarathustra's millennium

[28]It says in the Tradition: Their evil rule will end!

[29]A group will come with red signs, red banners, and will seize Pārs and the other provinces of Iran all the way to Babylon. They will weaken the Arabs.

[30]Then one will come from the area of Khorāsān, an evil man. He will push back the inhabitants of Mount Padishkhwār and wield his evil rule for some years. Under his leadership people will be destroyed

in Pārs, leaving only a few on the shores of the sea of Kāzerūn (the Persian Gulf).

³¹Then the Khiyonians and Turks will rush into Iran in large numbers with many banners and lay waste this prosperous, sweet-smelling Iran. They will ruin the houses of noblemen and perpetrate much evil and oppression upon the people of Iran. They will destroy their houses and seize property until God has mercy.

³²When the Romans arrive, they will rule for one year.

At that time one endowed with Fortune will come from the direction of Kāwarestān, kinsman of the gods. They will call him Kay Wahrām. All the people will rally to him, and he will also rule everywhere in India, Rome, and Turkestān. He will eradicate the ones of evil beliefs, restore the Mazdayasnian Tradition, and no one will be able to come forth with another belief.

³³In the same age, Pishyōtan, son of Wishtāsp, will come from Kang castle with 150 righteous men. He will destroy that idol temple of mysteries of theirs, enthrone the Wahrān fire in its place, and utter the entire Tradition correctly and redress it.

Millennia of the Revitalizers

³⁴Then the fifth millennium, that of Ushēdar, son of Zarathustra, begins.

³⁵Ushēdar will come from Ohrmazd to exhibit the Tradition and bring the right message. As Zarathustra brought it, he will bring it. Destitution and dryness will decrease, and generosity, peace, and absence of hate will be furthered in the whole world of the living; plants will stay green for three years. The river Wātaēni will flow deep as the height of a horse, and its springs will flow back to the Kiyānsī sea.

For ten days and nights the sun will stand still in the sky, and all the wolf species will be destroyed.

³⁶When the millennium of Ushēdar ends, Malkūs will arrive, that brood of destruction, of the lineage of Brātrōrēsh, Zarathustra's murderer. By his tradition, which is that of sorcerers, and by his desire, which is that of witches, he will produce that terrible rain which they call "that of

Malkūs." It will rain for three years, both in winter, when it is cold, and in summer, when it is warm, with enormous amounts of snow and hail to destroy the creation, so that all mankind except a few will be destroyed.

Then people and animals will be repopulated from Jam's bunker, which is in hiding for this very purpose.

[37]At that time the healing power laid down in the thousand kinds of plants to fight the thousand kinds of illnesses will come into two kinds of plants and one kind of land, and no one will die from illness, only from old age or if killed.

[38]Then the sixth millennium begins, the millennium of Ushēdar-māh.

[39]In that millennium, Ushēdar-māh, son of Zarathustra, will come from Ohrmazd to bring the right message. As Zarathustra brought the Tradition, he will send it forth in the world of the living.

For twenty days and nights the sun will stand still in the sky. Plants stay green for six years. The Lie, brood of Lust (*or*: vipers), will be destroyed—i.e., snakes and other evil animals will be destroyed.

[40]Close to the end of the millennium of Ushēdar-māh, Dahāg Bēwarāsp will come loose from his chains and will cause much damage to the creation by his demonic desire.

[41]And at that time Sōshāns, son of Zarathustra, will appear.

For thirty days and nights the sun will stand still in the sky.

[42]As the first of dead living beings, Garsāsp, son of Sām, will be resurrected. He will smash Bēwarāsp with his mace and kill him and thus keep him away from the creatures.

On Zarathustra's three eschatological sons

[43]About those three sons of Zarathustra, that is, Ushēdar, Ushēdar-māh, and Sōshāns, they say: Formerly, when Zarathustra was speaking, they deposited the Fortune of Zarathustra in the Kiyānsī sea for safe keeping, entrusting it to the Fortune of the waters, that is the divine Anāhīd. [44]Now, too, they say they keep seeing at night three lights that blaze at the bottom of the sea.

[45]And one by one, when their time comes, it will happen that a young woman will go to the water of the Kiyānsī to wash her head, and

the Fortune mingles with her body. She becomes pregnant, and those three will be born from her one by one in due course.

68 The coming of the wonder-working Shā-Wahrām

When will the messenger come from India? "The awaited Shā-Wahrām has come, he of the line (*dūdag*) of the Kays, with a thousand elephants with mahoots seated on their heads and with an uplifted banner that they carry before the army in the manner of the famed men of old."

The army leaders will need a messenger as skilled translator, who will go and say what we have suffered at the hands of the Arabs (*tāzīg*): They weakened our Tradition. They killed our king. An Iranian they hold to be no better than a demon, the Tradition no better than a dog. They have taken and eaten our bread. They have taken the kingdom from the famed men of old, not by skill or by valor, but by scorn and mockery.

They will take from men by violence their sweet women, properties, lands, and gardens.

They have imposed a poll tax to be paid by head count. They have demanded back the principal, a crushing amount.

Look how much evil that Lie has hurled into this world! Our homeland is now the worst in the world!

From us has come that wonder-working Shā-Wahrām, he of the line of the Kays!

We shall wreak our vengeance upon the Arabs, like Rōstam wrought a hundred-fold vengeance for Siyāwakhsh!

We shall let the mosques fall in ruin! We shall enthrone new fires! We shall erase the idol-temples!

And we shall clean them out the of world, so that the brood of the Lie may vanish from this world!

On the Resurrection and the Final Body

69 From "The day Hordad of the month of Frawardīn"

[31]On the day Hordad of the month of Frawardīn (= first day of the year), Sām Narīmān (= Garsāsp) will kill Azhidahāg and become king

of the seven continents until Kay Husrōy comes out of hiding. Then Sām will hand over the kingship to him, [32]and, for fifty-seven years, Kay Husrōy will be king of the seven continents and Sōshāns High Priest.

[33]Then, when they give King Wishtāsp back his body, Kay Husrōy will hand over the kingship to him, and Sōshāns will hand over the office of High Priest to his father, Zarathustra.

[34]On the day Hordad of the month of Frawardīn, Ohrmazd the Lord will perform the Resurrection and produce the Final Body. The world of the living will be deathless, ageless, free from harm and Opposition.

[35]Ahrimen and his demons and lie-demons and the other demonic brood, as well as the false teachers and evil priests, will be undone. The demon Lust will devour all the demons and lie-demons, and righteous Srōsh will undo the demon Lust. [36]Ohrmazd the Lord will strike down Ahrimen, stunned and undone, [37]so that, thenceforth, the Foul Spirit and his creatures will never again rule on the earth.

[38]They will lead Ahrimen to the hole through which he rushed in, cut off his head, and fill hell with seven metals.

[39]This earth will go up to the star level, and Garōdmān will go from where it is to the star level, and Garōdmān will be everywhere.

70 From Bundahishn 34

Mankind and food before the end of the world

[1]It says in the Tradition: As for Mashī and Mashiyānī, when they had grown up from the earth, first they drank water, then they ate plants, then milk, and then meat. People, too, when they are about to die, first stop eating meat and milk, then bread, and then, until they die, they drink only water.

[2]In this manner, in the millennium of Ushēdar-māh, the strength of the bodily needs will decrease, so that people will be satisfied with eating one meal every three days.

³After that, they will stop eating meat and eat plants and drink the milk of domestic animals. Next, they will stop drinking milk, too. Then they will stop eating plants, and drink only water. Ten years before Sōshāns comes, they will stop eating altogether and not die.

Then Sōshāns will raise the dead.

Zarathustra asks Ohrmazd about the resurrection

⁴As it says: Zarathustra asked Ohrmazd: "The body that the wind winnows and the water carries off, from where will they raise it and how will the Resurrection come about?"

⁵He answered: "The sky is set up without pillars, standing in the world of thought, with its borders in the distance, and from the essence of shining metal [cf. 17:2]. Similarly, when I set in place the earth, which carries the entire existence with bones, it had no support in the world of the living [cf. 17:9]. When I led the sun, moon, and stars into the intermediate space in the form of light; when I gave men grain for them to cast into the ground and it grows up again and becomes manifold, and also when I gave the plants colors of many kinds; when I gave the plants and other things fire so that it does not burn; when I established sons in the wombs of their mothers and protected them, and gave them individually hair, skin, nails, blood, sinews, eyes, ears, and the other limbs [cf. 17:11]; when I gave the water fattiness so that it flows; when I set in place the cloud in the world of thought to carry the water of the world of the living and to rain it down wherever it pleases; when I set in place the wind, which blows up and down as it pleases, as is plain to see by the power of the wind, and it is impossible to seize it with one's hands— every single one of these it was more difficult to set in place than performing the Resurrection, for in the Resurrection I have the assistance of those who were not when I did those other things.

Since I made that which was not, why should it not be possible to make that which was? For at that time I shall call the bones from the earth in the world of thought, the blood from the water, the hair from the plants, the soul from the wind, as they received them at the original creation."

The resurrection

⁶The first bones Sōshāns will raise are those of Gayōmard, and then those of Mashī and Mashiyānī, and then he will raise those of other persons.

⁷For fifty-seven years, Sōshāns will raise all the dead. Whether good or bad, everybody will be raised from wherever their soul departed or they first fell to the ground.

⁸Then, when they have restored the entire existence with bones in bodies, then they give them a frame (*ēwēnag*) [cf. 26:15]. Of the light which is with the sun, they give one half to Gayōmard and one half to the other people.

⁹Then people will recognize other people: souls will recognize other souls, bodies other bodies, thinking: "This is my father, this is my brother, this is my wife, this is one of my close relatives."

¹⁰Then the assembly of Isadwāstar will take place, that is, people will stand up on this earth. ¹¹In that assembly everybody will see their own good and evil deeds. The good will be apparent among the bad like a white sheep among the black. ¹²In that assembly, a good person who befriended a bad person in the world, that bad person will complain to the good one: "Why did you not tell me about the good deeds you yourself performed in the world?" If the good one informs him accordingly, then he has to experience shame in the assembly.

¹³Then the good are separated from the bad, and the good are led to paradise, and the bad are thrown into hell. For three days and nights, they experience in their bodies and souls the punishments of hell, while, for three days and nights, the good will experience in paradise bliss in their bodies.

¹⁴As it says: On that day, when the good and bad are separated, everybody's tears will reach as far as their calves, when sons are separated from their fathers, brothers from brothers, and friends from friends.

¹⁵Everybody will experience their own deeds. The good will weep for the bad. The bad will weep for themselves. It happens that the father is good and the son bad or one brother is good and one bad.

Those who committed egregious crimes, like Dahāg and Frāsiyāb and other high criminals of their ilk, undergo a ten-fold punishment of the kind no man undergoes, which they call "the punishment of four nights."

The final ordeal

¹⁶During that Perfectioning of the world, those good men, about whom it is written "they are alive," fifteen men and fifteen women (his Companions), will come to assist Sōshāns [cf. 64:88].

¹⁷Then the snake Gōchihr, which is in the firmament, will fall down to earth from the sharp edge of the moon. The earth will feel such pain as a sheep when a wolf tears off its fleece.

¹⁸The Fire and the divine Ērman (Airyaman) will melt the metal in the hills and mountains, which will stand on the earth like a river.

¹⁹Then all people pass through that molten metal and become pure. Whoever is good, to him it will seem like he walks through warm milk, but, if it is a bad person, then it will seem to him just like he walks through molten metal.

²⁰Then all people come together in great love for one another. Fathers, sons, brothers, all men who were friends, ask other men: "Where were you all those years, and what judgment did your soul receive? Were you good or bad?"

²¹First the soul will see the body and will ask it. When it answers, they will all shout loudly together and praise Ohrmazd and the Amahrspands.

The final sacrifices

²²At that time Ohrmazd's creation will be completed (*hangerd*), which means there will be no need for further action to restore the dead.

²³When Sōshāns and his helpers perform the sacrifice to raise the dead, they kill the bull Hadayansh, and from the fat of that bull they prepare an immortality drink, the white *hōm*, which they give to all people. People become immortal for ever and ever. [Cf. 71:100]

²⁴This too it says: If they have reached the age of "man," then they will be restored as forty-year-old. And the small children, who were not yet of age, them they will put back as fifteen-year-old. They give everybody a wife and children, and they enjoy their wives as they do now in the world, but there will be no children born.

²⁵Then Sōshāns, according to the command of the Creator, will give rewards and prizes befitting their deeds. There are some that are so good that they say: "Lead him to Ohrmazd's paradise!"—and he takes on a form as befits him and stays with that for ever and ever.

²⁶This too it says: He who performed no sacrifices, who ordered no services for his soul, gave no garment of goodness to the deserving, will be naked there, but, after sacrificing to Ohrmazd, the *Gāthās* in the world of thought will be his clothes.

²⁷Then Ohrmazd will seize the Foul Spirit, Wahman will seize Akōman, Urdwahisht, Indar, Shahrewar Sāwul, Spandarmad Tarōmad, whom some call Nānghaith. Hordad and Amurdad will seize Taurij and Zairij, True Speech False Speech, and Srōsh-ahlī will seize Wrath with the bloody mace.

²⁸Then two evil beings will remain in the world of thought: Ahrimen and Lust (Āz).

²⁹Ohrmazd goes down into the world, himself as officiating priest (*zōt*) with Srōsh-ahlī as assistant priest (*rāspī*), bringing the girdle in his hands.

³⁰The Foul Spirit and Lust will be greatly and exceedingly smashed by the magic power of the *Gāthās*, and they fall back to the darkness and gloom through the passage through the sky where they first rushed in.

³¹The snake Gōchihr will be burnt by that molten metal. The metal will flow into hell, and that stench and filth in the earth where hell was will be burnt by that metal and become pure. That hole through which the Foul Spirit rushed in will be closed by that metal.

³²That earth in which hell was located will be brought back to the expanse of the world of the living. The Perfectioning of the world will be in the two worlds according to the will of living beings for ever and ever.

³³This too it says: This earth will have no high or low spots and will become flat, and there will be no mountain ridges or deep valleys, nothing above to hold up and nothing below to prop up.

71 From the Dādestān ī dēnīg 36

¹The thirty-sixth question asked was: How will they perform the Resurrection, and how will they restore the dead? When they have restored the dead, how will they be? When they have finished, will the light of the stars, moon, and sun need to shine in the world or not? And will there be seas, rivers, and mountains in it or not? And will the world of the living be the same size as this world or will it be larger and wider?

⁹⁹In the end, the Fortune of the Creator and the gods will be victorious over the demons by their own weapons, by their own combating and fighting, and they will have no existence, and they will be left with no abilities whatever, being tied up and discarded. Then they will suffer torture in great pains and trials and be cast down, separated from their tools in the same way that those in this world who are mortal have their souls separated from their bodies, are scattered, separated from their tools, and have their strength (zōr) taken away from them. They will be stunned, unable to act and move, and as when this world is shaken in its innermost and one is buried and unable to reach the surface by one's will but is then thrown out by the quake.

Thus, no part or part of parts of demonhood, not even as much as the smaller of three parts that is bound in this light, will remain of demonhood.

¹⁰⁰The fortress Awareness-of-the-Righteous, made from the very Fortune of the Tradition in the other world, will be bound to that light form, endlessly, all around the sky [cf. 29:6a3]. When its depth on each side is three times as much as this earth set in place by Ohrmazd, he will re-order the creations he had set in place, and, according to his own wish and pleasure, he will reassemble the bodies. Then they will also have the comfort of righteousness and all other comfort from Mount Ush-dāshtār (Upholder of Dawn), and they will have moisture

from the purified water of Ardwīsūr the Unattached/Unblemished (*aniwast/awinast*). From the good Protector and the one connected with him and from the bull Hadhayansh, there will be strength providing satiety at all times, as well as immortality. [Cf. 70:23]

Life will be given back to the bodies, and their souls (*gyān*) will be eternally blessed. There will be no corrosion or rot, no old age or death, no harm or sickness, only eternal life and eternal benefit.

[101]After the Perfectioning, there will be no demons, no deceit, no lie-demons, for there will be no lying. There will be no *angra-manyu* as there is no "killing" (*angra*); no hell as there is no wickedness; no fighting as there is no Wrath; no vengeance as there is no injury; no pain as there is no illness; no grief as there is no fear (of dying); no need as there is no lust; no shame as there is no ugliness; and no lies as nobody will wish to lie. Nobody will adhere to evil traditions as nobody will speak lies, and nobody will be bad as its seed (*tōhmag*) has been cut off. As has been said: the seed of all evil thoughts, utterances, and actions of all evil people, which are the artless creations of the Foul Spirit, [102]everything bad will be overcome when he is. When all that is bad is overcome, goodness will be made complete. In the time of complete goodness, no pain or harm will in any way be able to affect any creature at all.

[103]At present, when a fist hits a body or a sharp, cutting instrument is struck against a limb, it is because something of different essence, namely the demon in the body, is mingled with the tool that cutting and wounds are born. In that time, when everything is joy, when a body hits another body, or, as in the case of a knife, sword, cudgel, stone, or arrow coming upon the body, there is no pain or discomfort. Instead, bliss comes upon the body against that new pain. For, as it is now, all pain from striking or hitting is from what is of different essence (*gōhr*) and transient, while, at that time, when all is of the same essence and fits together, there will be no harm.

[104]In that best of times, the sun, moon, and stars will be there, but with no need for day or break of dawn, for the world of the living will be all light, without darkness, and all the creatures will be light.

[105]Those other lights will be there, as well, blazing and full of bliss. And all creatures will have the same will and pleasure.

No mortals, whoever they may be, will envy the goodness of all other creatures, but rather rejoice in it.

[108]In the Creator's eternal capability is all that is the wish and pleasure of their souls (*ruwān*) and pre-souls. By the Creator's Fortune and the Creator's command, they will be without trouble and full of bliss.

[109]Like oceans, rivers, mountains, plants, and the other creations with forms from water, their souls and pre-souls are placed in comfort and made to shine. Even the small beings in the other world, all those with sensations, are made to be pleased and to rejoice in it. Eternally happy, they will be set up in that all-joy.

CHAPTER FIVE

✦

TEXTS ON BODY AND SOUL

From the Young Avesta

72 From Yasna 55

[1]All our beings (*gaēthā*), bodies, bones and life breaths (*ushtāna*), forms (*kerp*) and tissue strengths (*tawishī*), consciousness (*baodah*), and breath-soul (*urwan*) and pre-soul (*frawashi*) we place all around and make them known. Thus we make them known to the life-giving *Gāthās*, sustainers of Order, whose command is according to the models.

[2]The *Gāthās*, which are our guardians and protectors and food in the world of thought, which are for our breath-soul both food and clothing, they are for us the guardians and protectors and food in the world of thought, those are for our breath-soul both food and clothing. May they bring us good awards, great awards, the award of Order, for new Life in days to come, after the wrenching apart of bones and consciousness!

73 From Yasna 59

[21]Of the males and females, sustainers of Order, who were the first guides, the first to hear the commandments, here we offer up in sacrifice the life (*ahu*) and vision-soul (*daēnā*), consciousness (*baodah*), breath-soul and pre-soul of those who have always won for Order. We offer up in sacrifice the breath-soul of the cow which gives good gifts.

74 From Yasna 9

[28]Take away from us the hostilities of those hostile ones and the thought (*manah*) of those irate ones!

In this house or town, in this tribe or land, whatever sinful mortal there is, remove endurance (*zāwar*) from his feet, cover his inner hearing (*ushi*), shatter his thought!

²⁹May you not be able (to walk) forth with your crooked legs! May you not at all be able (to grasp) with your evil hands! May he not see the earth or the cow with his evil eyes, he who does sinful things to our thought or body!

75 From Yasht 10

²³May you, O Mithra, when undeceived, carry us out of all constrictions. Thereby you bring down fear upon the bodies of contract-belying men.

When enraged, you, having the power to do so, carry away the strength (*aojah*) of their arms and the endurance of their feet, the sight of their eyes and the hearing of their ears.

From the Old Persian Inscriptions

76 From Darius I's Inscription on his Tomb at Naqsh-e Rostam (DNb)

¹The great god is Ahuramazdā, who set in place this Perfection (*frasha*) that can be seen, who set in place peace for man, who bestowed upon Darius wisdom (*khratu*) and agility.

³I do not anger easily. Whatever conflict arises in me I control firmly by my thought. I am firmly in command of myself.

⁸Once it is clearly established in my understanding (*ushi*) whether what I see with my understanding and forethought (? *framānā*) is something conspiratorial, at that time I consider myself less fearful—when I *see* something conspiratorial—than if I do not.

[See [91]].

77 From Darius I's Inscription at Bisotun (DB)

³²King Dārayavaush announces:

Afterward, that Fravarti fled with a few horsemen and went as far as the land of Ragā in Media. Afterward, I sent an army after them. Fravarti was seized and brought to me.

I cut off his nose, ears, and tongue and gouged out one of his eyes. He was held bound at my gate. The whole people saw him. Afterward, I impaled him in Hamadān. And the men who were his foremost followers I hanged in the fortress in Hamadān.

From the Pahlavi Texts

78 From Selections of Zādspram 29

¹The bodily constituents are flesh, bones, fat, etc., which makes the body like a house whose constituents are clay, stones, wood, etc.

²The pre-soul (*frawahr*) is what makes growth. It makes hands and feet grow, makes manifest gender, fits together veins and sinews, gathers the bones, makes manifest paths and passages, opens doors and windows, like a builder who builds a house.

³The soul (*ruwān*), which keeps the body alive, is like a fire enthroned in a fire-temple. (...)

⁸When the body sleeps, the soul goes out, to near or far, and looks at things, and, when the body wakes up, goes back into it, like a fire that, when hidden behind the closed door of the fire-temple, goes to near or far.

79 Dādestān ī dēnīg 2

¹³When the most perfectly benevolent one put together the creation of the Lord in a fully miraculous manner, unmoving being became motion when the spirit that makes motion came upon it. The spirit of invisibility, not yet mingled, turned into visible being and a visible sign.

He made the soul (*ruwān*), which grows in the other world, the good master over the body as it fares in this world. In it he made the vital soul (*gyān*), which is what gives life; the pre-soul (*frawahr*), which is what upholds; perception (*wīr*), which is what obtains; the intelligence (*ōsh*; memory?), which is what preserves; wisdom (*khrad*), which discriminates; nature (*chihr*), which heals itself; and strength (*zōr*), which is what organizes.

He made the eyes from seeing, the ears from hearing, the nose from smelling, the mouth from identifying tastes, form (*kerb*) from touching and feeling, the heart from thinking, the mouth from speaking, the hands from making, and the feet from walking.

80 From Dēnkard VI

[1a]In men's mind (*okh*) there is a thought, speech, and action, where a god sits on the throne and a lie-demon bars the road.

[1b]In thought, there is the "core" (*wārom*), where Wahman sits on the throne and Akōman bars the road.

In the "core," there is desire (*kāmag*), where Srōsh sits on the throne and Wrath bars the road.

In desire, there is thought, where Spandarmad sits on the throne and Tarōmad ("scorn") bars the road.

In thought, there is speech, where Wisdom (*khrad*) sits on the throne and Greed (Waran) bars the road.

In speech, there is action, where the Tradition sits on the throne and Self-indulgence bars the road.

[2]Character (*khēm*) is best for causing one not to do to others what is not good for oneself.

Wisdom is best for making one eat the fruit of the goodness that has already come and not worry about the evil that has not yet come.

Perception (*wīr*) is best for making one know that one does not know what one does not know.

[55]One should tell the Word only to somebody reliable, one should discuss the Tradition only with those who have the same Tradition, and one should tell everybody about good and bad deeds and their respective merits.

[56]One should tell the Word only to somebody who has the perception (*wīr*) needed to grasp it, and the intelligence (*ōsh*) needed not to lie, and the wisdom (*khrad*) needed to be able to make others good.

[64]The task of perception (*wīr*) is to acquire things; that of intelligence (*ōsh*) is to store away and preserve what the perception acquires;

that of wisdom (*khrad*) is discernment: to recognize good and bad and do what is good, but leave alone what is bad.

[68]Man's essence (*gōhr*) is of three kinds: those that come from being of good or bad seed (*tōhmag*) and a third. He who comes from good seed, even when they do not educate him in the usual manner, yet he becomes good. He who comes from bad seed does not become good even with much education. The third becomes either better or worse by education: by morally good education he becomes better, and by morally bad education he becomes worse. Some of them apply morally good education to morally bad behavior, as when heretics enumerate the Tradition.

[217]Man's perception (*wīr*) has thirty seeds, of which the lowest is the one needed to learn and know the *Avesta* and *Zand*.

81 On man and the Gāthās (Shāyist nē shāyist 13)

[3]The following three *Gāthās* are said to have been made from the body of the Righteous Man [Gayōmard?].

Yasna 28, 29, and 30 have eleven strophes each, because eleven things from the other world run through the human body: the mind (*okh*), the consciousness, the vision-soul, the breath-soul, the pre-soul, thought, speech, and action, sight, smell, and hearing. The other creatures, too, were created from water, fire, and wind.

✦

CHAPTER SIX

TEXTS ON DEATH, REWARDS, AND PUNISHMENT

From the Young Avesta

82 From Videvdad 19

[27]Zarathustra asked Ahura Mazdā: "O you who established the world of the living with bones, O sustainer of Order! Where will those gifts be, where will they come together and be counted, which a mortal man gives away in this world with bones for the sake of his soul (*urwan*)?"

[28]Then Ahura Mazdā said to Zarathustra: "After a man is departed and has passed on, demons possessed by the Lie and giving bad gifts tear at the departed.

"As it becomes light after the third night, as the brilliant dawn lights up, well-armed Mithra ascends the mountains reaching up into the good breathing space of Order, and the sun comes up.

[29]"The demon Drag-off leads the soul bound, both that of the demon-sacrificers possessed by the Lie and the short-lived humans. It comes along the paths set in place by Time—for both the one possessed by the Lie and the sustainer of Order—to the Ford of the Accountant set in place by Ahura Mazdā. There, they ask back the consciousness and soul, the share of living beings laid down in the existence with bones.

[30]"Then *she* will come with her dogs, beautiful, firm, well-shaped, with her brilliant crown, and her arts and talents. She drags the vile souls of the wicked into darkness. With the breath-souls of the sustainers of Order, she rises above tall Mount Harā, stretches them across the Ford of the Accountant, where those worthy of sacrifice in the world of thought cross over."

³¹Up rose Good Thought from his golden throne, saying: "When did *you* come hither to us, O sustainer of Order, from that dangerous existence to this existence without danger?"

³²Thus welcomed, the souls of the sustainers of Order go forth to the golden thrones of Ahura Mazdā and the Life-giving Immortals, to the House of Song, the abode of Ahura Mazdā, the Life-giving Immortals, and the other sustainers of Order.

³³After the sustainer of Order who is to be purified has passed on, the demons possessed by the Lie and giving evil gifts fear his smell just like a ewe frightened by the wolf fears the wolf.

From the Old Persian Inscriptions

83 From one of Xerxes's Inscriptions at Persepolis (XPh)

⁷If you who come hereafter should think "May I be blessed while alive and one with Order when dead!" then behave according to the law which Ahuramazdā set down.

You should sacrifice to Ahuramazdā (Avestan:) *according to the Order up on high!*

The man who behaves according to the law which Ahuramazdā set down and sacrifices to Ahuramazdā *according to the Order up on high*, he will both be blessed while alive and one with Order when dead.

From the Middle Persian Inscriptions

84 Inscription of Kerdīr at Naqsh-e Rajab

I, Kerdīr, have lived in truthfulness in the land and have served the gods well and obtained their favor.

I prayed to the gods as follows: If you gods once made me, Kerdīr, outstanding in this life, then do show me, too, in the afterlife, the appearance (*chihrag*) of heaven and hell! And show me, too, how it will be in the afterlife with respect to these services as they are performed in the land, so that I may be more confident about them!

And as I had prayed to the gods and had indicated, so they did show me heaven and hell and these services and the appearance of righteousness and wickedness.

Because the gods did show me in this manner how it is in the afterlife, I served the gods even better and obtained greater favor from them, and I was even more generous and truthful for the sake of my own soul (*ruwān*). I also became much more confident about these sacrifices and other services that are performed in the land.

Whoever sees and reads this inscription, let him be generous and truthful with respect to the gods and the rulers and his own soul, and let him be confident about these sacrifices and other services and the Mazdayasnian Tradition that are performed in the land! Let him not be agnostic (?) about the afterlife, but let him know well that heaven and hell exist! And he who is righteous will go to heaven, but he who is wicked will be thrown down to hell. And he who is good and behaves well, fame and prosperity will come upon this his body with bones, and oneness with Order will come upon that soul with bones of his, as it did me, Kerdīr.

85 Kerdīr's Vision

[22]When I asked the gods for help, I pointed out:

"If it is possible for you gods, then show me the appearance of heaven and hell. And in the way it says in the *nask* (*Avesta*), namely, that (*Zand:*) *When people pass on, then* [...], *and he who is good, his* dēn *will come toward him in the form* [*of a young woman*]. *And he who is righteous, his* dēn *will lead him to heaven, but he who is wicked, his* dēn *will lead him to hell*, let it be revealed to me in the same way here in life. In this way, when I pass on, then my own *dēn* may come toward me in that same way. And if I prove to be righteous, then let my own *dēn* appear like the one who leads to paradise! But, if I prove to be wicked, then let my own *dēn* appear like the one who leads to hell!"

[23]When I had inquired from those in the beyond regarding the sacrifices and religious services and the Mazdayasnian Tradition as it is performed here among the living [...], then I performed many

services, and in Pārs, Sagestān (Sistan), and other places, many priests were rendered happy and prosperous.

After I had asked the gods for help as is written in this inscription, [24]then, [at the time(?)] of Shābuhr, king of kings, I made a séance (?) for the sake of the gods and my own soul (asking): "Let me prove to be righteous! But if I do prove to be bad, then let me take this faith in you, gods!"

I also insisted that: "If I prove to be good, then, O gods, show me now how those who are good fare in the beyond, so I may hold on to this faith in you! And if I prove to be bad, then, O gods, show me now how those who are bad fare in the beyond, so I may, for all time, hold firmly on to this faith that I received from you, gods!"

[25]Then those youths who had been put in a trance (?) in that séance spoke as follows:

"We see a resplendent, princely horseman seated on an excellent horse with a banner in his hand. Now a man has appeared, sitting on a throne with golden ornaments, who looks like Kerdīr's double, and a page stands [behind him].

[26]"Now a woman has appeared, coming from the east, and we have seen no woman more beautiful than her. The road she is walking on is [very] luminous. Now she comes forth, and she and the man who is Kerdīr's double touch heads [and . . .]. And that woman and the man who is Kerdīr's double hold hands and proceed toward the east on that luminous road where the woman came. That road is very luminous, indeed.

[27]"And on that road, where that man who is Kerdīr's double and that woman are walking, now a princely man appears, sitting on a throne with golden ornaments. A balance stands before him, just like [a man who] weighs [. . .]. Now that woman and the man who is Kerdīr's double stand before that princely man [. . .]."

And they said:

"That woman and the man who is Kerdīr's double are now passing that princely man [. . .] and keep walking on that [very luminous] road.

²⁸"Now another resplendent, princely man has appeared, [...] and [...] on a throne with golden ornaments. He has a ladle (for firewood) in the hand, and he is more excellent than the ones we saw first."

And when they [had ...], they said:

"The ladle has become [extended downward] like a bottomless pit (*chāh*), and it is full of serpents, scorpions, lizards, and other evil animals."

²⁹But those youths that had been put in a trance in that séance, when they saw that [horrifying] structure of hell, became very alarmed. But [... said] to them: "[Be not afraid!" But] there is no other way for you than [across that bridge that goes] over that well! But you, just keep telling (us) what you see!"

³⁰And they said:

"A wooden beam goes over that well like a bridge. Now that woman and the man who is Kerdīr's double are [coming] forth [to the bridge], where a [...] is standing. That bridge is [now] becoming wider and is now greater in width than in length. And that woman and the man who is Kerdīr's double [have now come to the bridge]."

³¹And they said:

"Another resplendent, princely man has appeared, even more excellent than the ones we saw first. He is coming forth to the bridge from the other side, and now he has arrived at the bridge. Now [he has crossed] the bridge to this side, and he has taken the hands of that woman and the man who is Kerdīr's double. And that princely man [...] goes forth to the bridge and walks before the man who is Kerdīr's double, while the woman walks behind (cf. [59:62]). Now they have crossed the bridge over to the other side and are proceeding toward the east. [And the...] is excellent and beautiful.

³²"And now a palace has appeared, [and a ladder] has appeared in the sky. That princely man is walking before the man who is Kerdīr's double, and the woman walks behind him. [Now] they have arrived [at a palace], and [all three] together enter that palace."

³³And they said:

"We have seen nothing more excellent and more luminous than this! [. . . Now . . . has appeared . . .], and that princely man goes forth. A throne with golden ornaments stands before that palace. [. . .] back [to. . . . Now the man who is] Kerdīr's [double] and the woman in front are walking upward to the heights.

"Far up [. . . another palace has appeared, and] a throne with golden [ornaments stands before that palace. . . . The man who is Kerdīr's] double [. . .] and the woman have entered and have sat down in the (celestial) window of Warahrān.

34"Now that man who is Kerdīr's double has taken meat and wine. [Now] a great [throng] is coming forth, and that man who is Kerdīr's double is portioning out the food to them.

"That [woman?] and that princely man [. . .], and he keeps pointing toward that man who is Kerdīr's double and smiles, [and that man who is Kerdīr's double] paid [homage to him (?)]."

From the Pahlavi Texts

86 On Death (Mēnōy Khrad 1)

110Do not rely on life, 111for death will finally come upon you. 112Dogs and birds will tear your corpse, 113and your bones will fall to the ground.

114For three days and nights, the soul sits at the head-rest of the body, 115but, on the fourth day at dawn, it goes accompanied by Srōsh-ahlī, good Wāy, and mighty Warahrām, but opposed by the Bone-untier, the bad Wāy, the demons Drag-off and Drag-away and exposed to the malevolence of evil-doing Wrath with the bloody mace, up to the terrifying, high Chinwad bridge, where every good and evil person will come 116and many opponents are waiting.

117There it goes exposed to the malevolence of Wrath with the bloody mace and the Bone-untier, who swallows all creation and, yet, is not sated, but with the mediation of Mihr, Srōsh, and Rashn.

119Then comes the weighing by Rashn the Straight 120on a balance in the world of thought that dips to no side, either for the good or the bad, either for lords or rulers. [121]It does not diverge as much as a single hair's breadth and has no respect for anybody, [122]but holds a lord and a ruler to be equal by the law to the least of men.

87 On the Chinwad Bridge and the souls of the departed
    (Bundahishn 30)
[1]It says in the Tradition: There is a ridge a hundred men high in the middle of the world of the living that they call the Ridge of the Law, which is the yoke of the balance set in place by Rashn. One edge is at the bottom of Mount Hariburz on the northern side, and one edge is at the top of Mount Hariburz on the southern side. In the middle is the Ridge of the Law.

[2]In the middle of it there is a sharp place like a sword nine spears long and wide.

[3]There stand the gods in the world of thought who purify the souls of the Righteous by means from the world of thought. A dog from the world of thought is at the end of that bridge, and Hell is below that bridge.

[4]When people pass on, for three nights the soul sits near the body where the head used to be. In that night it experiences much torment from the demon Drag-off and his collaborators, and it keeps turning its back to the fire that is lit there.

[5]Therefore, for three nights until daybreak, they keep a fire burning there where his head used to be. Without that fire, he turns his back to the Warahrām fire or the ever-burning fires.

[6]In those three nights, when the body is cut apart and destroyed, it seems as hard to him as to a man whose house they demolish.

[7]Those three nights the soul sits at the top of the bed with the body hoping: "If it comes to pass that the blood flows and the wind enters the body, then maybe it will be possible to go back!"

[8]On the third night at dawn, if the soul is Righteous, it says: "Lucky him from whom there is goodness!" That is, I am good, from my goodness everyone is good. And Ohrmazd has made me king.

⁹If that soul is wicked it says: "This is that body, breath-soul (*gyān*), and form in which I used to run about, so from here where shall I run?"

¹⁰If he is Righteous, no sooner are those words said than a wind comes toward him which gladdens the soul, a wind better, nicer, and more sweet-smelling and victorious than all winds in the world of the living.

¹¹If he is wicked, a wind comes toward him that makes the soul unhappy and frightened, a wind fouler and more rotten and non-victorious than all winds in the world of the living.

¹²Then they carry off all those souls, whether Righteous or wicked.

¹³If that soul is Righteous, then, on the way, a cow-shape comes toward him, fat and full of milk, from which the soul gets prosperity and fattiness.

¹⁴Next a woman-shape comes toward him, well-shaped, with white garments, fifteen years old, and beautiful from all sides, at which the soul is gladdened.

¹⁵Next a garden-shape comes, full of water, fruits from trees, and prosperity, from which the soul receives gladness and prosperous thoughts. Some say: it is the land of paradise. He sees this in the world of the living, before the accounting, as signs. Some say: that soul asks them one by one. When they come toward him he asks: "Who are you who seem to me to contain all happiness and comfort?"

¹⁶In this way they answer him one by one: "I am your Righteous *dēn*, the deeds you performed when you did that goodness. It is because of you that I am here."

¹⁷If that soul is wicked, then a cow-shape comes toward him, dry, scrawny, and terrible, from which the soul gets dryness and un-fattiness.

¹⁸Next a woman-shape comes toward him, terrible, ill-shaped, covered in reproach, and terrible from all sides, at which the soul is frightened and terrified.

¹⁹Next a garden-shape comes, devoid of water, trees, and comfort, from which the soul receives bad thoughts. Some say: it is the land of

Hell. He sees this before the accounting as signs. Some say: It asks them one by one. When they come toward him he asks: "Who are you, the most evil I have ever seen in the world of the living?"

²⁰It answers him: "O you wicked one, I am your *dēn*, the bad deed you performed. It is because of you that I am here."

²¹So it is clear that everybody's deeds come toward him.

²²Then they convey that soul to the foot of Mount Hariburz, above which there goes the edge of a yoke up to the top of the ridge, where that sharp edge is.

²³If he is Righteous, that sharp edge remains as wide as it is. The Farnbay fire strikes the darkness and, in the form of fire, conveys that soul over that ridge, and the gods in the world of thought purify it. It conveys it over another yoke up to the top of Hariburz, and good Wāy takes it by the hand and brings it to his own place, that is, he who receives the soul, delivers it there.

²⁴Also when they purify a body in the world of thought, they proceed as in the world of the living.

²⁵If that soul is wicked, when it comes over that yoke up to the ridge, that sharp edge becomes a sharp blade and does not give passage, and, unwillingly, he must go over that sharp blade. After taking three steps forward, that is, his evil thoughts, speech, and deeds, it cuts him down and he falls headlong down to Hell and suffers every evil.

²⁶It says this too: he who has been Righteous in generosity, when that wind comes toward him, in that wind he sees a woman-shape, and he asks her. The woman then shows the way and brings him to a ladder, which has three levels. By that ladder he goes to paradise in three steps, that is, good thought, good speech, and good action. The first step takes him to the star level, the second to the moon level, and the third to the sun level, where paradise is.

²⁷If he has been wicked and niggardly, when that wind comes toward him, in that wind he sees a woman-shape, and he asks her. There are some who say: that action becomes like a sharp edge. It says to that soul: "O you wicked one, whether you wish or not, you must step on this edge."

²⁸Then the soul says: "Were you to cut me with a very sharp knife, it would seem better to me than to step on this edge."

²⁹A second time it says the same. He answers: "If you were to shoot me with an arrow, it would seem better to me than to step on this edge."

³⁰A third time it says the same. He answers: "If you were to strike my soul out of my body, it would seem better to me than to step on this edge."

³¹But his deeds become like a wild untamed beast and stands before the soul, and that soul becomes so afraid that it steps on that edge, and it cuts him down, and he falls to hell.

³²Those whose sins and good deeds are equal they consign to the Intermediary place, ³³about which it says that it is a place like the world of the living.

88 From Mēnōy Khrad 6

⁹Paradise is, firstly, from the star level to the moon level, ¹⁰secondly, from the moon level to the sun level, ¹¹and, thirdly, from the sun level to Garōdmān, where Ohrmazd resides. ¹²It is reached by stepping through good thoughts, good speech, and good deeds.

¹³The Righteous in paradise know no old age, death, fear, hostility, or Opposition. ¹⁴All the places—fragrant, blissful, peaceful— are full of Fortune and goodness, ¹⁵and, at all times, a fragrant wind and a scent like that of flowers meets them that are more pleasant than every other delight and smells better than every other good smell.

¹⁶They do not get enough of being in paradise, ¹⁷where they sit, walk, see, and take pleasure together with the gods, the Amahrspands, and the Righteous for ever and ever.

¹⁸Regarding the intermediate stage, it is revealed that it is from the earth to the star level, ¹⁹and their only Opposition is cold and heat.

²⁰Hell is reached through bad thoughts, bad speech, and bad deeds. ²¹At the fourth step, the wicked one arrives in the darkest hell, ²²where they lead him to the wicked Ahrimen, ²³and Ahrimen and the demons ridicule and mock him, saying: ²⁴"What did you have to complain and

lament about Ohrmazd and the Amahrspands and the fragrant, peaceful paradise, that you longed to see Ahrimen and the demons and the dark hell? [25]For we will harm you and not forgive you, and you will suffer evil for a long time!"

[26]Then they punish and hurt him in various ways. [27]There is one place which is as cold as the coldest ice and snow, [28]another which is hot like the hottest and most burning fire, [29]another where an evil animal tears at them as dogs tear at a bone, [30]and yet another where the stench is such that they tremble and fall.

89 On hell (Bundahishn chapter 27)

[53]About hell they say that its darkness is so thick one can take it with one's hands and its stench so thick one can cut it with a knife. When they are punishing a thousand men within a yard, these will think they are alone, for solitary punishment is the worst of all.

CHAPTER SEVEN

✦

TEXTS ON ETHICS

From the Young Avesta

90 On the Heavenly Girdle (Yasna 9)

²⁶Mazdā brought you, O Haoma, the girdle with knots, star-adorned, fashioned in the world of thought, the good Mazdayasnian Daēnā [cf. 101:15]. With that you are girded on the heights of the mountains, (enabling you) to hold the reins and chariot-handles of the Life-giving Word.

From the Old Persian Inscriptions

91 Darius's Testament II: Tomb of Darius at Naqsh-e Rostam (DNb)

¹ = [76:1]

²King Darius announces: By Ahuramazdā's greatness, I am such that I favor what is straight/true, not what is devious. It is not my wish that a poor man should be wronged on account of the mighty, nor that the mighty should be wronged on account of the poor. What is straight, that is my wish. I am not a friend of the one who lies.

³ = [76:3]

⁴I treat according to his achievement the man who exerts himself. I punish according to his evil deed him who does evil. It is neither my wish that a man should do evil, nor that a man who does evil should not be punished.

⁵I do not believe what a man says against another man until I hear the testimony of both.

⁶I am satisfied with whatever a man does or brings about according to his capabilities. That is what I really wish and what pleases me.

⁷My understanding and intent are of such a sort as you see or hear from what I have done, both at home and abroad. This is my agility in thought and understanding.

⁸This, in addition, is the agility of which my body is capable: As a battle-fighter I am a good battle-fighter.

= [76:8]

⁹I am in control of my hands and feet. As a horseman I am a good horseman; as an archer a good archer, both on foot and on horseback; and as a spear-man a good spear-man, both on foot and on horseback.

¹⁰I was able to carry these skills that Ahuramazdā bestowed upon me. By Ahuramazdā's greatness, what I have done, I did with these skills that Ahuramazdā bestowed upon me.

¹¹Young man, make it perfectly clear to yourself of what sort I am! Do not let it seem [. . .] to you of what sort your skills are and of what sort your behavior is!

From the Pahlavi Texts

92 From The Book of Advice of Zarathustra
¹The teachers of old, who have the foremost knowledge of the Tradition, have said that, at the age of fifteen, one should know the following:

Who am I, and to whom do I belong? Where did I come from, and to where will I go back? And of what lineage (*paywand*) and family (*tōhmag*) am I?

And what are my duties in the world of the living, and what is my reward in the world of thought"?

And did I come from heaven, or have I always been on earth? Do I belong to Ohrmazd, or do I belong to Ahrimen, to the gods or to the demons, to the good or the bad? Am I a human or a demon?

How many are the paths, and which is my Tradition?

What is good for me, and what is bad? Who is my friend, and who is my enemy?

Are the Origins one or two? From whom is goodness and badness? From whom is light and darkness? From whom is fragrance and stench? From whom is right and wrong? From whom is forgiveness and mercilessness?

²Now, he who can explain the meanings has taken this firmly in hand, and this is his conviction, as it has been transmitted to him by the path of wisdom, that one should have no doubt about the following:

I have come from heaven, I have not always been on earth.

I am something created (*āfrīdag*), not something that has always been.

I belong to Ohrmazd, not to Ahrimen, to the gods, not to the demons, to the good, not to the bad.

I am a human, not a demon, the creature of Ohrmazd, not of Ahrimen.

My lineage and family is from Gayōmard. My mother is Spandarmad and my father Ohrmazd.

My humanity is from Mahlī and Mahliyānī, the first of the lineage and seed (*tōhm*) of Gayōmard.

³My duties and obligations are to think about Ohrmazd that he is, has always been, and will always be, that he is the immortal ruler, boundless, and pure, while Ahrimen is not and shall be destroyed.

I have to consider myself as the property of Ohrmazd and the Amahrspands and separate myself from the demons and consideration of the demons.

⁴On earth, firstly, I have to ally myself by my praise to the Tradition, perform and sacrifice according to it, and not turn away from it, but believe in my mind in the Good Tradition of the Mazdayasnians. I have to distinguish what is good for me from what is bad, evil-doing from well-doing, goodness from badness, and light from darkness, and one who sacrifices to Ohrmazd from one who sacrifices to the demons.

⁵Secondly, I have to take a wife and see to my lineage on earth diligently and constantly.

⁶Thirdly, I have to plow the earth and cultivate it. ⁷Fourthly, I have to tend cattle according to the rules.

⁸Fifthly, I have to go to school (*hērbedestān*) one-third of the day and one-third of the night in order to ask about the wisdom of the righteous; to cultivate the land one-third of the day and one-third of the night; and to eat, have a good time, and rest one-third of the day and one-third of the night.

⁹I have to have no doubt that good deeds are good for me and bad deeds bad for me; that my friend is Ohrmazd and my enemy Ahrimen; and that the path of the Tradition is one:

¹⁰The one path is that of good thought, speech, and action; paradise is the light and purity and limitlessness of Ohrmazd the Creator, who has always been and shall always be.

¹¹Another is the path of evil thought, speech, and action. This is the darkness, boundedness, all evil and destruction, and badness of the wicked one, the Foul Spirit, who once upon a time was not in this creation and who once in the future shall not be in the creation of Ohrmazd, but in the end will be annihilated.

¹²I have to have no doubt about this too, that the Origins are two: the Creator and the Destroyer.

¹³The Creator is Ohrmazd, from whom all goodness and all light emanates.

¹⁴The Destroyer is the wicked Foul Spirit, who is all badness and full of death, wicked and deceiving.

¹⁵I have to have no doubt about these things, that, other than Sōshāns and the seven Kays, every person is mortal; ¹⁶that the soul (*gyān*) is expelled and the body destroyed; that the accounting takes place at the third dawn (*sidōsh*); that the Resurrection and the Final Body will come about; that one must cross the Chinwad Bridge; and that Sōshāns will come and make the Resurrection and the Final Body.

²³Zarathustra received the Good Tradition of the Mazdayasnians. I have no doubt about that, and I shall not forsake the Good Tradition of the Mazdayasnians for love of body and soul (*gyān*), for good life or

long life, or when my consciousness is wrenched from the body. I will not praise or exalt teachings different from this, and I will not believe in them.

²⁴For it is manifest that, of thoughts, words, and actions, count the action, ²⁵for the thought, which is not supported (on anything concrete), is intangible, while the action is tangible.

³⁰I must be grateful, for by gratitude one turns one's soul away from hell.

³¹For when a person goes from the father's loins to the mother's womb, then the Bone-untier throws a bond (*band*) around his neck in the world of thought, and, as long as he lives, no one in that world, either good or bad, can remove that bond from his neck. ³²But after his passing, that bond falls off the neck of the righteous on account of his own good actions, while the wicked are led to hell by that same bond.

³³Also, I have to go to school and learn the *Zand*.

³⁴Parents should teach their child all these good actions before it is fifteen. If they do, then all good actions by the child reflect on the parents, but if not, when the child becomes an adult and commits a sin, this goes to the parents' account.

⁴¹Be diligent in the acquisition of education, for education is the seed (*tōhm*) of knowledge, and its fruit is wisdom, which governs all things in the two worlds.

⁴²It is said that learning is an adornment in times of plenty, protection in times of hardship, a helping hand in misfortune, and an occupation in times of dearth.

⁴⁵Every day you should go to the house of Fires and recite the hymn to the Fire. For he who goes most frequently to the house of Fires and most frequently recites the hymn to the Fire, to him (the gods) give most wealth and righteousness.

⁴⁸It is well-known that, three times daily, the sun issues its commands to mankind. ⁴⁹At dawn it says: "Ohrmazd says to you all: 'Be diligent in your performance of secular and religious work, so that I can produce life in the world among you!'"

⁵⁰At noon it says: "Be diligent in acquiring a wife, making children, and your other duties, for the Foul Spirit and his brood will not leave this creation until the Final Body."

⁵¹In the evening it says: "Confess the sins you have committed, so that I may forgive you!" For it is well-known that in the same way that the light of the sun arrives upon earth, so also its speech comes down to earth.

93 *From Mēnōy Khrad*

On good and bad behavior (chapter 1)

¹The wise man asked the divine wisdom: ²How can one maintain and make the body prosper without harming the soul (*ruwān*) and save the soul without harming the body?

³The divine wisdom answered: ⁴Regard the one inferior to you as equal and the one equal to you as superior; ⁵the one superior to you as your chief and your chief as your ruler! ⁶Be loyal and obedient to rulers, and speak the truth! ⁷Be humble, gentle, and benevolent to your opponents!

⁸Do not commit slander, ⁹lest dishonor and sin come upon you!

¹⁰For it is said that ¹¹slander is more grievous than witchcraft, ¹²and, in hell, every lie-demon moves forward, but the lie-demon of slander, because it is such a serious sin, moves backward.

¹³Do not harbor lusty desire, ¹⁴lest the demon Lust (Āz) deceive you ¹⁵and the things of the world of the living become tasteless to you and those of the world of thought be destroyed for you!

¹⁶Do not harbor wrath, ¹⁷for a man who becomes wroth forgets to do work and good deeds and homage and service to the gods, ¹⁸and every kind of sin and crime comes to his mind until his wrath subsides. ¹⁹Indeed, Wrath is said to be the equal of Ahrimen!

²⁹Do not procrastinate, ³⁰lest the work and good deeds you have to do remain undone!

³¹Choose a wife of good stock (*gōhr*), ³²for, in the end, that one is the better who has the better reputation!

[33]Do not talk while eating, [34]lest you incur a serious transgression against Hordad and Amurdad!

[35]Do not walk about with your *kusti* untied, [36]lest harm befall your men and animals and injury your children!

[37]Do not walk with one shoe, [38]lest your soul incur a serious transgression!

[39]Do not urinate standing, [40]lest you become captive of the law of the demons [41]and the demons drag you off to hell!

[42]Be diligent and moderate, [43]eat by your own effort to do good, [44]and give their share to the good gods! [45]Such behavior is the best good deed you can do within what are your proper duties.

[46]Do not steal from others, [47]lest your own effort to do good be destroyed for you! [48]For it is said: [49]He who does not eat by his own effort to do good, but by that of another, is like one who holds a human head in his hand and eats human brains.

[50]Stay away from other people's wives, [51]lest these three be destroyed for you: wealth, body, and soul!

[64]Be diligent and devoted in giving thanks to the gods, in sacrifice and singing hymns, in sacrificing and invocation, and in getting education.

[91]All this is well and true and all the same, [92]but one's proper duties and watching one's tongue are above all else.

[96]Be diligent in storing good deeds, [97]so that they may help you in the world of thought.

[98]Do not rely on any goodness in the world of the living, [99]because the goodness of this world is like a cloud that comes on a spring day and does not linger on any mountain.

[100]Do not be too preoccupied with this world, [101]because such a man ruins the other world.

[102]Do not rely on much property and wealth, [103]because in the end you have to leave it all.

[104]Do not rely on kingship, [105]because in the end you have to be without a king.

[106]Do not rely on respect and love, [107]for in the other world respectfulness is of no help.

[108]And do not rely on a large lineage (*paywand*) and much offspring (*tōhmag*), [108]for in the end you must lean on your own deeds.

The greatest virtues (chapter 2)

[1]The wise man asked the divine wisdom: [2]"What is best: generosity, truth, [3]gratitude, wisdom, [4]perfect thought, or contentment?

[5]The divine wisdom answered: [6]For the soul generosity is best. For all living beings truth is best; [7]toward the gods gratitude; for a man's body wisdom; [8]for all deeds perfect thought; for the comfort of the body and for striking down Ahrimen and the demons contentment is best.

The greatest virtues (chapter 3)

[1]The wise man asked the divine wisdom: [2]Which good deeds are greatest and best?

[3]The divine wisdom answered: [3]The greatest seven good deeds are: generosity, truth and marriage within one's closest family (*khwēdōdah*), [4]observing the religious festivals, the entire Tradition, [6]sacrificing to the gods, providing lodging for travelers, [7]providing happiness for all, [8]and being benevolent toward good people.

94 Some sayings of Ādurbād son of Mahraspand

[1]These are some sayings that Ādurbād son of Mahraspand of immortal soul uttered and taught to those in the world of the living as he passed away. Remember this, and learn something from it!

Do not hoard things, so that you may not feel need! For hoarding things does not lead to less need. [2]Strive only to store up more righteousness, that is, in deeds and good works, for the only good thing you should store up is righteousness.

[3]Do not think of vengeance, so that enemies may not rise up against *you*. [4]Keep in mind what kind of hurt and harm and destruction may befall you for slaying an enemy as vengeance. Keep vengeance for yourselves, and do not strike an enemy as vengeance, for it is revealed that he who forgets the smallest vengeance will be saved at the Passage of Lamentations.

⁵Speak the truth when litigating, so that you may be more often saved by the law! ⁶For it is by giving truthful testimony that a man becomes Righteous. He who has information he does not give becomes wicked.

⁷Eat in moderation, so that you may be long-enduring! ⁸For eating in moderation is best for the body and speaking in moderation best for the soul. ⁹The man who has least wealth is rich if he is moderate of character. ¹⁰Think more about your souls than your bellies! For the man who accumulates for the stomach ruins the spirit.

¹¹Take a wife from your own lineage, so that your lineage may go farther. ¹²For the most ruin and vengeance and harm came upon the creation of Ohrmazd when they gave away their daughters and they asked for other people's daughters in marriage for their sons, so that the family (*dūdag*) was completely spoiled.

¹⁶Receive traveling people well, so that you may be well received both here and there. ¹⁷For he who gives also takes and will grow thereby. At receptions, sit wherever they seat you. The most important position is where a good man sits.

¹⁸Do not fight for position, for a man who fights for position ruins the other world (for himself).

¹⁹Go along with good deeds, oppose sinful action, be grateful for goodness, and be content in adversity, stay away from enemies, do not harm good deeds, and do not befriend someone bad!

²⁰When the most terrible things happen, do not harbor doubt about the gods and the Tradition. ²¹Do not be too happy and content when goodness befalls you, ²²and do not be too offended when evil befalls you!

²³Be content in adversity, patient in misfortune! Do not trust in life, but in good actions! ²⁴For a person's good actions are his defenders, while a person's bad actions are his accusers. ²⁵Of thoughts, words, and actions, actions are best.

⁴⁸Do not trust women, because you may come to shame and regret. ⁴⁹Tell no secrets to women, because you may have no profit from your toil!

[60]Do not be too happy when something good happens to you, and do not be too upset when something bad happens to you, [61]for both good and bad things are bound to happen to people. [62]Thank the gods for whatever good has happened to you and give the gods and good people a share of it. Leave it to the gods, for gifts come by themselves, wherever they come from.

[63]Cultivate the earth well, for all men live and are nourished by cultivating Spandarmad, the Earth.

[64]Do not sin against water, fire, cattle, sheep, or dogs, and do not harm animals of the dog family, so that the road to paradise and Garōdmān may not be closed to you.

[65]When it comes to doing good deeds, keep your door open to whoever comes from near or from afar. For he who, when doing good deeds, does not keep his door open, will find the door to paradise and Garōdmān closed to him.

[66]Be diligent in seeking culture, for in times of comfort education is an adornment, in times of difficulties it is a refuge, in misfortune it lends a helping hand, and in hard times it is a trade.

[67]Act as you know is best. But knowing more and believing less makes for greater sins. [68]Wisdom with much knowledge unaccompanied by goodness will turn perception (*wīr*) to heresy and wisdom to false teachings.

[69]Do not despise anybody, for he who despises shall be despised. His fortune will be struck down, and he will be cursed and have fewer children destined to be warriors.

[70]Every day you should go to the assembly to discuss with good people, [71]for he who most often goes to the assembly to discuss with good people will acquire most good deeds and righteousness.

[72]Every day you should go three times to the house of Fires and pray to the Fire. [73]For he who most often goes to the house of Fires and most often prays to the Fire, will receive the most good deeds and wealth.

[74]Be very careful to keep your bodies away from deceitful evil actions, from menstruating women, and prostitutes, so that your bodies may not be polluted or, even worse, evil may befall your souls.

⁷⁵Never neglect any sin for which penance is demanded, even for a moment, so that the pure Tradition of the Mazdayasnians may not be your opponent.

⁷⁶The body is mortal. Look after your souls, and perform good deeds. For the soul *is*, not the body. The other world *is*, not this world. ⁷⁷Do not relinquish or forget your souls for love of the body. Do not set your hearts on something for the love of people or things, for it will bring your body to expiation and your soul to punishment. ⁷⁸Do not let go of your love of your souls for the love of a person, so that you may not have to suffer cruel punishments.

95 *About protecting oneself from evil (Dēnkard V, 7)*

²One must know how Ahrimen and the demons deceive and lead astray; how they are mixed into every part of the good creatures; how they hide the straight and true road and way; how they crookedly exhibit what is as what is not; how they act as highwaymen in the minds, thoughts, words, and deeds of beings in the existence with bones; and how they untiringly comply with the commitment of crimes.

³We need the prophets to bring what is straight and true, as well as the secrets of the other world and what is here to be seen in this world, to seize that passageway and guard that protection untiringly.

⁴Rub the demons from the body and do not let them into the body. In the constant struggle against the lie-demons, specifically keep the demon of all demons, the Foul Spirit, scorned and struck down, as well as his mighty giant demons: Akōman, Indar, Sāwul, Nānghais, Tawrij, Zairij, Aktash, Lust, Wrath, and so on.

⁵However much one exercises protection against all those, one needs to exercise even more protection against Greed (Waran), which leads on roads that are no roads, and, in particular, to raise up Wisdom (*khrad*) against Greed.

⁶And, likewise, in order to set up Wahman against Akōman and the other good beings in the other world against the individual lie-demon that is their special opponent, one must invite them into oneself and firmly exercise protection for as long as one's soul is in one's body.

96 About gift-giving (Dēnkard V, 17)

²There are many kinds of gifts, the following in particular.

³To those deserving liberality one should give great gifts and, for one's soul, more to those abiding by the Tradition, but also to anybody following the good Tradition.

⁴Keep hunger and thirst, heat and cold away from those who suffer unjustly from them.

⁵Of the annual surplus of the various fruits and produce that it is the religious duty of the giver to distribute among those for whose upkeep he is responsible, and even more than that, two meals yearly should be given to the poor as their share.

⁶Give to those of evil tradition when they fear being wounded, and keep hunger and thirst, heat and cold away from them.

⁷It is permitted to give even to those guilty of a capital crime when it is in obedience to a higher law or fear (that they may die) or because one can do nothing else.

⁸It is not permitted that one should not eat oneself in order to give food to those deserving, except when giving to keep those alive for whose upkeep one is responsible and whose guardian one is by virtue of abiding by the Tradition.

97 About khwēdōdah (Dēnkard III, 80)

⁰About how a Jew lamented to a Zoroastrian priest (hērbed), seeking to know the reason for the sin of performing khwēdōdah and the priest's answer as exposed in the Tradition.

¹In the same way that it is the law that a plaintiff who has suffered harm from a wound or other damage should, in accordance with the law, sue the defendant and that the totality of what is comprised (parwand) in the opposition of the innocent man has a name—the Law; in the same way, prosperity means tying (paywand-) one's own power (nērōg) to his fellow creatures and one's own in order to protect and deliver them, and the totality of what is comprised in people's helping one another has a name—khwēdōdah.

²The *khwēdōdah* of someone is when he "gives of/to his own" and ties the power of his position to his own fellow creatures in order to protect and deliver them, so that his own people, in particular, are tied to one another, males to females, and are organized so as to be tied to the Perfectioning.

³For that tie (*paywand*) to be immeasurably firmer, people of the same species should unite with their closest relatives and those who are close relatives with those to whom they are most closely tied. And the most closely tied relationships are the following three relationships involving being tied together: father and daughter, son and birth mother, and brother and sister. These are the ones I have concentrated on in this chapter after the oral exposition and guidance of a knowledgeable teacher of the Tradition.

⁴Of the creatures god created some are male, others female. The male son is the sibling of the female daughter. He himself is the father of all, and Spandarmad, the Earth, is the female one of the Creation.

⁵He created Gayōmard male, whose name is explained as "First Man," especially since Gayōmard's special definition is as a living, speaking, and mortal being. For these three words, living, speaking, and mortal, are his definition. Two of them, "living" and "speaking," he had by the Creation from his father, the Creator; the third, "mortal," was adventitious and came from the Assault. His is the same definition (*wimand*) of all humans, who are tied to the tie of that man until the Perfectioning.

⁶Also, now, whenever a father creates a male from his daughter, this is called the *khwēdōdah* of father and daughter.

⁷Let me also say this as exposed in the good Tradition that, when Gayōmard passed on, his semen (*shusr*), which is called seed (*tōhmag*), was enveloped (*parwand-*) by Spandarmad, the Earth, who was his mother, and from it there came into being Mashī and Mashiyānī, Gayōmard and Spandarmad's son and daughter, which is called the *khwēdōdah* of mother and son.

⁸Mashī and Mashiyānī, desiring offspring, had intercourse and produced children, which is called the *khwēdōdah* of brother and sister. A great family (*dūdag*) was born from them, who, having paired up, became husbands and wives. And so, all humans who have been or are came from the original seed (*tōhm*) of a *khwēdōdah*.

⁹It is manifest that this was the natural (*chihrīg*) reason why the creation came from god, seing that his plan was to increase the population of the entire world.

¹⁰Let me also say that the demons are the enemies of humans and that they strive to apply their evil desire against them.

¹¹But, when *khwēdōdah* is performed, they remember how those *khwēdōdah*s were performed in the beginning, from which there came humans enough to fill an army to fight against them. This thought causes them heavy fear, harm, and pain, their powers diminish, and they have less reason to oppose humans and cause them damage.

¹²Thus, it is certain that it is a good deed to cause the demons harm, pain, and fear and lead them astray, and, for those who practice good deeds in this manner, this is the road to making recompense and repayment their "own."

¹³Let me also say that what is good is appearance (*chihrag*), form, and soul (*gyān*). And wisdom, character, decency, love, and artistry are the powers of what is good and various other things, too. For the closer one's children are to the original seed (*tōhmag*) of the ones who give them birth, the more firmly they receive (these qualities).

¹⁸Let me also say that a brother and a sister have a loving relationship of, as it were, six reeds (wide/long?) with those born to them: one in that it is her brother's child and a brother; another in that it is her brother's son and their sister; yet another in that it is the sister's child; and, finally, in that it is her brother's child.

¹⁹For the same reason, their love, wishes, and endeavors are four reeds, and, by raising the child, their hope for it is four reeds. The fit between the children and those who have given birth to them is the same.

²⁰Those are the two roads to the love that increases: good up-bringing and more guidance.

²¹It is likewise with a son born from a father and his daughter. It is crystal clear to be seen in this age that he is very happy and joyful who has a child from his child. What happiness, sweetness, and joy he experiences from a son whom a man has with his own daughter and who is also the mother's brother!

²²And if it is a child born from a son and his mother, he is also the father's brother. This is the road to more joy and bliss. And there is no harm from it greater than the benefits from it, nor any blemish greater than the beauty of it.

²³If someone says that it is ugly, let him consider the following. If the mother, sister, or daughter has a wound on her genitals, then there is no way a doctor, a man, could apply any medication to them directly. And if her father, son, or brother is trained in medicine, which would be the uglier procedure: that *they* should touch the area while applying the medication or that man from outside?

²⁴When it is appropriate for them to consummate their union, what is less ugly: that they are united in their building, so that they have affirmed the contract to be wife and husband in the presence of witnesses, or it is announced in the whole land: "Know ye, people, that such and such a Roman wishes to do such and such with the daughter, sister, of such and such a Persian man!" This is why there is not only little ugliness, but even beauty in this action.

²⁵So one can see both how useful it is in daily life to cover one's modesty, sharing what is useful and what is harmful, being happy with everything that has happened, and helping people together.

²⁶On the other hand, in the case of wives from outside, one can see their subservience and helplessness; how eager they are to serve their husbands so that they do not commit any offense; the patience they muster against the husband's harshness, and many other things.

²⁷Nor are they happy in this way, for, when it comes to covering themselves with ornaments, wearing excellent garments, having serv-

ants, making up their faces and wearing perfumes, and living in large mansions, and all the other things affected by ladies of the house, then, when she does not get what she wants and she has no other recourse, she calls him bad names and heaps upon him foulness and bad language.

²⁸She has accumulated by trickery the things she owns. Secrets she divulges. Night and day she bickers and finds fault with him, she attacks his parents' household, drags her husband to court, and incites the town against him. She will say: "Release me from this marriage!" and many other various bad, harmful, evil, ugly sins connected with this.

²⁹Those three kinds of women are destined to do nothing that manifestly has great power to generate profit, a good life, a full stomach, dignity, and absence of sin.

³⁰If someone says that, in spite of all this that he adduces, there is still something ugly to imagine, they should know that ugliness and beauty are mostly so, not in themselves, but in people's actions, appearances, beliefs, and dispositions (*khōg*).

³¹There are many ugly children who, to their parents' mind, are mostly beautiful. And there are many with beautiful bodies who, to the minds of "the others," are mostly ugly.

³²Similarly, when, according to the Tradition of our enemies, someone walks about in the town naked, we hold it to be ugly, but the town of those whose skin is naked calls those beautiful, while those who are dressed (?) seem ugly to them.

³³To our mind, someone with a completely flat nose is ugly, while *they* consider a high nose ugly and say: "Gee, he has a wall between the eyes!" To them people with blemishes are beautiful.

³⁴Ugliness and beauty are so, not in themselves, but in people's actions, appearances, and beliefs and are bound to change with place and time.

³⁵For our ancestors, to whom a shaved head was ugly—and it was laid down in the law as a sin worthy of death—rather did not order people's heads to be shaved according to the custom of the land.

Currently, a wise man will consider it beautiful and even a good deed, and it is not obvious to him that it is ugly.

³⁶As for what one group of people may think, that it is not in itself, but in one's own actions that they seem ugly, then we consider it something worth knowing, namely, that it was fashioned by the Creator as it is, as a good deed for which you get a reward, a guardian of the seed, and something that makes the essence (*gōhr*) firmer.

³⁷Since it is free, causes love, is a benefit for the children, stretches the lineage, its essence being hope, causes joy, sows sweetness, reaps bliss, causes little damage and more benefit, overcomes blemishes, has many virtues, produces beautiful people, guarantees salvation, accumulates friends, pushes back harm, stops grief, causes less fear, and is in itself resplendent and enduring, why abandon it?

³⁸It is beautiful to have in the house all the benevolent fathers and grandfathers, whose complaints by the law are merely pleasing, and to think of it as the human way.

³⁹But, as for salvation, there is one clear and firm reason, witnessed by wisdom, that proves it: If one does not practice (*khwēdōdah*), then one is not worthy of salvation.

⁴⁰If someone says that, from then on, god ordered us not to perform it and that it is something everybody should know and abide by, then, to us, that order would not be something we should know and not something to guide our behavior.

⁴¹Let him look closely at this and examine it truly. All human knowledge is produced by *khwēdōdah*. For knowledge is born from the union of the inborn wisdom and the wisdom acquired-through-hearing. And the inborn wisdom is female and the wisdom acquired-through-hearing is male, and, because they both came from the Creator's Creation, they were sister and brother.

⁴²Everything in this world that comes into existence, ripens, and is organized (into a living being) is from the measured union of the female water and the male fire, which are thought to be sister and brother from the way they unite.

98 Spandarmad and the kusti (Selections of Zādspram 4)

⁰About the coming of the Tradition into time.

¹Its analogy is like the birth of of a child, which happens through there being two shared forces (zōr): the females receive the seed, and at birth the child is handed over to the fathers.

²The struggle of the Mixture in time is essentially by two means: one is rulership not connected to the Tradition by the same umbilical cord (nāf?), and one is the Tradition that has been connected to rulership by the same umbilical cord (?).

³The Mazdayasnian Tradition, when time came for it to be turned from arranging the world of living beings back to its nature (chihr) as something from the other world, became visible on earth first in Spandarmad, then in Ohrmazd, as when children are received by their mothers, then handed over to the fathers.

⁴The appearance of the Tradition in Spandarmad was at the time when Frāsiyāb withheld water from Iran. In order to return the water, she became visible in the form of a young woman in the house of Mānush-chihr, who ruled the land of the Iranians and answered the non-Iranians.

⁵She wore a garment of light that shone out to all sides as far as one league, i.e., about one frasang.

⁶Around her waist she had bound a golden girdle that was none other than the Mazdayasnian Tradition. For the Tradition is a cord to which are attached 33 other cords tied over 33 sins, of which all sins have a share.

⁷After that, the young women who saw Spandarmad with her *kusti* tied on, because it seemed beautiful to them, became fervent in tying on the *kusti*.

99 On the shirt and the kusti (Dādestān ī dēnīg 39)

¹The thirty-ninth question asked was: What kind of goodness can there be or not in the *kusti* and the shirt for it to be a sin not to wear them when one is up and about? (. . .)

²The answer is as follows. It is proper that the shirt should be completely white, made whole and in one piece (without seams), just as

Wahman in the same manner was the first single creation/fabric (*dām*). After that, it is the garment that is called the innermost and hidden.

As for wearing the Tradition as a belt, whole, but with two folds and two layers, those two layers are the wisdom of the Tradition that is thus bound around the works of those who have awareness. It is nothing but the two divisions of wisdom that are called "inborn" and "heard by the ear." Since a man, by tying the *kusti*, has closed the body to sin, it has been explained as a mark that the body has been closed to sin.

100 From "The Meaning of the Kustī"

[27]The *kusti* serves principally to show by a mark the border between the two (worlds), [28]because, also in the human body, which, among those who know, is called the little world, [29]the upper half is like the lights which inhabit the uppermost (part of the world).

[44]And the lower half, which is all aridity and desolation, is similar to hell.

[45]And the belly, which is between, is the world of mixture and separation, the power that attracts, seizes, digests, and throws back. [46]There it is like the mixed world of the living.

[47]Showing the two parts (of the world), which is the meaning of wearing the *kusti* in the middle (of the body), [48]is also like showing and making manifest the sign of duality also on one's own (body) sphere.

[55]Wearing the *kusti* of the Zoroastrians is a custom and fashion (designed) to show the Way [56]and a sign to serve as a mark of someone of the Tradition (saying): [57]"I am someone of discernment, not someone without discernment."

[58]For we have discerned what is the seat of the lights up above and what is the seat of the darkness down below, [59]and what is the place of mixture and separation in the middle.

101 The reason for the homage and the kusti (Dādestān ī dēnīg 38)

[1]Question. Why tie the *kusti*? For it is said that those who tie it are deserving of such great (rewards), while those who do not are committing such grievous sins.

²Answer. The all-good spirit (*mēnōy*) of spirits and lord of lords, the creator of all that is good, has no need for the poor humans in any matter or thing, for they are all his already, and he rules over them at will and omnipotently. But he requires of humans that they stay within firm limits in true bondedness, but with no bond indicating bondedness nor any other visible sign of bondedness.

³As it is to be seen and is clearly manifest, in all men's laws, traditions, and beliefs, in serving god by name, the homage is what is most essential, most compulsory, and most indispensable. Every day, in serving god, they regard the homage as the greatest deed.

⁴When one scrutinizes this world and the essence (*gōhr*) of what comes into being to find the reasons (for all things), no benefit in this world is apparent from doing homage, different from the way fruits come from trees, taste from foods, fragrance from flowers, brightness from colors, beauty from blossoms, healing from medicinal plants, and discernment from words.

⁵But the singular act of bringing one's head low is a proof (*nishānag*) of lowliness. For, as the head, which is on top of the body and its highest point, is brought down in humility to the low level in the body, which is the undermost point in the thought, when serving god by name and doing homage, and is placed on the ground, it is a way of indicating (*nimāy-*) on oneself that there is at least bondedness.

⁶Together with the fact that there is much apparent benefit in this world—food from trees and so on, as was just enumerated—from doing homage, that is (by itself) a manifest proof and indication and, consequently, a great sign (*nishān*) of lowliness and bondedness.

⁷Most people regard doing homage to the Radiant One (= sun) to be the most compulsory. By planting a tree in the name of god and eating its blessings and by performing the other work in this world that brings benefit in this world, they consider all belief to have been instituted for this one purpose: that the world of the living should do this.

⁸In the innumerable things one does, it is apparent in reliable fashion that in the service to those in the other world it is a

mark (*dakhshag*) and sign of a great work, by which there is great deliverance.

⁹The reasons why this bond, which is called *kusti* and is bound about the middle (of the body), is deliverance are many.

¹⁰Its first deliverance is this: the servant of the gods from the deception-less Tradition, who shows it from knowledge and also gratifies (the gods) with certainty (*tāshtīg*) by the wisdom that guides the Tradition on the straight path—this is the reason for his deliverance in a manner that obeys the commands: that he has something on the body that shows his belief in the other world and his way (*ristag*) and that he expresses therewith his religious allegiance and his bondedness to the gods as someone who observes the words of the Tradition, and also that he commands the followers of the Tradition in the same way that the Beneficial Teachers commanded us to observe the Tradition of the gods.

¹¹Also how it is firmly true that it is proper for both the smallest bondsman and the greatest lord to keep on their bodies the bond that is the sign of bondedness. For it is not the custom even for a very short time to leave bondedness, as if he had no master, nor is it proper to go about other than with the mark of bondedness to one's lord, as if he were not a bondsman.

¹²Also that it is commanded in the Tradition that one should keep one's thought, speech, and action bound from (= closed to) sin by the bond, as if they were one's bondsmen, and also to bind one's sins (away from) from the purity of one's thought, whose dwelling is the heart. This bond of bondedness is to be kept as a mark and sign around the middle of the body and before the heart. This sign and mark that one binds the sins should be seen before one's eyes as an eternal reminder to one's thought.

That it is appropriate to keep one's thought, speech, and action bound from sin is evident also from experience and from the amount of protection one receives from wearing this bond. By providing the reason and purpose of protecting from many sins, it is more of a reminder of that against which it protects in this way.

[13]Also that those who were before and who were well-acquainted with the Tradition connected these words they had heard with those who were before us, as well as with us. When the Assault came upon the creation, demons and witches in very great numbers ran all over the earth, in the intermediate space, and up under the place of the stars.

[14]There they saw many lights and also the Fortune of the Tradition/ Dēn, which is a bond and fastness and enclosure for (?) all desires and good deeds, shining like a bright *kusti*. It enclosed (*parwand-*) all the lights by an enclosure. For it is by the all-aware gods that this enclosure of all-aware wisdom is being enclosed.

[15]That great doubt-resolving Fortune of the pure Tradition was as beautiful and shone as far as it is said in the divine word: The good Mazdayasnian Tradition is a Girdle (*aibyānghan*), star-adorned and fashioned in the world of thought [cf. 90].

[16]All the demons were afraid of the great Fortune of the Tradition. It is said that all the demons will be frustrated by the memorizing, practicing, and propagating this way of the wise Tradition, and, then, the Perfectioning will be established at will in the two worlds.

[17]Because of that fear, none of the demons, even the most giant of the demons, will be able to run up to the creations of the uppermost third, which is in purity without the Assault.

[18]He commands in the Tradition that men, especially the bearers of the Tradition, should tie on that enclosing bond of that Tradition as a *kusti* around the middle third of the body, close to the uppermost third.

[19]As for this story that radiant Jam, son of Wiwangh, who was the most Fortunate in the works of this world as it progressed and kept terror and death away from all seven continents and set them up without old age and death—when he was deceived by the lie-demon, he desired to rise from being Ohrmazd's bondsman to the highest lordship [cf. 33; 34; 47:4].

[20]So he said he was responsible for the creation, and, for that lie, he was removed from wealth and Fortune and they rent him apart, both demons and men. In that rending, he was cut off (= destroyed).

²¹He then pleaded for forgiveness frrom the beneficent Creator, and, as atonement for having left the bondedness of the Creator, he spoke to and instructed those who came after him from the teaching of the gods with many good deeds, in which the power of Terror is explained and the road of moderation is strengthened. He did this when he commanded people to wear the bond about the middle of their body. They also command that that Fortunate ruler, lord of the world of the living, also by his being so Fortunate, should be a good example for his own.

²²Also that, since it was commanded from the gods that it should be tied for that reason and be worn as the *kusti*, even before Zarathustra of the Spitāmas arrived, afterward, that bringer of the word of the gods, Righteous Zarathustra, who commanded the good command of those in the other world, taught the Tradition while uttering the *Avesta*, which praises the gods, about how to commit oneself to the praise of the good Tradition.

This belt of the Tradition is girded around the body, accompanied by rituals (*nīrang*) from the Tradition, over the garment of Wahman, ²³like wisdom, which is girded on all sides, whose seed is the Tradition.

²³That word is told truly that men in general, in accordance with the same way, wear this good belt, the Tradition, which shows their ritual bondedness to the Creator: the Girdle, around the middle of their body, as it has more power to break evil, bind (= close) the road to sin, and to diminish the wish of the demons.

✦

CHAPTER EIGHT

RITUAL TEXTS

From the Old Avesta

102 Yasna 33: Prayers

[11]You, who have the greatest life-giving strength, who are Lord and All-knowing, and you who are Humility and you who are Order, which furthers the herds, listen, all of you, to my good thought and command! Be merciful in return for my every presentation!

[12]Rise up before me now, O Lord (Fire)! Through Humility (the earth) receive strength! By your most life-giving spirit, O All-knowing one, receive quickness by my good presentation, forceful violent power by the Order (of my ritual), creative power (?) by my good thought.

[13]You shall show me now, as support for the far-seeing sun, your path, by which I shall cross over. Along that (path?) of my/your command, O Ahura, along which the reward of (= for) my good thought shall arrive, launch, O Humility, our vision-souls through life-giving Order!

[14]Thus, Zarathustra is giving as gift the life breath of nothing less than his own body as the foremost share of his sacrifice and of his good thought to the All-knowing one, as well as what is the foremost share of his action through Order and that of his utterance: his readiness to listen (*sraosha*) and the command of his sacrifice.

103 Yasna 34: Concluding prayer

[13]Teach us that road which you, O Lord, told me is that of good thought, the well-made one along which the vision-souls of the

revitalizers strode, precisely the one through Order, toward the fee which was first assigned to those giving good gifts and whose depository you are, O All-knowing one.

[14]For, O All-knowing one, that is the well-deserved fee you all shall give for my life breath and bones on account of the action of my good thought. For, to those who are in the household of the fertile cow, you all give *your* good insight of guiding wisdom. Through your Order, O Lord, you further the households.

[15]O All-knowing one, thus say *my* poems conferring fame and my actions are the best! Say, you, that my repayment in the form of praises is best on account of that good thought of mine and the Order of my ritual!

You now make by your command, all of you, O Lord, this Life Juicy in exchange value, the *real* one.

104 Yasna 54: The Airyamā Ishiyō

[1]Let speedy Airyaman come here as support for our men and women, as support for Zarathustra's good thought, by which his vision-soul may gain a well-deserved fee. I am now asking for the reward of Order, which Ahura Mazdā shall deem (?) worthy of being sped hither.

From the Young Avesta

105 Yasna 1: Litanies

[1]I announce (them to you)! I am assembling (the sacrifice) to/of Ahura Mazdā, who has set (everything in its place), the wealthy and munificent one, the greatest, the best, the most beautiful, the firmest, the one with the best guiding wisdom, the best shaped, the one who gets closest to Order, the one of good creations, of wide support, who has set us in place, who has fashioned us, who has put us together, who is the most "Life-giving" Spirit.

[2]I announce (them to you)! I am assembling (the sacrifice) for (regenerating) Good Thought, for Best Order, for Well-deserved Command, for Life-giving Humility, for Wholeness and Immortality,

for the Fashioner of the Cow, for the Soul of the Cow, and for the Fire of Ahura Mazdā, the one of the Life-giving Immortals who most often takes up his (ritual) position.

[10]I announce (them to you)! I am assembling (the sacrifice) for all these models, which are the models of Order, thirty-three, the nearest, those surrounding the hour of the *haoma* pressing, which are those of Best Order, ordained by Ahura Mazdā, spoken by Zarathustra.

[11]I announce (them to you)! I am assembling (the sacrifice)

to the two exalted ones, Ahura Mazdā and Mithra, unthreatening sustainers of Order,

to the stars, the creations of the Life-giving Spirit,

to the star Tishtriya, wealthy and munificent,

to the moon containing the seed of the cow,

to the radiant sun with speedy horses, the eye of Ahura Mazdā, and to Mithra the land-lord of lands.

I announce (them to you)! I am assembling (the sacrifice)

to Ahura Mazdā, wealthy and munificent.

I announce (them to you)! I am assembling (the sacrifice)

to the pre-souls of the sustainers of Order (etc.).

106 Yasna 1: Safety precautions

[21]If I have ever offended you in thought, speech, or action, whether because it pleased me or not, I say it forth in my praise to you to atone for it, I make it known to you, if I have ever omitted anything from this your sacrifice and hymn.

[22]O all greatest models! O model of Order, sustainer of Order! If I have offended you, either in thought, speech, or action, whether because it pleased me or not, I say it forth in my praise to you all to atone for it, I make it known to you all, if I have barred you from this your sacrifice and hymn.

107 Yasna 8: The purpose of the ritual

[5]May you, Ahura Mazdā, now rule over your creations at will and according to your wish!

You, O waters, you, O plants, you, O all good things with the appearance/brilliance (*chithra*) of Order, place the sustainer of Order in command, the one possessed by the Lie out of command!

⁶May the sustainer of Order have command at will! May the one possessed by the Lie have no command at will! May he be gone, discomfited, removed from the creations of the Life-giving Spirit, restrained, commanding nothing at will! [Cf. 64:96]

⁷May I, too, (a) Zarathustra, now make the foremost people of the houses, towns, tribes, and lands help my vision-soul and that of Ahura Mazdā along with their thoughts, words, and actions.

⁸I invite expanse and comfort for the entire existence of the sustainer of Order. I invite constriction and discomfort for the entire existence possessed by the Lie.

108 Yasna 9: Zarathustra praises Haoma

¹⁶Then Zarathustra said: Homage to the haoma! Good is the haoma. Well set up is the tawny-colored haoma, with pliable twigs, set up straight and well-shaped, healing and invigorating, providing obstruction-smashing strength. For the drinker he is the best drink and for the breath-soul the best flight-maker.

¹⁷I call down, O tawny one, your intoxication, your force and your obstruction-smashing strength, your talent and healing, your furthering and increasing, your strength of the whole body, your all-adorned learning. I call down all that so that I may go forth among living beings commanding at will, overcoming hostilities, conquering the Lie!

¹⁸I call down all that so that I may overcome the hostilities of all those hostile to us, of evil gods and men, sorcerers and witches, evil teachers, poetasters, and mumblers, of the villains on two feet, of those on two feet who darken Order, of wolves on four feet, and of their deceiving, scrambling, disorganized army.

¹⁹This I ask you as my first request, O death-averting Haoma: the Best Existence of the sustainers of Order, which is light and all comfort.

This I ask you as my second request, O death-averting Haoma: health of this body.

This I ask you as my third request, O death-averting Haoma: long life for my life breath.

²⁰This I ask you as my fourth request, O death-averting Haoma: that I may stand forth upon the earth strong, forceful, satisfied, overcoming hostilities, conquering the Lie!

This I ask you as my fifth request, O death-averting Haoma: that I may stand forth upon the earth smashing obstructions, conquering in battles, overcoming hostilities, conquering the Lie!

²¹This I ask you as my sixth request, O death-averting Haoma: May we be the first to notice the thief and the robber, the first to notice the wolf! May no one notice us first! May we notice all first!

²²Haoma bestows endurance and strength on the rapid horses that run in pairs around the race-course. Haoma gives radiant and Orderly sons to those in labor. And Haoma bestows life-giving wisdom and learning on those who sit in their homes consulting the Tradition.

109 Yasna 11-12: The Frawarānē declaration

¹⁹I praise Order! ¹I scorn the evil gods!

I shall choose to sacrifice to Ahura Mazdā, like Zarathustra, discarding the evil gods and with Ahura Mazdā as my guide.

110 Yasna 27: Pressing of the haoma

Purpose of the ritual

¹This (we do), for him to be established as the greatest new life (*ahu*) of all and its model: Ahura Mazdā, for him

to strike the Evil Spirit, possessed by the Lie,

to strike Wrath with the bloody mace,

to strike all the evil gods, the giant evil gods and the greedy ones, possessed by the Lie,

²to further Ahura Mazdā, wealthy and munificent,

to further the Life-giving Immortals,

to further the star Tishtriya, wealthy and munificent,

to further the Man Sustaining Order,

to further all the Creations of the Life-giving Spirit, sustainers of Order.

Filtering of the haoma

⁶The *haomas* are about to be filtered, containing the command of Ahura Mazdā, containing the models of Order. Let good Sraosha, followed by Ashi who bestows riches, also be present!

⁷We assign to them the accompaniment of the good creative magic of change (*māyā*?) of the *Ahuna Wairiya*, proclaimed in Orderly fashion; of the mortar and the pestle, moved in Orderly fashion; and of the words correctly spoken. For, in that way, they shall have even greater creative magic of change for us.

The Ahuna Wairiya

¹³*In as much as (a new Life)* is a worthy one by (the example of the first) new Life, so its Model is just in accordance with Order.

The Model of good thought and of the actions of the first new Life is always established for him who is All-knowing, and the (royal) command is always assigned to him who is Lord, whom one shall thereby establish as pastor for the poor.

The Ashem wohū

¹⁴*Order is the best good* (reward/possession) *there is. There are wished-for things in his wish for this one when his Order is for the best Order.*

¹⁵We offer up in sacrifice the *Ahuna Wairiya*. We offer up the *Ashem vohū*, the most beautiful life-giving Immortal.

The Yenghyē Hātām

Thus, he among those that are, as well as the women, *in return for whose sacrifice the better good is to be given,* him (and them) *Ahura Mazdā knows to be according to Order—to those men and those women we sacrifice.*

111 Yasna 55: Offering of the Gāthās

[2]The *Gāthās*, which are our guardians and protectors and food in the
world of thought, which are for our breath-soul both food and clothing,
they are for us the guardians, protectors, and food in the world of
thought. Those are both food and clothing for our breath-soul.

May they bring us good rewards, great rewards, the reward of
Order, for tomorrow's new existence, after the wrenching apart of
bones and consciousness!

[3]By that force and obstruction-smashing strength, by that mastery
and remedy, by that furthering and growth, by that good existence and
rejuvenation, by that good gift-giving and righteousness, by that
generosity and distribution, may they come up for us, the *Texts of
Sacrifice and Praise*, as Mazdā brought them forth, he the richest
in life-giving strength, the obstruction-smashing furtherer of living beings, for the protection of the living beings of Order, for
guarding the living beings of Order, both those to be Revitalized and
those who shall Revitalize and the entire existence of the sustainer of
Order!

112 Animal sacrifices (Yasna 11)

[3]Haoma curses the eater: "May you have no offspring and be
pursued by bad fame, you who keep me for yourself when filtered, as
if I, the death-averting Haoma, sustainer of Order, were a thief whose
head is forfeit. But my head is not forfeit.

[4]My father, Ahura Mazdā, sustainer of Order, sent up to me as my
meat offering the cheeks together with the tongue, as well as the
left eye.

[5]He who robs me of that offering, steals or withholds it, the cheeks
together with the tongue, as well as the left eye, [6]in his home no priest,
charioteer, or husbandman will be born, only all kinds of stinging and
crawling things!

From the Pahlavi Texts

113 Animal sacrifices (Shāyist nē shāyist 11)

⁴When an animal is slaughtered and cut in pieces, then the meat offering should be apportioned as follows:

The cheeks, tongue, and left eye go to the divine Hōm, the neck to Ashwahisht, the head to the divine (good) Wāy, the upper right arm to Ardwīsūr, the left to Druwāsp, the right thigh to Wishtāsp's pre-soul, the left to Jāmāsp's pre-soul, the back to the Exalted Model, the flank to those in the other world, the belly to Spandarmad, the testicles to Wanand, the kidneys to the Big Dipper, the breast to the priests' pre-souls, the lungs to the warriors' pre-souls, the liver for mercy and protection of the poor, the spleen to the Life-giving Word, the forelegs to the waters, the heart to the fires, the fatty entrails to the pre-soul of the sustainers of Order, the fat-tail to the pre-soul of Zarathustra of the Spitāmas, the … (?) to the righteous Wind, the right eye to the Moon, and anything left over to the other Amahrspands.

⁶Any part one offers to another god is fine, exept for the cheeks, tongue, and left eye, for those belong to the divine Hōm, as is evident from the Avestan passage [cf. 112].

From the Avesta and Zand

114 Pollution (Videvdad 3)

What makes the earth happy or unhappy

¹Creator of the world of the living with bones, sustainer of Order! Where firstly in this earth is there most happiness? Ahura Mazdā said: Wherever, Zarathustra of the Spitāmas, a man, sustainer of Order, goes forth with firewood in his hands, with *barsom* in his hands, with milk in his hands, with the *haoma* mortar in his hands, pronouncing in peace words according to the Tradition and beseeching Mithra who provides wide pastures and Peace with good pastures.

²Creator . . .! Where secondly in this earth is there most happiness? Ahura Mazdā said: Wherever a man, sustainer of Order, sets up a house with fire, cattle, wife, sons, and good herds. Then afterwards that house has in abundance cattle, Order, pasture, dogs, women, children, fire, and all things for good living. (. . .)

⁴Creator . . .! Where thirdly in this earth is there most happiness? Ahura Mazdā said: Wherever one sows barley, grass, and food-bearing plants the most, when one irrigates dry land or drains waterlogged land.

⁵Creator . . .! Where fourthly in this earth is there most happiness? Ahura Mazdā said: Wherever animals, small and large, defecate the most.

⁶Creator . . .! Where fifthly in this earth is there most happiness? Ahura Mazdā said: Wherever animals, small and large, urinate the most.

⁷Creator . . .! Where firstly in this earth is there most unhappiness? Ahura Mazdā said: On the ridge of (Mount) Arzūra, O Zarathustra of the Spitāmas, because there the evil gods run together from the lair of the Lie.

⁸Creator . . .! Where secondly in this earth is there most unhappiness? Ahura Mazdā said: Wherever dead dogs and men lie interred the most.

⁹Creator . . .! Where thirdly in this earth is there most unhappiness? Ahura Mazdā said: Wherever most funerary mounds are built in which dead men are laid down.

¹⁰Creator . . .! Where fourthly in this earth is there most unhappiness? Ahura Mazdā said: Wherever the lairs of the Evil Spirit are the most numerous.

¹¹Creator . . .! Where fifthly in this earth is there most unhappiness? Ahura Mazdā said: Wherever a man, sustainer of Order, and his woman and child are dragged captive along the road, raising plaintive voices with mouths dry with dust.

¹²Creator . . .! Who firstly satisfies this earth with greatest satisfaction? Ahura Mazdā said: Wherever they most dig up places where dead dogs and men lie buried.

¹³Creator ...! Who secondly satisfies this earth with greatest satisfaction? Ahura Mazdā said: Where they dig out the most funerary mounds in which dead men are laid down.

On the undertaker

¹⁴Let no one carry alone what is dead! If he does, for certain the corpse will contaminate him via the nose, eyes, tongue, jaw, penis, and anus. This lie-demon, the corpse, will then rush upon the nails of such men. Afterward they become impure for ever and eternity.

¹⁵Creator ...! Where shall the place of this man be, the corpse-cutter? Ahura Mazdā said: Wherever this earth is most devoid of water and plants, where the earth is the most purified and dry, and where animals, small and large, the Fire of Ahura Mazdā, the *barsom* spread out in Orderly fashion, and a man sustaining Order most rarely walk along these paths.

¹⁶Creator ...! How far must the *barsom* spread out in Orderly fashion and the men sustaining Order be from the Fire of Ahura Mazdā? ¹⁷Then Ahura Mazdā said: Thirty steps from the fire, thirty steps from the water, thirty steps from the *barsom* to be spread out, three steps from men sustaining Order.

¹⁸Here these Mazdayasnians should build enclosures of earth for him. Afterward they should approach with foods and clothes. ¹⁹Among the poorest and the most emaciated let him eat these foods and don these garments, ever until he becomes old, senile, and his bodily fluids have come to rest. ²⁰Then the Mazdayasnians, as strongly and as quickly and as expertly as possible, should shave (?) his head the width of his... [cf. 97:35].

One should expose the body to the most ravenous of the living beings of the Life-giving Spirit, the scavenging vultures, saying: "No bad thought, word, or deed remains with him!" ²¹And if he has committed other bad deeds, he is aquitted of this penalty, and if he has committed no other bad deeds, then that man is aquitted for ever and eternity.

²²Creator . . .! Who thirdly satisfies this earth with greatest satisfaction? Ahura Mazdā said: Where they dig out the most funerary mounds in which dead men are laid down.

115 From the Pahlavi commentary on Videvdad 3.7

Creator . . . unhappy? i.e., from what does the spirit (*mēnōy*) of this earth receive most discomfort?

Ohrmazd said: On the ridge of Arzūr, at the door to hell, *in which the evil gods rush together,* i.e., when they rush back (to hell), that is where they rush back, *from the lair of the Lie,* i.e., when they rush up (from hell), that is where they rush up.

There is one who says that, when they "rush about," they have male-to-male intercourse.

Hell is below the earth, above the (lower sky), and it has a door into the earth. Whether this is outside the sky or not is not clear to me. That is where they rush back from the lair of the Lie when they rush back.

What we call "demons" (*dēw*) and "lie-demons" (*druz*) are both the same, but there is one who says that they are male and female, while another says it is *all* sinfulness! When they say "male" and "female" it means that "demons" are male and "witches" (*parīg*) female.

116 Pahlavi commentary on Videvdad 3.14

. . . *He then becomes ritually impure forever and ever.*

It is well-known from the *Avesta* that this is the case when they *know* it is a dead body and they *know* it has not been seen by a dog. If they move it then, it is a sin "worth death" (*marg-arzān*).

If someone takes it alone and carries it out and moves it by intimately touching it, then one need not *know* that it has *not* been seen by a dog, for it is not different: it is pollution, and he is guilty of death. And there is no effective washing. He must be put to death by the ritual that was described before.

Abarg said: One should *not* take into account means and possibility.

Gōgushasp said: True, but it *will* be "by means and possibility." And he does not need to know that it is a sin worth death. For, if they know that it is any sin at all, and still do it, then too it becomes "worth death" in the usual manner.

Rōshn said: It means that they need to know the *size* of the sin when it has not been seen by a dog and the dead body is any measure at all (cf.) *not fly-borne* [117:3]. When it has been taken up and put down several times, each time it becomes "worth death" in the usual manner. If one has taken it up with one hand and another puts it down with the other hand it is "worth death," it means that, if they see that it has been tied down intimately once but he then took it up, it is not *more* than "worth death."

So, anyone intimate with the (dead) man, if one moves him, one's body is polluted, and one becomes "worth death" in the usual manner.

And if the corpse is moved by a man's foot, his body is polluted, and because of what he has done he incurs the sin of "one's body is forfeited" (*tanābuhl*) in the usual manner.

. . .

A corpse that has not been seen by a dog, when it has been moved by two men, both men must be cleansed by a *barshnūm* ceremony and their clothes by the six-month wash. It is not different in the case of intimate touch.

A corpse that has been seen by a dog, when it is moved by one man alone, his body must be washed by *barshnūm* and his clothes by the six-month wash. If there is intimate touch, then also with water and cow's urine.

If his body is made so polluted that he must wash it by *barshnūm*, then he is guilty of one *tanābuhl*.

. . .

If he is certain that, yes, it is a "dead body," but he is in doubt whether he bumped into it, then too he should wash in the usual way. If he is in doubt whether it is a "dead body," but he is certain he bumped into it, then he should not wash. And if he is in doubt whether it was actually there, then it is just like if it were doubtful whether it was "dead body."

117 Pollution (Videvdad 5)

[1]A man dies there, in the deepest river bed. A bird flies up there, from the highest mountain and down to the deepest river bed. It nibbles at the body of that dead man. The bird flies up, from the deepest river bed to the highest mountain. It flies up on some tree, hard or soft. It vomits, urinates, or defecates on it.

[2]A man goes forth there, from the deepest river bed to the highest mountain. He goes to that tree where that bird was, seeking firewood for the fire. He strikes it, cuts into it, and cuts it down. On it he lights the fire, the son of Ahura Mazdā. What is the penalty for it?

[3]Ahura Mazdā said: Dog-borne, bird-borne, wolf-borne, wind-borne, or fly-borne corpse (*nasush*) does not make a man guilty.

[4]For, if these dog-borne, bird-borne, wolf-borne, wind-borne, and fly-borne corpses were to make a man guilty, right away the Order of my entire existence with bones would be crippled by the large amount of these corpses lying dead upon this earth. Every soul would be shuddering (in fear), every body would be forfeit.

118 Pahlavi commentary on Videvdad 5

Abarg said: This question is about *hikhr* (dead matter), but the decision was about *nasāy.* (corpse). For, when a bird has eaten it, it becomes *hikhr.*

Mēdōmah said: This question is about both, but the decision was about *nasāy.* For, until the bird digests it, it is regarded as *nasāy.*

In both teachings they agreed that, when a heavier sin has been committed, it also implies the lighter sin.

When a man goes to fetch firewood it does not matter where he gets it from. (...)

A piece of wood on which there is *nasāy* cannot be used. And if there is *nasāy* on wood that has been used to destroy something, on which they have hanged, it someone, which fat has gotten into, or a menstruant woman has touched, it cannot be burnt except when it is a matter of death or bodily harm. If they burn it, it is a matter of a *tanābuhl* sin, except when fat has gotten into it, in which case it is a sin "worth death" if one burns it.

. . .

If a *nasāy* gets onto a road, a town gate, or into a canal where there is always water, then, according to the good teachers of old, the outermost door should be left to be used for the same purpose. But the door of a privy should be used for a hut for menstruant women, and the door of a hut for menstruant women should be used for a place where corpses are kept. Something producing a heavier sin cannot be used for something producing a lighter sin.

✦

CHAPTER NINE

TEXTS ON KINGSHIP

From the Old Persian Inscriptions

119 *From Darius's inscription at Bisotun (DB)*

[1]I am Dārayavahush, the great king, king of kings, king in Pārsa, king over the lands, the son of Wishtāspa, the grandson of Ershāma (Arsames), a descendent of Hakhāmanish.

[7]King Dārayavahush announces: These are the lands that came to me by Ahuramazdā's greatness. They were my bondsmen. They brought me tribute. Whatever was announced to them from me, that they would do.

[8]King Dārayavahush announces: In these lands, any man who was outstanding, him I treated well. Whoever sided with the Evil One, him I punished well. By Ahuramazdā's greatness, these lands behaved according to *my* law. As was announced to them from me, thus they would do.

[9]King Dārayavahush announces: Ahuramazdā conferred the royal command upon me. Ahuramazdā brought me support until I held this royal command together. By Ahuramazdā's greatness, I hold this royal command.

Machinations of the Lie: The story of the false Smerdis

[10]King Dārayavahush announces: This is what I have done after becoming king.

Before, Kambūjiya (Cambyses), son of Kurush (Cyrus), of our family, was king here. That Kambūjiya had a brother called Berdiya

(Smerdis), with the same mother and father as Kambūjiya. Then Kambūjiya killed that Berdiya. When Kambūjiya killed Berdiya, the people/army did not realize that Berdiya had been killed.

Then Kambūjiya went to Mudrāya (Egypt). When Kambūjiya had gone to Mudrāya, then the people sided with the Evil One, and the Lie became rampant in the lands, both in Pārsa and Māda (Media) and in the other lands.

¹¹King Dārayavahush announces: Then there was a man called Gaumāta. He rose up from Mount Arakadri in Paishiyāuvāda. It was on the 14th of the month of Viyakhana that he rose up.

He lied to the people as follows: "I am Berdiya, son of Kurush, brother of Kambūjiya." Then the people in its entirety conspired against Kambūjiya. They went over to that other one, both Pārsa and Māda and the other lands. *He* seized the royal command.

It was on the 9th of the month of Garmapada that he seized the royal command. Then Kambūjiya died in an accident caused by himself.

¹²King Dārayavahush announces: This royal command that Gaumāta the priest (*magu*) took from Kambūjiya had been in our family from old. Gaumāta the priest took it from Kambūjiya. He appropriated Pārsa and Māda and the other lands. He made them his own. He became king.

¹³King Dārayavahush announces: There was no man, either from Pārsa or Māda, or anyone of our family, who could have taken the royal command from that Gaumāta the priest. The army feared him strongly, seeing that he would kill in large numbers the people who had known Berdiya in the past. He would kill people lest they learn he was not Berdiya son of Kurush. Nobody dared say anything about Gaumāta the priest until I arrived.

Then I called upon Ahuramazdā for help. Ahuramazdā brought me support. On the 10th of the month of Bāgayādi I killed that Gaumāta the priest with just a few men, as well as the men who were his foremost followers. I killed him in the fortress of Sikayauvati in the land of Nisāya in Māda. I took the royal command from him.

By Ahuramazdā's greatness, I became king. Ahuramazdā conferred the royal command upon me.

Darius restores the empire

[14]King Dārayavahush announces: I set back in its place the royal command that had been taken away from our family. I set it in its proper place, just like before. I did the same for the temples that Gaumāta the priest had destroyed. Throughout the homelands that Gaumāta the priest had taken from them, I restored to the people the pastures, cattle, and household (slaves). I put back in place the people, both in Pārsa and Māda and the other lands, just like they were before. I brought back whatever had been taken away.

By Ahuramazdā's greatness, I did this. I exerted myself until I had set back in its place our homeland, just like it was before. In that manner I exerted myself by Ahuramazdā's greatness so that Gaumāta the priest did not take away our homeland.

Darius's advice to his successors

[54]King Dārayavahush announces: These lands which conspired, the Lie made these men conspire so that they deceived the people. Then Ahuramazdā placed them in my hands. As was my wish, thus I did to them. [Cf. 6:8]

[55]King Dārayavahush announces: You who shall be king hereafter, guard strongly against the Lie. The man who is a liar, punish him well if you think: "May my country be healthy!"

[58]King Dārayavahush announces: By Ahuramazdā's and my greatness, much else has been done that has not been written in this inscription. It has not been written, lest what I have done seem much to him who reads this inscription hereafter and he may not believe it, but think it is all a lie. (...)

[60]King Dārayavahush announces: Believe now what I have done! Likewise, do not hide it from the people! If you do not hide this testimony and tell the people, may Ahuramazdā favor you, and may you have much family, and may you live long!

⁶¹King Dārayavahush announces: If you hide this testimony and do not tell the people, may Ahuramazdā strike you down, and may you have no family!

⁶²King Dārayavahush announces: That which I did in a single year I did by Ahuramazdā's greatness. Ahuramazdā bore me aid, as well as the other gods who are.

⁶³King Dārayavahush announces: For this reason Ahuramazdā bore me aid, as well as the other gods who are, so that I should not side with the Evil One. I was not a liar and did nothing crooked, neither I nor my family. I wandered in rectitude. I did wrong to neither the poor nor the mighty. The man who exerted himself in my homeland, him I treated well. Whoever did evil, him I punished well.

⁶⁴King Dārayavahush announces: You who shall be king hereafter shall not favor the man who is a liar or does crooked deeds, but shall punish him well!

120 Darius's Testament I: Tomb of Darius at Naqsh-e Rostam (DNa)

⁴King Dārayavahush announces: When Ahuramazdā saw this earth in turmoil, he gave it to me. He made me king. I am king. By Ahuramazdā's greatness, I set it down in its place. They did whatever was announced to them from me, as was my wish.

And if you think: "How were those countries that King Dārayavahush held?"—then look at the figures that carry the throne. Then you will know, then you will realize how far the spear of the man from Pārsa has gone. Then you will realize how far the man from Pārsa has fought battles (keeping enemies) away from Pārsa.

⁵King Dārayavahush announces: All this that has been achieved I did by Ahuramazdā's greatness. Ahuramazdā bore me aid until I got it done. Let Ahuramazdā protect me from the Foulness, as well as my home and this land. This I ask of Ahuramazdā. Let Ahuramazdā give this to me!

⁶O man, let not Ahura Mazdā's forethought (?) seem evil to you! Do not leave the straight path! Do not rebel!

121 *Darius's Prayer I, from an inscription at Persepolis (DPd)*

¹The great Ahuramazdā, the greatest among the gods, set Dārayavahush in place as king. He gave him the royal command. By Ahuramazdā's greatness, Dārayavahush is king.

²King Dārayavahush announces: This land of Pārsa, which Ahuramazdā gave to me, is beautiful and has good horses and men. By the greatness of Ahuramazdā and me, King Dārayavahush, it fears no other.

³King Dārayavahush announces: Let Ahuramazdā together with all the gods bring me aid! Let Ahuramazdā protect this land from armies, famine, and the Lie! May neither armies, famine, or the Lie come upon this land!

⁴This I ask of Ahuramazdā together with all the gods. Let Ahuramazdā together with all the gods grant me this!

122 *Darius's Prayer II, from an inscription at Susa (DSk)*

¹I am Dārayavahush, the great king, king of kings, king over lands, the son of Wishtāspa, a descendent of Hakhāmanish.

²King Dārayavahush announces: Ahuramazdā is mine. I am Ahuramazdā's. I have sacrificed to Ahuramazdā. Let Ahuramazdā bring me aid!

123 *Darius's Prayer III, from the building inscription at Susa (DSf)*

¹¹King Darius announces: Much Perfection (*frasha*) was commanded at Susa. Much Perfection was made. Let Ahuramazdā protect me, my father Wishtāspa, and my land!

124 *Inscription of Artaxerxes II at Susa*

¹The great king Artakhshassa announces, king of kings, king over lands, king over this earth, the son of King Dārayavahush;

of Dārayavahush, the son of King Ertakhshassa (Artaxerxes I);

of Ertakhshassa, the son of King Khshayarsha (Xerxes);

of Khshayarsha, the son of King Dārayavahush;

of Dārayavahush, the son of Wishtāspa, a descendent of Hakhāmanish.

²Dārayavahush, my great-grandfather, made this colonnade. Later on, under Ertakhshassa, my grandfather, it burnt down. By the greatness of Ahuramazdā, Anāhitā, and Mithra, I ordered this colonnade to be made. Let Ahuramazdā, Anāhitā, and Mithra protect me from the Foulness! Let no sorcerer or magician destroy this that I have made!

From the Middle Persian Inscriptions

125 The conclusion of the inscription of Shāpūr I at Naqsh-e Rostam

Now, in the same manner that We exerted Ourselves in the matters and services of the gods (*yazd*) and are the property of the gods, so that, with the help of the gods, We sought and held all these lands and obtained great fame, in the same manner, let him who comes after us and is fortunate also exert himself in the matters and services of the gods, so that the gods may help him, too, and make him their property!

From the Pahlavi Texts

126 Kingship and priesthood (Dēnkard III, 129)

The one thing the Foul Spirit labors against more violently than anything else is the coming together in the strongest degree of the Fortunes of kingship and the good Tradition in one person, because then he will be destroyed by this combination. For, if the Fortune of superior strength of the good Tradition had come together with the Fortune of kingship in the strongest degree in Jamshēd, or if the superior strength of kingship as it was in Jamshēd had come together with the Fortune of the good Tradition in the strongest degree in Zarathustra, then the destruction of the Foul Spirit, the deliverance of the creation from the Assault, and the Perfectioning in the two worlds would quickly have come about.

As long as, in the world of the living, the good Tradition and good kingship are as one and the one of good Tradition and the good king come together, sinfulness will weaken and good behavior increase,

Opposition will diminish and helpfulness grow, and righteousness will increase and wickedness decrease among mankind. Good people will experience expanse and good rule, while evil people will have constriction and no rule. And prosperity will be arrayed and adorned in the world of the living, bliss in the whole creation, and goodness in the general population.

CHAPTER TEN

✦

TEXTS ON DOCTRINAL ISSUES

Diverging Practices in the Yasna

127 *The standard order of the ritual models (Yasna 6)*

[1]We sacrifice to Ahura Mazdā, who has set (all things) in their places.

We sacrifice to the Life-giving Immortals, who bestow good command and give good gifts.

[2]We sacrifice to the daily models of Order, sustainers of Order.

We sacrifice to the Haoma-pressing Hour, sustainer of Order, a model of Order.

We sacrifice to the Hour of Life-giving Strength, sustainer of Order, and the (Protector) of the House, a model of Order.

128 *An earlier order (Yasna 71)*

[1]Frashaoshtra, sustainer of Order, asked Zarathustra, sustainer of Order:

Answer me about the former things, O Zarathustra. What was the enumeration of the models (then)? What was the assembling of the *Gāthās*?

[2]Zarathustra answered:

We sacrifice to Ahura Mazdā, sustainer of Order, a model of Order.

We sacrifice to Zarathustra, sustainer of Order, a model of Order.

We sacrifice to the pre-soul of Zarathustra, sustainer of Order.

We sacrifice to the Life-giving Immortals, sustainers of Order. (etc.)

On Right Practices and Foreign Worship in the Old and Middle Persian Inscriptions

129 Xerxes's dealing with foreign gods (XPh)

[4]King Xerxes announces: When I had become king, there was among the lands that are written above one that was in turmoil. Then Ahuramazdā brought me aid. By Ahuramazdā's greatness, I struck down that land and set it in its place.

[5]And in these lands there was a place where previously they sacrificed to foreign gods (*daivas*). Then, by Ahuramazdā's greatness, I destroyed that lair of foreign gods and proclaimed: "The foreign gods are not to receive sacrifices!" Where previously the foreign gods had received sacrifices, there I sacrificed to Ahuramazdā *according to the Order up on high*.

[6]And there was much other evil that had been done, which I made good. All this that I did, I did by Ahuramazdā's greatness. Ahuramazdā bore me aid until I had successfully done it all.

[7]= [83]

[8]King Xerxes announces: Let Ahuramazdā protect me from evil Foulness, as well as my house and this land! This I ask of Ahuramazdā. Let Ahuramazdā grant me this!

130 From Kerdīr's inscription on the Ka'ba of Zardosht

Career under Shāpūr I (242–72 CE)

[1]And I, Kerdīr, High Priest (*mowbed*), served the gods (*yazd*) and Shābuhr, king of kings, well and received their good favor. [2]And in return for the service I had performed for the gods and Shābuhr, king of kings, Shābuhr, king of kings, gave me among all the other priests full control and authority over the services to the gods, both at the court, and throughout the realm.

At the order of Shābuhr, king of kings, and with the help of the gods and the king of kings, the number of services for the gods was increased, many Victorious Fires were established, many priests were rendered prosperous, many fires and priests received official letters of recognition, and, altogether, there was great profit for Ohrmazd and the gods, while Ahrimen and the demons (*dēw*) suffered great distress.

³For all these fires and services that are listed in this inscription, Shābuhr, king of kings, appointed me in particular, stating: "Let this be your capital! Keep doing that which you know is best for the gods and Us!"

⁴On the various documents that were issued at that time under Shābuhr, king of kings, at the court and throughout the realm, it was written "Kerdīr, the Teacher (*ēhrbed*)."

Under Ohrmazd I (272–73 CE); Warahrān I (273–76 CE)

...

⁸On the various documents issued at that time under Ohrmazd/ Warahrān, king of kings, at court and throughout the realm, it was written "Kerdīr, High Priest (*mowbed*) of Ohrmazd" [cf. 2:22].

Under Warahrān II (276–93 CE)

⁹When Warahrān, king of kings, son of Shābuhr, went to the place of the gods (*bayān gāh*) and his son Warahrān, king of kings, son of Warahrān, ascended the throne and was generous, truthful, friendly, beneficent, and a well-doer in the land, then, out of love for Ohrmazd and the gods and his own soul, he elevated my position and honor in the land. And he gave me the rank of a Grandee. He gave me still greater control and authority over the services to the gods, both at the court, and throughout the entire realm, than I had at first.

¹⁰And he made me High Priest and Judge of the whole realm, made me Master of Customs, and placed me in charge of the fire of Anāhīd-Ardakhshahr at Stakhr.

He gave me the title "Kerdīr, High Priest of Ohrmazd, whose soul was saved by Warahrān."

¹¹Throughout the entire realm, the services to Ohrmazd and the gods were heightened; the Mazdayasnian Tradition and the clergy

were greatly honored; and great blessing came to the gods, the water, the fire, and the cattle.

Throughout the realm, Jews (*yahūd*), Buddhists (*shaman*), Hindus (*braman*), Nazoreans (*nāzarā*) and Christians, Baptists (*magdag*), and Manicheans (*zandīg*) were struck down, idol temples were destroyed, and the lairs of the demons were ruined and turned into thrones and seats for the gods.

¹²Throughout the realm, the services to the gods were greatly increased, many Victorious Fires were established, many priests were rendered prosperous, and many fires and priests received official letters of recognition.

¹³On the various documents issued at that time under Warahrān, son of Warahrān, king of kings, at the court and throughout the realm, it was written "Kerdīr, High Priest of Ohrmazd, whose soul was saved by Warahrān."

Kerdīr's achievements

¹⁴From the beginning, I, Kerdīr, have labored hard for the sake of the gods, the rulers, and my own soul, and I have made many fires and priests prosperous in the realm.

¹⁵Also in the neighboring lands [*list*], wherever the horses and men of the king of kings went to pillage, burn, and lay waste the land, by the order of the king of kings, I organized the fires and priests who were there in that land. I did not allow any of them to come to harm or be taken away as captives, and whoever had already been made captive, those I sent back to their own lands.

¹⁶I furthered the Mazdayasnian Tradition and the good priests in the land and honored them. But the heretics (*ahlomōg*) and (sexual?) deviants (*gumarzāg*) among the clergy who did not live correctly by the Mazdayasnian Tradition and the services to the gods, those I punished and reprimanded until I had made them better.

¹⁷I issued official documents for many fires and priests, and, with the help of the gods, I managed to have many Victorious Fires established in the realm. Many marriages between close relatives

(*khwēdōdah*) were celebrated, and many whose allegiance was not (with the Tradition) changed their allegiance. There were many who held belief (*kēsh*) in the demons (*dēw*), but I managed to have them give up the belief in the demons and receive the belief in the gods.

I undertook the sacrifice of many *ratus* [see p. 35] and enumerated the Tradition by categories (? *gōnag*). Many other services to the gods have been increased and heightened as well, which are not mentioned here, because if it had been written down, it would have been too much.

¹⁸From my own funds I established many Victorious Fires in various places, and, at all those fires that I had established from my own funds, I sacrificed at each seasonal festival (*gāh*) 1133 *ratus*, and in one year it was 6798 *ratus*. I performed many other various services to the gods, too, from my own funds, which it would have been too much to mention in this inscription.

From the Pahlavi Books

131 True speech and the Messiah (Dādestān ī dēnīg 36)

⁷²One is this, that the evilest weapon was obedience to the law of the demons and lying to oneself, since the souls are made wicked thereby, because that made it seem to imply great victory to themselves, but complete damage to the gods.

⁷³In the great Fortune of the pure, straight Tradition of the gods there is as much power as in the all-crooked Demon, who observes no laws, and is full of hostility. For "Right (*arsh*) speech" is nothing but the good true speech; every truth bears witness to that, and no truth is defeated by someone speaking lies. There are many whose speech is good and are enemies of speaking good speech, and even then truth does not prevail in the discussion.

⁷⁴For its analogy is when the truthful say of something that is white that it is white, while, among those speaking lies, some say it is black, others dark blue, blue, or green, and others again red or yellow.

⁷⁵Each single utterance by all speakers of truth bears witness that the utterances of those speaking lies simply are not so, like the

opposing speech, contrary to our custom, [76]of the Christians, who also call their Word Mashīhā, whom they regard in such a way that they hold him to be the son of god, but not less than his father and himself an undying god.

[77]One group says about this Mashīhā that he died, while another group says he did not die. [78]They discuss this back and forth, but, contradicting one another, they oppose what they say themselves. [79]For, when *one* says he died to the one who says he did not and when *one* says he did not die to the one who says he did, by their disagreement, they ruin the position that the *dēw*s (?) are good. By the strength and united power of its truth, the good Tradition of the Mazdayasnians is as powerful and fully endures and is empowered by the disagreements of the others. Thus, this word, the law of the Lie, is confounded and rendered ineffective all by itself. For the firmness of supremacy is seen to be above change, the victory of those with united powers above those whose strength is divided, the final destruction above the destruction of selfhood.

132 *The transmission of the Life-giving Word by different prophets and in different languages (Dēnkard III, 7)*
[1]Another heretic asked:

If the divine words (*mānsr*) are manifest in speech, some spoken by Frashōstar and some by Jāmāsp, some by Wohunam and some by Saēn, some by those before Zarathustra but after Saēn, was it all spoken by Ohrmazd to Zarathustra? [2]As far as we are concerned, we have considered that what Ohrmazd spoke to Zarathustra was the voice (*ēwāz*) of the *Gāthās*, while the rest, what Zarathustra and his pupils fashioned out of speech here in this world, belongs to what is unorganized and subject to change.

[3]Answer.

That may be so, but the other divine words, separate from the *Gāthās*, which were fashioned from the *Gāthās* and the *Yatā-ahū-wairiyō*, also the divine words separate from those whose testimony is above, their testimony is with Ohrmazd himself; they were fashioned by the power of his all-awareness, not by human knowledge, which does not get close to even the smallest part (of his knowledge). The divine words are spoken in many voices, and Ohrmazd did not speak it all to Zarathustra in those voices.

⁴In view of the many different voices of speech in which the divine word is spoken, it should not be said that Ohrmazd spoke it to Zarathustra in those sounds of speech. Rather, it is manifest from what was spoken by Ohrmazd that this and that divine word as uttered by Zarathustra and other good and bad people, even by demons including the Foul Spirit, those utterances, even the (un)divine words of the Foul Spirit and the demons and the *Law for keeping the demons away* would have been spoken by the same demon.

⁵The divine words of Ohrmazd to Zarathustra were in many voices, but it is all something that can be relied on and in no way contradictory. For the *Gāthās*, which you too regard as in their entirety spoken by Ohrmazd to Zarathustra, were some of them spoken in the voice of Zarathustra, some in that of the Amahrspands, some in that of Gōshurūn, some in that of the other gods, yet in no way contradict the fact that they were all spoken by Ohrmazd to Zarathustra.

133 The certainties in the sayings of the teachers of old (Dēnkard III, 94)

These things are certain:

The Creator does not wish anything bad, but there are bad things. What the Creator does not wish, however, *he* did not create or even attempt to.

The Creator is knowledgeable, and someone who is knowledgeable does not strike at someone who is his own friend or even attempt to.

Innumerable people are useful to the Creator. Innumerable people are harmful to that which is useful to him and also harm his wish.

134 Why we are right and those who say against us are in error
*   (Dēnkard V, 22)*

²When (the Tradition) had been organized so as to be manifest through the righteous Zarathustra from the miracles he had worked,

the acts of Fortune, to all of which the Amahrspands had been witness, as well as other wonders of that kind, including some quite unprecedented ones, ³then the things that happened in period after period and could be seen in the other world, as well as perfectly clearly (in this world), were also seen by the bringers of the Tradition from then on.

⁴It was during the reign of King Shābuhr (II), son of Ohrmazd, that Ādurbād, son of Mahrspand, underwent the ordeal by molten brass and emerged unscathed from the battles and attacks of the opponents in the entire continent of Khwanirah.

⁵Other things, too, became miraculously evident from several ritual ordeals of that kind that were practiced until after the end of the reign of His Majesty Yazdegerd, King of Kings, son of Shahriyār.

These other evident matters went out together with others that went out for the same reason. This every person should study for his own sake.

⁶But a little has remained (unexplained), which provides a path for those who now oppose that kind of teaching to express their disbelief. But, in that case, one should cite the *Avesta*, which is supreme and uncontested, against them, and the many writings that are to the point, as well as the judgements of wisdom, with which one cannot disagree. With the weakening to the point of extinction of those who defend the *Avesta*, however, those who contest it have grown numerous.

⁷And so, when this beneficent majesty of immortal soul and superior Fortune, the king of kings, issues orders, our banners are raised against the destructive heretics other than the Muslims, and all the others who wished to contest it.

Thus, we wish that the power of truth of the uninterrupted Mazdayasnian Tradition, the principle of speaking in moderation, the Life-giving Word of great Fortune, and the writings of the *Avesta* and the goodness of the *Zand* may be what decides, what is considered to be informed, and what provides increase!

135 Discussion between Abālish and a high priest

In the Name of the beneficent gods.

[1]It is said that Abālish the accursed was a heretic from Stakhr. He was a good man, who did well for his soul. One day, being hungry and thirsty, he came to the fire temple of Pusht intending to take the blessing (*wāj*) before the meal. But there was nobody to give him the blessing, and he went out again.

There was a man in whose body Wrath resided, and he approached him and said: "What good is it to perform these rituals and wish people well when a good man like you comes and they do not give him the blessing, because they think he is lazy and lowly and deserves no respect?"

In Abālish's tradition, the first name was Ohrmazd, but he got confused, and Wrath scuttled into his body, so that he refrained from doing good and sacrificing to the gods, and the demon made him dispute with all learned people in Pārs—Mazdayasnians, Arabs, Jews, and Christians.

[2]Finally, he set out for Baghdad and the court of Ma'mūn, Amīr of the Faithful, who ordered that all of his own learned men, as well as those of the Jews and Christians, should be asked to come before him and dispute with Abālish.

After Ma'mūn, Amīr of the Faithful, had ordered thus, Ādurfarnbay, son of Farrokh-zād, leader of the Mazdayasnians, the Qādī (judge), and Ma'mūn himself sat down together.

Abālish said: "Mowbed (High priest), will you or I ask first?" The Mowbed said, "You ask, and I shall explain!"

[3]Abālish the accursed asked: "Mowbed, who created water and fire?" The Mowbed said: "Ohrmazd." Abālish said: "Then, why do they strike and kill one another?"

The Mowbed answered: "We know from what we experience that there is nothing created by the Lord Ohrmazd to which the accursed demon Ahrimen has not brought an Opponent, and to the water he brought wetness and to the fire the ability to burn. When they come together, the demon which is with the fire comes to the water like a father and a son who each have an enemy who holds them captive. When they meet, the enemy with the father strikes the son down, but we cannot say that the father has struck his own son."

Ma'mūn, Amīr of the Faithful, was very pleased with this, considered it good, and much enjoyed it.

⁴Abālish the accursed asked: "If one were to strike the water and the burning fire, would that be a greater sin than bringing dead matter (*nasāy*) onto them and leaving it there?

The Mowbed said: "Water and fire are like bulls or horses who are taken outside their herds and are brought to a flock of sheep. There they find grass and water and are protected by them. If one brings dead matter to the fire or water, it is like sending the bull and horse into a pack of lions and wolves: they strike them down, kill them, and devour them."

Ma'mūn, Amīr of the Faithful, was pleased.

⁵The third question was this: "Does Ohrmazd or Ahrimen order the wounding and punishment of humans? For, when the lords order men to be struck, wounded, or killed as punishment for their sins and have their hands cut off or have them beaten with sticks, does the order come from Ahrimen? If so, with what wisdom can people whom Ohrmazd punishes believe (in him)? If it was Ohrmazd who ordered the punishment, then no violence comes to us from Ahrimen."

The Mowbed said: "This law is like a child when a snake bites it in the finger and the father, in order for the poison not to spread throughout the body and kill the child, cuts off the child's finger. One should not therefore regard the father as ignorant or an enemy, but as a wise friend. It is just like that with priests, teachers, and judges. When people commit sins themselves, they wound their souls and block the path to paradise, and for that reason, lest their souls fall into the hands of demons and lie-demons, they are punished in this world. Those who punish them must not be regarded as ignorant or enemies, but as friends wishing them well."

Ma'mūn and the Qādi were both amazed and pleased.

⁶The fourth question was this: "Is washing the hands with cow's urine more purifying than washing with water? If cow's urine is more purifying, then one should not need to wash a second time with water?"

The Mowbed said, "When some excrement or something smelly and polluted lies about in your house, do you take it out yourself, or do you order servants to take it out?"

Abālish, Ma'mūn, and the Qādi said: "Everybody orders the servants to take care of something like that!"

The Mowbed said: "During the night, the demon of filth (*nasrusht*) reaches our body, so, in the morning, we order it to be taken away by means of cow's urine or the sap of plants, but we do not order pure, clean water to do it, since the filth reaches everybody's body, as everyone agrees. Do not Jews, Christians, and Arabs, every morning when they get up, wash their hands, do homage to god and praise god before they lay their hands on any food? If somebody does not, will they not count him as an ignorant sinner?"

Ma'mūn, Amīr of the Faithful, was pleased, thought it was good, and much enjoyed it.

⁷The fifth question was this: "What about doing homage to the Victorious Fire and asking it for a reward, saying: "Give me wealth, friend, son of Ohrmazd, and instant comfort, protection, and good living!" when it is well-known that the fire itself is so weak, powerless, and poor that it will die if people do not feed it firewood for one day. Asking rewards from someone who cannot move himself is proof of poor discernment."

The Mowbed said: "The judgement is like a city in which there are all the trades: a blacksmith, a shoemaker, a carpenter, and a tailor. The shoemaker asks the blacksmith: "Blacksmith, make my tool such that I can make good shoes for you!" and so on. The shoemaker sews shoes for the tailor, and the tailor makes clothes for the shoemaker. In the same way, the fire, when made into a body, is in need of us to obtain libations, perfumes, and firewood. Thus, we too need the fire to perform what needs to be done in the other world—striking the demons in the other world, e.g., illness, fever, terror, and anger, just as masters need servants and servants need masters."

Ma'mūn, Amīr of the Faithful, was pleased, thought it was good, and much enjoyed it.

[8]The sixth question was this: "The following is clear as the day, and everyone agrees that the bodies of the righteous, who perform good deeds, are cleaner and purer than those of the wicked and sinful. You, however, say that the (dead) bodies of the wicked are cleaner, (even) those of the sinful non-Iranians are cleaner than those of the righteous. This is unreasonable and unacceptable."

The Mowbed said: "This is not the way you think! For, when the wicked die, the demon that was with them in life seizes them and leads them to hell into Ahrimen's presence, and there is then no demon left with the corpse, so it is pure!

When the righteous, whose deeds are good, pass away, the Amahrspands seize their souls and receive them and lead them back before Ohrmazd, the Lord; but the demon of filth, which was with the body, by its contamination, takes up residence (?) in the house of the body, and that makes the corpse polluted.

It is like an enemy who has come into a city. If the king of that city falls into the hands of the enemy, the enemy seizes him and binds him and brings him into the presence of his own king. If they cannot seize the king of that country, they enter the city at an unexpected (?) place and lay waste the city."

When Ma'mūn, Amīr of the Faithful, heard this, he was was very pleased and quite amazed.

[9]The seventh question was this: "Why do you tie the *kusti*? For, if there is merit in tying the *kusti*, then asses, camels, and horses, who night and day have (a belt) tied seven times tightly around their bellies, will go to heaven before you."

The Mowbed said, "It is not something we do for no reason. It only seems unreasonable to the unaware who know the wrong things, to those who are unaware and do not know the reason for anything, and to whom the reason for nothing is clear. But I will make it clear.

We say, as we believe in two origins, that this is made visible on our bodies. Ohrmazd's share is the light and Garōdmān. In the same way, all that is in the upper half of the body, such as hearing and smell—the place of wisdom, the soul (*gyān*), the mind (*okh*), thought, intelligence (*ōsh*), perception (*wīr*), the inborn wisdom and that acquired-through-hearing —is the place of the gods and the Amahrspands. When people regard the upper half as being like heaven, the original creation is not at issue.

The lower half is like a place of stench and pollution, a place containing urine, excrement, and stench, like the lair and place of Ahrimen and the demons. If one regards this as obvious, one makes it a foundation and regards it as one would a house.

The *kusti* makes a boundary in the bodies, which is why it is called *kusti*. For by it, it is shown that the body clearly has two sides (*kust*). In the same way, if you squat somewhere, that is where urine appears. So the *kusti* is, in fact, a dividing wall."

Ma'mūn, Amīr of the Faithful, and the Qādi were pleased, thought it was good, and much enjoyed it.

[10]Then, afterward, they said to Abalish: "Go! For you are unable to dispute! For the more you ask, the better, clearer, more well-reasoned the other explains it."

Thus, the wicked Abālish was as if crushed, broken, bound, and damned.

136 Discussion between a Christian and a Zoroastrian
(Dēnkard V, 23–24)

What the Christian Bōkht-Mārē asked in a recent discussion and Ādurfarnbay son of Farrokh-zād's answer:

Because he is so little aware of our discussions, the many fundamentals of what I have to say would need to be exhibited at length, and he would have to be informed about how knowledgeable men have questioned and explained what I have to say, in other words, the book which we have named *Dēnkard*, because everything is in it.

If I need to show him in detail, as a friendly proof, the way all of it has been written and arranged, according to what he has selected (to discuss, there is) that which is inevitable only because obvious from knowledge; that which is certain by actual awareness; that which is certain because it is the way it is; and that which is within the boundaries of the faith and that it is the custom to accept abundantly and in undiminished fashion from analogies.

[1]From what is God's and the Opponent's existence evident?

God's existence is evident from many things. One is the fact that the world of the living was made and that the Opposition appeared. Another is the reason why the creation was needed.

[2]From where came that Opponent?

Because he moved from place to place, he came into the Emptiness.

[3]For what reason did he come? From the beginning, the Opponent ran about without intent and purpose, just because he could move. It was not because he was seeking something in particular that he came to the border of this essence of light. So the Opponent has no purpose, and his acts are those of an idiot. As he had happened upon it in unawareness, he had to be counted as something of a different essence.

[4]By what pretext did he struggle to mingle (with God's creation)?

The pretext was uncustomary hatred, lust, greed, envy, shame, thievishness, quarrelsomeness, arrogance, scorn, lack of foresight, his lying speech about being able to destroy the foundation whose essence is light, his desire to do evil, his lawless nature, his foolish struggling, and the combination of all these.

[5]Why did he not come earlier?

This needs no reason, unless you wish me to speak about it at greater length. You do not consider closely the notion of "ability," which can only be applied to "doing", not to "not doing," just like "not doing" and "refraining from doing." Then that too is a way to say it: "he was able not to come earlier." Why do you keep harping on that "beforeness," when, in the end, he will not be able to return through time, which will then be limitless!

[6]Was God able to hold back that Opponent or not? And if he was able to hold him back, why did he not hold him back?

God was able to hold the Opponent back and stear him away from his own border, and he did so repeatedly, but he kept returning to do battle. Also now, if he needs to expel someone, he can easily do so, but he does not let him move about to the farthest limits so that they might meet. Thus he cannot be inside, not because he is "unable," but because he could not be inside any power (*zōr*). It is hard to imagine what "within the limits of ability" is left over from (= is not covered by?) "one can" and what "within the limits of un-ability" is left over from "one cannot" and in what way.

⁷Why did he let him in?

Because it benefited his creatures, and because the Opponent would then be tested in sectioned time so that it would seem to the Opponent, steeped in his habit of crooked lying speech, that he would win a victory. The evident conclusion of this struggle, the extent to which he would suffer pain from us in the mixture, the visibility of all kinds of victories by the gods, and the fact that he would not be capable of returning to the struggle, and everything else one could enumerate are also exposed in this *Dēnkard*. One reason for not expelling him before that time was in order for this activity, on account of which there was a reason to let him in, should not be prevented from being led to a good conclusion.

⁸Why did he accept the damage to his creatures? And if he was not able to hold him back, how will he be able to hold him back in the end?

The fact that, in the Mixture, there would be damage was as inevitable as not to smell stench in something mingled with dead matter.

⁹By what power (*nērōg*) will he throw him back?

It is by that same power of God that he will be cast out and fall back into the Emptiness, having been fully tested and completely defeated, helpless, completely crippled, incapacitated, his color drained, having been submitted to the most grievous oppression, dressed in the most horrible fright, and that Fortress of Victory will be called "non-victory," having had his struggle cut off, and without hope.

¹⁰Did he come back or not?

One reason why he ought not to be capable of coming back to struggle is that he ran back earlier and ought not to be capable of coming back. And there is no analogy. And no fear of him remains here, no mourning, no concern. Also, he is completely bound in that Fortress of Victory in terror and dread by chains and ropes. So, it is reasonable to conclude that he will in no way be capable.

¹¹If he is not able, why is he not able? And if he is able, why does he not come?

The reason for the "able/not able," "comes/does not come" that you keep harping on is evident from what was written above about "how?" and "in how many ways?"

¹²Why did God utter this Tradition in the unknown and hidden language called *Avesta*?

This divine word of the Tradition, the *Avesta*, containing all awareness, by being in a form close to the good beings in the other world, in all the voices of beings in this world, is so amazing that it has passed beyond the grasp of humanity. But the *Zand* is spoken in such a manner that it can spread more easily and be better known in this world. The *Avesta* itself has a great mark showing that it was brought by Zarathustra from Ohrmazd. It contains no deception, stupidity, or anything reflecting the desire of the demons; rather, it has all been spoken truly, in obedience to a higher law, so as to win the gods' favor. It is not maintained in the voice of any lie-demons, and, because they cannot turn anybody away from it, the demons have no hope of attaining it. However it is spoken, it terrifies the lie-demons, but is bliss for the gods. Because the *Avesta* comes truly and equally to all the regions, as is proper, and because the *Zand* is sent by tongue into the world of the living so as to make it known, it is evident that it leads to full salvation among whomsoever.

¹³Why did he not assemble it completely in writing, but commanded us to learn it by heart in speech?

He commanded that this Tradition, the divine word, and all that is by tongue, be written down from beginning (to end). Now, too, it is mostly preserved in written form, as is well known among those who are aware. But there is great benefit in learning by heart, especially (?) in making the masses aware of how to sacrifice to the gods and how to praise them, but, above all, one gets to know things from it. Also, because it is possible to transmit the words conveying such deep meanings truly according to custom and without introducing changes, the law spoken by voice is superior by far to the written one. For these and many other reasons, it is reasonable to consider the word of living speech more essential (*mādagwar*) than that in writing.

[14]Why did god send the Tradition to the land of the Iranians only and leave the others to the teaching of the demons? And does he not consider the other gods deserving, or can he not exhibit it to them?

Ohrmazd the Creator did not send this Tradition only to the land of the Iranians, but to the entire world of the living and to all kinds (of people), and it was set in motion throughout this world, in both pure and mixed form. In the other world, it goes forth by natural (*chihrīg*) knowledge and true thought and speech and in this world by true deeds among whomsoever. It goes forth in such a way that even someone of the most evil tradition sets great store (?) by this Tradition. But in this Mixture such as it is now, it cannot go forth entirely in pure form, but by struggling, and it will keep increasing and its opponent keep decreasing until the Tradition is spread everywhere and, thereby, the world of the living becomes all pure.

God does not leave anybody to the teaching of the demons. For there is not only one kind of reason why there are, among those in this world, those who do not receive the Tradition of the gods in purity and do not practice it or who leave it or turn away from it—that the Tradition is un-"deserving," has the most blemishes, or has some kind of error (*ērang*). Rather, it is because they are led astray by demons and because the lie-demon in their bodies fights battles and wins victories because they have not sought or examined the customs; because they have surrendered their bodies and do not care about their illnesses, and so stay weak; or because they have discarded the commands, take pleasure in leading an easy life, are given over to indolence; and so on.

[15]Why is homage performed not only to god, but also to the sun and many other heavenly lights?

It is the custom to perform homage to the sun, moon, and fire, to the other luminaries, and to all the good creations. These are various customs performed in a spirit of brotherhood and family. There are some that should receive greater homage because superior, others again as equals, in the same way that men greet one another. Most often, those among them who are superior compared with us are greeted with more words. It is not a service or respect that is rendered to God alone and for himself, as those of evil tradition wickedly say about us, since they themselves in their basic custom believe that the gods ought to perform homage to men![1]

[17]Why do we need *barsom* and *drōn* and the other objects used in the sacrifice?

Barsom, drōn, and the other things that are offered in the service to the gods are, by carrying their names, miniatures (*nihang*?) of the totality of all creatures in this world, which have been entrusted to mankind in guardianship. The demons fight over them to absorb them, and people, unwillingly, fight to expel the demons in their thoughts, words, and deeds with their bodies and souls, by thinking complete thoughts and, by their superior love, offer themselves as the property of the gods and praise the gods with them and scorn the demons with them, wherefrom the greater sovereignty of the gods and the demons' lack of sovereignty is especially evident.

[18]What benefit do the gods derive from the sacrifice?

Even if it were merely the diminished sovereignty of the demons over the sacrificer himself, freedom from their greater sovereignty should also be counted as a benefit to the gods from the sacrifice.

[19a]Why is the body more polluting (*rēman*) when dead than while alive?

Pollution is all demonic and comes from the demons. Wherever there are more demons abiding, the greater the pollution. It means that, when a body is dead, then the demon that causes death stops the

---

1. Sura 2, *The Cow* 34 "And behold, We said to the angels: "Bow down to Adam' and they bowed down. But Iblis refused and was haughty, being of the non-believers (*kāfir*)."

body from functioning. That is, the Bone-untier comes upon it in supremacy, overcomes and chases the soul (*gyān*) from the body. Then it takes back the life in place after place and brings its brothers into the body to abide in it, producing stench and rot, as well as the other demons who render it useless. And each of them rejects from the body his own opponent, for instance, fragrance, cleanness, good behavior, beauty, and other decent things. And they prosper as inhabitants in the same body to such a great extent that they breathe to the outside, too, stench, dead matter, and all the illnesses. It hardly seems disputable that, where the demons inhabit in that manner, it should be called pollution.

[19b]So let us talk about the pollution of the parts of the body that die and are separated from the body while the main part of the body is still alive, not only the flesh, but also semen and blood, as well as the other things, too, that are called *hikhr*. And the most serious of all is menstrual matter and the dead part of that which is connected (*niwast*) with the binding together of the child (= the afterbirth?), on account of which that lie-demon, too, which destroys good delivery and damages and prevents birth, the greatest adversary of females, the whore-species, finds an abode in the body together with those lie-demons I mentioned above.

[19c]And what is even more (polluting) even than a woman who has aborted or one even (who pollutes) by striking things with the evil eye? One is the supremacy in her living form of the demon of the whore-species which breathes into her vinegar-smelling (?) poison, as can be seen both in this world and in the other world by him who has a visionary twin. For this reason it is possible for those with vision to know and keep away from the other demons in the other world. One must put one's trust in those who are aware of things in the other world and the Tradition that has been chosen with knowledge. It is for him to explain who says for certain there are none, while he who says it as a point of faith must compare his faith with this Tradition that has been chosen with knowledge and has been received through (our predecessors'?) ability to see in the other world and from which its existence is evident.

[20]Why is menstruation polluting? And why is the entire body polluting and to be avoided when it comes out of just a hole?

The menstrual matter that comes out of that one hole comes out also with the vinegar-smelling (?) poison of that demon and with all of her own stench and the pollution of both worlds that she pours out. For that reason one must keep as far away from the corpse as the corpse has the strength to blow. And the purer and cleaner something is, because of its sensitivity, the more one must keep away from the pollution. This holds for the various specific objects used in the sacrifice to the gods, as well.

[20a]And because menstrual matter is also of different color from the other blood, because of its grievous stench, and because it soils everything, the body itself in which it has this destructive effect also causes water and plants to diminish and foods to lose their taste and smells bad. And even in conversation with a menstruating woman there is damage from it to intelligence, perception, wisdom, and so on, as is perfectly clear among those who know.

[21]Why are demons born when someone speaks while eating, walks without shoes, urinates standing up, and all the other similar things? And if these demons are born, how come they do not swallow the entire world of the living?

Whoever thinks the birth of demons is amazing should first have a look at how it is with the birth of anything else and will then see that the main characteristic is that there are more births in certain places, which also means that the demons obviously tend to congregate where typically greater lawlessness and disregard for custom is rampant, where semen is wasted, where there is ingratitude toward the gods and scorn of the gods and deliberate speaking while eating and other things wherefrom a demon is said to be born. Certainly, nobody doubts that one recognizes law and custom by lawlessness and disregard for custom.

[21a]The demons destroy the world of the living in a great many ways, but the gods' protection is greater still, for they do not permit the demons' power (*zōr*) to prevail or let them swallow the world in

their supremacy. For, to the degree people act lawlessly in that manner and gain confidence and come forth, so also, when struck by law-abiding people, they run back terrified. And, all the time, the will of the gods is performed more often in the world than that of the demons.

[22]Why should one wash a woman who has had an abortion? If washing is needed, why is it a man who washes and not another woman?

A woman who has had an abortion and a man who has been close to the corpse need to be washed when the pollution of the dead fetus is quite clear and innumerable people are witnesses. There is nothing to be amazed about. So, it is something to be suitably believed in, and one should think suitably about whether it is of greater or lesser importance. If what I say seems ugly, a thing "seeming ugly" is not something in itself, but is according to what one does. Learned men consider the reason for something to be in itself rather than by what has been done. Even if they do not look at the genitals, their existence is still perfectly clear to those of intelligence, as if they saw them all the time. And if learned men approve of having her examined by many doctors when she has some illness, how much less is it a blemish to look when the purpose is to purify her from the corpse demon which causes her harm.

[22a]And one reason the purification is to be performed not by a woman but by a man is that the Righteous Man (i.e., a good Zoroastrian) is stronger and frightens the demons with greater terror, while women also have the adversary of their species harnessed to their nature (*chihr*). Also, because those lie-demons, too, are male, they fear females less. Also, in other activities that are not that important, a man can perform them better than a woman. In conclusion, the argument of "seem ugly"—see above—should not be used as a reason to refrain from something.

[23]When a sheep is to be killed, why must it be struck with a stick before it is cut with a knife?

The reason for bringing a stick before the knife as well as the other activities in that chapter, aside from rubbing a number of demons from the body and making it clean, is especially because of the great dread and bad taste it imparts (without it). One reason is that, by these rituals, the sheep is less often killed lawlessly and stupidly, and, by this procedure, one has mercy on the sheep, the sheep is less frightened when the knife is brought, and sheep are not killed hurriedly, stupidly, and on the spur of the moment.

[26]How do the departed come back during the Frawardīgān festival?

At Frawardīgān and other such times, it is proper for the souls (*ruwān*) of the righteous to "come." Look at what is the case now (in life)—what with having to carry our bodies and several parts of the demons being mixed with the body, nevertheless, "coming and going" for all to see should not seem so amazing. Whoever gives body and soul (*gyān*) complete to the gods sees the souls (*ruwān*) of the righteous even more (clearly) than the proofs in these answers we now give to the many who ask.

[26a]Among them, there is this, that the time of Frawardīgān is the fullness of the year, since the assembly of the year comes about by assembling the daily good deeds and ceremonies, services to God and praise of his good creations, among which man is the principal one. For that reason, at that time, the souls of the righteous and other good entities in the other world come most frequently to receive these offerings in return (for their gifts).

[27]Why should one wash one's hands with urine and moist plants?

A hand that is soiled with blood, semen, or other discarded parts (*hikhr*) of the body, should not first be rubbed with water, which is the most sensitive, but with something else, which, because it is mixed, is less so. Then it is to be washed with water, which is the best cleansing agent, both in order to protect the water better and to keep it pure from the pollution of the corpse demon. Thus the water and the fire are our essence and in many ways our parents, and it is our special duty to keep our own essence healthy by purifying it, too.

[28]Why must one show a dog to a dead body?

Showing a dog to a corpse is part of the ritual. One reason is the following: Those inseparable lie-demons that incapacitate the body, who are themselves corpse demons, can hold a place in the body until it changes from being a corpse and returns to perform useful work for living beings.

[28a]For, before the corpse comes back to the clean fire, wind, earth, and clay and becomes active in giving new birth to what is born, to provide more help and benefit for the creatures according to the custom, it is better for it to be digested and burnt in the body of dogs and birds. Therefore we should think of it as food for them and make it clear that it is a duty to hand it over to them to make it clean. In this way, they have been made useful and become kinsmen.

[28b]As the dogs or birds look at the corpse, they reckon that those lie-demons are no longer able to hold their place. They start to shake and move, and their share of residence in the body diminishes, and that corpse demon weakens to the same degree.

[30]Why must one hold the Tradition oneself and have faith in something?

This is evident by the wisdom and the authority from the other world: the Tradition is appropriate, it possesses good knowledge, good beliefs, and discernment in matters of the Tradition, and knowledge is sought with discernment, as is belief in what is circumscribed (*parwand*) by the Tradition. Among those who know how to look, even those who look forward to salvation (as taught by) Bōkht-Mārē, there are more than a few.

[30a]Thus, those familiar with the Tradition do not fall blindly into the pit (*chāh*) of the wicked [cf. 85:28]. Someone among those in this world whose belief is good, is among those who will save (others) from the pit. And they have adversaries who deceive and lead astray, whose surrogate (*guharīg*) knowledge is crooked and merely a semblance of knowledge. Even in the name of belief, they present a non-path in the semblance of the Path to those who study little and do not discriminate between things. Thereby, they make them come to eternal evil. And lucky the person adorned with omniscience, familiar with the Mazdayasnian Tradition, who can show the way!

137 The path of Order (Yasna 72.11)

> One is the path of Order.
> Those of the others are all non-paths.
> The Vision-soul of the Evil Spirit
> is the one that leads the most astray.
> Destruction to those who sacrifice to the evil gods!
> Fame for our men!

SELECT BIBLIOGRAPHY

The Literature of pre-Islamic Iran. Companion volume I to A History of Persian Literature, ed. R. E. Emmerick and M. Macuch; gen. ed., E. Yarshater (London and New York: I.B. Tauris, 2009).

Texts

Gershevitch, I. The Avestan Hymn to Mithra (Cambridge: Cambridge University Press, 1967).

Hintze, A. Der Zamyād-yašt (Wiesbaden: Dr. Ludwig Reichert Verlag, 1994).

——. A Zoroastrian liturgy: The Worship in Seven Chapters (Yasna 35–41) (Wiesbaden: Harrassowitz, 2007).

Humbach, H., and P. Ichaporia. The Heritage of Zarathushtra. A New Translation of his Gāthās (Heidelberg: C. Winter, 1994).

Jaafari-Dehaghi, M. Dādestān ī dēnīg (Paris: Association pour l'avancement des études iraniennes, 1998).

Malandra, W. W. An Introduction to Ancient Iranian Religion. Readings from the Avesta and the Achaemenid Inscriptions (Minneapolis: University of Minnesota Press, 1983).

Menasce, J. de. Le troisième livre du Dēnkart (Paris: Klincksieck, 1973).

Molé, M. La légende de Zoroastre selon les textes pehlevis (Paris: Klincksieck, 1967).

Panaino, A. Tištrya, pt. 1: The Avestan Hymn to Sirius (Rome: IsMEO, 1990).

Schmitt, R. The Bisitun Inscriptions of Darius the Great (Corpus Inscriptionum Iranicarum; London, 1991).

——. The Old Persian Inscriptions of Naqsh-i Rustam and Persepolis (Corpus Inscriptionum Iranicarum; London, 2000).

——. Die altpersischen Inschriften der Achaimeniden. Editio minor mit deutscher Übersetzung (Wiesbaden: Reichert Verlag, 2009).

Shaked, S. The Wisdom of the Sasanian Sages (Dēnkard VI) (Boulder, Col.: Westview Press, 1979).

Williams, A. V. The Pahlavi Rivāyat Accompanying the Dādestān ī Dēnīg I–II (Copenhagen: Munksgard, 1990).

History

Lamberg-Karlovsky, C. C. "Archaeology and Language," Cultural Anthropology 43 (2002): 63–88.

Skjærvø, P. O. "The Avesta as Source for the Early History of the Iranians." In G. Erdosy, ed., *The Indo-Aryans of Ancient South Asia* (Berlin–New York: Walter de Gruyter, 1995): 155–76.

Waters, M. W. "The Earliest Persians in Southwestern Iran: the Textual Evidence," *Iranian Studies* 32 (1999): 99–107.

Wiesehöfer, J. *Ancient Persia from 550 BC to 650 AD* (London and New York: I.B. Tauris, 1996).

Religion

Boyce, M. *Zoroastrianism* I–III (*Handbuch der Orientalistik*; Leiden–Cologne: Brill, 1975, 1982, 1991 [with F. Grenet]).

Herrenschmidt, C. "Once upon a Time, Zoroaster," *History and Anthropology* 3 (1987): 209–37.

Kotwal, F. M., and Boyd, J. W. *A Persian Offering. The Yasna: A Zoroastrian High Liturgy* (Paris: Association pour l'avancement des études iraniennes, 1991).

Kreyenbroek, G., and Sh. N. Munshi. *Living Zoroastrianism. Urban Parsis speak about their religion* (Richmond, Surrey: Curzon, 2001).

Rose, J. Zoroastrianism: An Introduction (London and New York: I. B. Tauris, 2011).

Skjærvø, P. O. "Avestan Quotations in Old Persian?" In S. Shaked and A. Netzer, eds., *Irano-Judaica* IV (Jerusalem, 1999), 1–64.

——. "Zoroastrian Dualism." In E. M. Meyers et al., eds., *Light Against Darkness: Dualism in Ancient Mediterranean Religion and the Contemporary World* (Göttingen: Vandenhoeck & Ruprecht, 2011), 55–91.

——. "Zarathustra: A Revolutionary Monotheist?" In B. Pongratz-Leisten, ed., *Reconsidering the Concept of Revolutionary Monotheism* (Winona Lake, Ind.: Eisenbrauns, 2011), 325–58.

Stausberg, M. *Zarathustra and Zoroastrianism. A Short Introduction*, transl. M. Preisler-Weller with a postscript by A. Hultgård (London and Oakville, Conn.: Equinox Pub., 2008).

Websites

http://www.iranica.com/newsite/ : *Encyclopaedia Iranica*, London, 1982–.

http://avesta.org/ : contains the translations in the Sacred Books of the East and others and literature on rituals.

LIST OF TEXTS TRANSLATED

Numbers in bold, followed by paragraph numbers, refer to chapters and paragraphs in published editions of the source texts. In the case of some long texts that are not numbered in the editions, I have provided subdivisions (e.g., *Dēnkard* III). Numbers in [ ] refer to chapters and paragraphs, occasionally also to pages, in this book.

GLOSSARY

Languages are abbreviated as Av. = Avestan; Pahl. = Pahlavi; Pers. = Persian (Fārsi); OPers. = Old Persian. Most references are to the Introduction, where references to the texts can be found.

Artaxerxes, name of several
  Achaemenid kings 5, 29, 232
Aryan Expanse, Av. *airyanam vaējō*,
  Pahl. Ērānwēz, mythical homeland
  of the Iranians 22
asha (Av.), the cosmic and ritual Order;
  Pahl. *ahlāyīh* "righteousness" 10
Asha Wahishta, see Best Order
ashawan, Av. "sustainer of Order"; also
  as title and term for those who will
  go to paradise: "Righteous";
  OPers. *ertāwan*, Pahl. *ahlaw*,
  ardā(w), later also *ashō*, typical
  epithet of Zarathustra 10
Ashem Wohū (Av.), a sacred formula
  (prayer) 4, 219
Ashi (Av.), Pahl. Ard, Arshishwang,
  Ahlishwang (Av. Ashish wanghwī
  "good Ashi"), a female deity,
  divine charioteer 16
Ashwahisht, see Best Order
Asnwend (Pahl.), a mythological
  mountain, in the *Avesta* associated
  with Kawi Haosrawah 141
Assault, the Evil Spirit's attack on
  Ohrmazd's world 12, 21
Astōwidātu (Av.), Pahl. Astwihād, see
  Bone-untier
Astwad-erta (Av.), "he who gives Order
  bones," Pahl. Sōshāns,
  Zarathustra's 3rd eschatological
  son 19, 29
Astwihād, see Bone-untier
Avesta, the collection of Avestan texts
  2–4
Avestan, the language of the Avestan
  texts 1–5
Awareness-of-the-Righteous (Pahl.),
  name of a heavenly fortress 19
Āz (Pahl.), "Lust (?)," a demon 21
Azhi Dahāka (Av.), "the Giant (?)
  Dragon"; Pahl. Azh(i)dahāg,
  Dahāg; Pers. Zohhāk 23–4

Babylon 23, 163
baga (Av.), "Distributor," epithet of a
  deity; OPers. "god"; Pahl. *bay*,
  epithet of gods, "Lord," and kings,
  approximately "Majesty" 12

barshnūm (Pahl.), a purification
  ritual 37
barsman (Av.), Pahl. *barsom* 36
Best Existence, Av. *wahishta ahu*,
  Pahl. *wahišt*, Pers. *behesht*
  "paradise" 33
Best Order, Av. *asha vahishta*, Pahl.
  Ardwahisht (Urdwahisht),
  Ashwahisht, one of the Life-giving
  Immortals 14
Bisotun (Behistun), a rock containing
  an inscription by Darius 5
body 30–2
Bone-untier, Av. Astōwidātu, "the
  bone-untier," Pahl. Astwihād, a
  demon 21
bones 30
bones, Order having 11, 29-30
bones, the world with 8, 10, 34
Brādrōkhsh, Brādrōrēsh, Brādrēsh
  (Pahl.), Zarathustra's murderer
  148, 153, 156
Bud, see Butī
Bull, set in place alone, ancestor of good
  animals 20–1
Butī, a demon; Pahl. Bud, interpreted as
  Buddha; Pers *bot* "idol" (often
  used of beautiful women) 78, 104,
  136, 138, 150

Caspian Sea 2
Chistā (Av.), a female deity 27, 135
Complete Thought, Pahl. explanation of
  "Ārmaiti" 109, 111
creation (process) 11–2
creation (thing created), see
  dāman

Dādestān ī dēnīg, "Judgments according
  to the Tradition," a Pahlavi
  text 6
Dādestān ī mēnōy xrad, "Judgements of
  the Divine Wisdom," a Pahlavi
  text 6
daēnā (Av.), "(vision-)soul" 31
daēnā (Av.), Pahl. *dēn*, the totality of a
  person's thoughts, words, and
  deeds; meets the soul of the dead
  in the beyond 32

gētīy, see world of living beings; cf. *mēnōy*

girdle, Pahl. *kusti* 19, 34, 208–13, 246–7

Girdle, the heavenly/cosmic; see Daēnā māzdayasni

Gōchihr, heavenly dragon 29

god, see Ahura Mazdā, *baga*, *yazata*

gōmēz, see *gao-maēza*

Good (Best) Thought, one of the Life-giving Immortals 14

Good Lawful River (Av.), Pahl. the good Dāitī, river in the Aryan Expanse 22

Gōshurūn, see soul of the cow/bull 20

Greed (Pahl. Waran), a demon 21

guiding wisdom, guiding thoughts, Av. *khratu*, Pahl. *khrad* 32, 34

Haēchad-aspas (Av.), family name 128

Haētumant (Av.), a river, modern Helmand in southern Afghanistan 2, 159

haoma (Av.), Pahl. *hōm*, a sacred plant and the drink made from it 17–8, 27, 35–6

Haoma (Av.), Pahl. Hōm, the divinity of the *haoma* 2, 17–8, 27, 35

Haoma (Av.), Pahl. Hōm, slayer of Frangrasyān 25

Haoshyangha (Av.), first mythical sacrificer; Pahl. Hōshang, legendary king 22–3

hell 21, 33, 36

Helmand, see Haētumant

hērbedestān, religious school 194

Hērbedestān, an Avestan and Pahlavi text 6

Heshm, see Wrath

hōm, Hōm, see *haoma*, Haoma

homage, Av. *nemah*, Pahl. *namāz* 37, 75–6, 209–10, 245, 251–2

Hordad (Pahl.), Av. *haurwatāt*, see Wholeness

Hordad, first day of the month 166–7

Hōshang (Pahl.), see Haoshyangha

House of Song, Av. *garō dmāna*, Ahura Mazdā's abode, Pahl. Garōdmān, paradise 14, 26

Hudōs, see Hutaosa

Humāyā (Av.), Pahl. Humā, Dārāy's mother 28

Humility, see Life-giving Humility

Hutaosā (Av.), Pahl. Hudōs, Wishtāspa's (Wishtāsp's) wife 27–8

Huwagwas, family name, see Frashaoshtra, Jāmāspa 26

Hwōwī (Av.), Pahl. Hwōw, Zarathustra's wife 27

Indar, see Indra

Indo-Aryan, Indian speaking an Indic language of the Indo-European family 1, 2, 18

Indo-European, the proto-language (and its speakers) from which Indo-Aryan, Iranian, and most of the European languages are descended 1, 11, 22

Indo-Iranian, the common language from which Indo-Aryan and Iranian are descended 1, 13, 22

Indra (Av.), Pahl. Indar, a demon 20

Iran, Pahl. Ērān (šahr), "(land) of the Iranians"

Isad-wāstra (Av.), Pahl. Isadwāstar, eschatological son of Zarathustra 29

Jam, Jamshīd, see Yima

Jāmāspa (Av., OAv. Djāmāspa), brother of Frashaoshtra, of the Huwagwa family; Pahl. Jāmāsp 26

Juicy, see *frasha*

Kang castle (Pahl.), mythical castle built by Kay Siyāwakhsh 117, 121, 160, 164

Kansaoya (Av.), Pahl. Kiyānsī, mythical sea where Zarathustra's sperm is preserved; now identified with Lake Hamun in south-east Iran 28, 29

Karsāsp, Karisāsp, see Kersāspa

kawi (Av.), Pahl. *kayg*, poet-priest; in the plural evil priests or bad poets 11

Kawi (Av.), title of a series of mythical

poet-priests; Pahl. Kay, title of
mythical-legendary kings 18, 24–5

Kawi Haosrawah (Av.), Pahl. Kay
Husrōy, Pers. Kay Khosrow, last of
the great Kawis 25

Kawi Kawāta (Av.), first of the Kawis 24

Kawi Usan (or Usadan, Av.), Pahl.
(Kay) Kāy-Us (Pers. Kāvūs,
Qābūs), one of the Kawis 25

Kawi Wishtāspa, Kay Wishtāsp, see
Wishtāspa

Kerdīr, 3rd-century priest 2, 5, 6, 33, 38

Kersāspa (Av.), Pahl. Kar(i)sāsp, Gar(i)
shāsp, Garsāsp; Pers. Garshāsp,
Sām (Narīmān), youthful dragon
slayer 24, 29

Khiyonians (Av. Khiyaona, Pahl.
Khiyōn), people who go to war
with the Iranians under King
Wishtāspa (Wishtāsp) 25, 28

Khorāsān, estern Iran 119, 163

Khorde Avesta, collection of Avestan and
post-Avestan texts 4

khratu, khrad, see guiding wisdom,
guiding thoughts

khshathra wairiya (Av.), Pahl. *(kh)
shahrewar*, see Well-deserved
Command

Khwaniratha (Av.), Pahl. Khwanirah,
the central one of the seven
continents 41, etc.

khwarnah (Av.), Pahl. *khwarrah*, see
Fortune

Khwarshēd-chihr (Pahl.), Av. Khwar-
chithra "who has the splendor of
the sun" or "whose seed is from
the sun"(?), one of Zarathustra's
eschatological sons 160

khwēdōdah (Pahl.), marriage with
members of one's closest family
(parents, children, siblings) 33–4

kusti, the sacred girdle; see girdle, *Daēnā
māzdayasni*

Law for keeping the demons away, see
Videvdad

life-giving, Av. *spenta*, epithet of good
entities in the world of thought
implying fertility and growth;

Pahl. *abzōnīg* "making (things)
increase" 9

Life-giving Humility, Av. *spentā ārmaiti*,
Pahl. Spandarmad,"the Earth,"
one of the Life-giving Immortals
13–5, 31

Life-giving Immortals, Av. *amesha
spenta*s, Pahl. *amahrspand*s,
*ameshāspand*s 13–4, 16, 19

Life-giving Spirit 4, 9, 19

Life-giving Word, Av. *manthra spenta*,
Pahl. Mānsr-spand, Mahr-spand, a
divinity 19, 37

Luhrāsp (Pahl.), Wishtāsp's father 25

Mahr-spand, Mānsr-spand, see
Life-giving Word

Manushchihr, high priest and author 6

Manushchihr, Mānushchihr (Pahl.,
Av. Manush-chithra), mythical-
legendary king 24, 103,
116–7, 208

manyu (Av.), a mental force originating
in the other world, "spirit,"
inspiration 8–9

Mazandaran, today the area in northern
Iran south of the Caspian Sea 121

Mazdaism = Zoroastrianism 1

Mazdak, a heretic during the reign of
Kawād I (late 5th cent.) 119

Medes, ancient Iranian people in
north-western Iran; dynasty
preceding the Achaemenids 2

mēnōy, the world of thought, the "other"
world; epithet of entities in the
other world; cf. *gētīy, manyu* 9, 12,
16, 31

Mihragān festival 4

Millennium, thousand-year period; the
Pahlavi texts count 4x3 = 12
millennia 12, 22, 29

Mithra (Av.), Pahl. Mihr, deity
overseeing agreements, precedes
the sun at dawn 4, 13, 16–7, 19

Mixture, the state of the world
after the forces of Evil infected
it 12

mowbed, mowbedān mowbed (Pahl.),
high priest 42, etc.